MANAGEMENT OF WATER PROJECTS

Decision-Making and Investment Appraisal

ORGANISATION FOR ECONOMIC CO-OPERATION AND DEVELOPMENT

Pursuant to article 1 of the Convention signed in Paris on 14th December, 1960, and which came into force on 30th September, 1961, the Organisation for Economic Co-operation and Development (OECD) shall promote policies designed:

- to achieve the highest sustainable economic growth and employment and a rising standard of living in Member countries, while maintaining financial stability, and thus to contribute to the development of the world economy;
- to contribute to sound economic expansion in Member as well as non-member countries in the process of economic development; and
- to contribute to the expansion of world trade on a multilateral, non-discriminatory basis in accordance with international obligations.

The Signatories of the Convention on the OECD are Austria, Belgium, Canada, Denmark, France, the Federal Republic of Germany, Greece, Iceland, Ireland, Italy, Luxembourg, the Netherlands, Norway, Portugal, Spain, Sweden, Switzerland, Turkey, the United Kingdom and the United States. The following countries acceded subsequently to this Convention (the dates are those on which the instruments of accession were deposited): Japan (28th April, 1964), Finland (28th January, 1969), Australia (7th June, 1971) and New Zealand (29th May, 1973).

The Socialist Federal Republic of Yugoslavia takes part in certain work of the OECD (agreement of 28th October, 1961).

Publié en français sous le titre:

**GESTION DES PROJETS
D'AMÉNAGEMENT DES EAUX**
Prise de décision et évaluation
des investissements

The present book is the result of work undertaken by national teams nominated in most OECD Member countries and of an international team of multi-disciplinary experts.

Members of the national teams belonged to different government institutions involved in the planning and management of water resources. They met regularly to exchange views and improve the present text in the light of their experience.

The international team was composed of Professor Heinz A. Becker, State University of Utrecht (Netherlands); M. Jean-Pierre Bourgin, Ingénieur en Chef du Génie Rural, des Eaux et des Forêts (France); M. Jean-Marc Boussard, Maître de Recherche, Institut National de la Recherche Agronomique (France); Professor Charles W. Howe, University of Colorado (United States); Mr. Josef van Doorn, Associate Professor, Catholic University of Tilburg (Netherlands) and Mr. Frans van Vught, Associate Professor, Twente University of Technology (Netherlands).

TABLE OF CONTENTS

Part I

BASIC CONSIDERATIONS

Part II

ECONOMIC CONSIDERATIONS AND FINANCING

Part III

SOCIAL CONSIDERATIONS

Chapter XVI

      DEALING WITH RESETTLEMENT

Part IV

ENVIRONMENT

Chapter XVII

      THE BASIC ENVIRONMENTAL QUESTIONS IN WATER PLANNING PROJECTS

Chapter XVIII

      GENERAL TECHNIQUES FOR ENVIRONMENTAL STUDIES

Chapter XIX

      PRESENTING THE RESULTS OF THE ENVIRONMENTAL STUDIES

Annexes:

List of Tables

List of Figures

PREFACE

The beginnings of this book date back to 1970 when the OECD observed that the Southern European countries were about to embark upon a large number of irrigation projects without adequate concern for the return they would yield and without attempting to define what markets there might be for the production the projects would make possible.

It was recognition of these facts that prompted the holding of the seminar in Athens in 1971 as a result of which an international team of experts was set up and national teams formed in seven Member countries that together tested and developed a "Guide to the Economic Evaluation of Irrigation projects".

From the outset, however, it was clear that, given the one-dimensional approach, then taken, this could only be a first stage that would need fuller development thereafter: the Guide dealt only with the problems connected with irrigation projects and their economic appraisal whereas other dimensions are also involved, such as sociology and, above all, the environment, whose role is just as important as purely economic factors for the success of the projects and for regional development in general.

The present publication covers a broader spectrum than just irrigation. It analyses and orders the factors to be taken into account for decision-making and appraisal in large-scale investment projects under the general heading of water management. In recent years, changes have taken place in the running of large-scale projects in Member countries. Previously, both political authorities and government departments tended to consider water projects as necessary for economic development. Nowadays it seems preferable as well to take account, at the appropriate time, of the effects that such projects may have on the environment and society. It was also felt that decision-making and appraisal in the case of large-scale water projects provided a good example that would illustrate and help solve the complex public management problems associated with large-scale investment projects.

Whilst it is generally accepted that the economic and social situation has changed considerably in the Member countries over the last decades, the capacity of governments to take and effectively apply the appropriate decisions seems to need improving. Aside from the essentially political issues, decision-making requires that governments and promoters of large-scale investment projects need to be provided with a larger range of criteria for evaluating public action.

The all-embracing approach on which this book is based meets the need to take into account a whole series of social and economic aspects bound up with water management. It came up against the same conflicts, of course, as those that are familiar problems in the design, appraisal and construction of large-scale water management projects. Each expert is generally convinced of the pre-eminence of his own field, seeking to ensure that his own viewpoint prevails, and each is tempted to cover only part of the problems. But avoiding or ruling out every repetition, every duplication and every contradictory opinion would mean that, in the multicriterion appraisal system, only one viewpoint could be right and fair, which surely can not be the case.

No-one will find, in this book, an "ideal" solution in which all the criteria are finally brought together in a single figure enabling the decision-making authority to make a final choice among the various alternatives. This would mean that the authority would have practically no power because everything would already have been resolved by the appraisal calculus. On the contrary, the book is for the use of policy-makers and members of the pluridisciplinary teams responsible for appraising projects, and its purpose is to make them aware of the complexity of the subject, the viewpoints and criteria of the various scientific disciplines involved in the appraisal process and the paths to follow when taking the decisions that have to be made as the studies and the project progress.

The book was written by an international, pluridisciplinary team working in close co-operation with the national teams and covers a broad range of situations and problems observed in various Member countries and in many non-Member developing countries. It defines the consequences projects can have, builds them into global, long-term planning strategies and sets them in the context of the institutional relations between the bodies concerned, the different levels of government and the various interests of the populations, which often surface with violence and when least expected.

In addition to the meetings held with the national pluridisciplinary teams, when they regularly compared progress, the authors had the benefit of case studies produced by the national experts. In particular, the members of the Finnish, Italian, Portuguese and Turkish teams tried out the proposed procedure and appraisal model whilst the other countries studied certain specific aspects of decision-making and appraisal for large-scale water management projects. These contributions furnished illustrations of possible application potential, problems and difficulties that may be encountered, and possible effects on management practice and were useful in refining the methodology and producing the final version of this text.

As Chairman of the meetings of the group of experts I would like to pay my thanks to all those who kindly co-operated in producing this book and particularly the consultants, the members of the national teams and the OECD Technical Co-operation Service and the Agricultural and Environment Directorates. The exercise has been extremely interesting and enriching for me and I hope that this book may contribute to the development of the OECD countries in the broadest sense of the term.

Hellmuth Bergmann
Chairman of the OECD Steering Committee of the Joint
Activity on Multipurpose Hydraulic Projects
Chief Technical Adviser, European Investment Bank, Luxembourg

Chapter I

INTRODUCTION

1.   The development of multipurpose hydraulic projects exemplifies the kind of complex public management problem with which Governments are faced today. They reflect remarkably well the difficulties of co-ordinating the various private agencies involved in the planning and execution of projects, as well as in their subsequent day to day maintenance and operation. Whilst this constitutes the main justification for the elaboration of this document, its objectives have, however, evolved during its development.

2.   Originally, the main output was planned to be a guide for the evaluation of multipurpose hydraulic projects. The first drafts of this document were based on the idea that the decision to go ahead with a project is essentially unique: before the decision, a team of experts prepares an evaluation report. The latter merely presents a choice between a few project alternatives. At the time of decision, a decision-maker chooses one of these alternatives, on the basis of some utility function. After the decision, the project alternative chosen is implemented according to the plans previously prepared in the study phase.

3.   Numerous contacts with the experts forming the steering committee of the activity, many field-visits, various discussions even within the team of consultants showed that these views were somewhat simplistic and naïve. The above mentioned decision schema works only in the case of very small projects, which are not within the scope of the present study. In the case of multipurpose hydraulic projects, the final shape of the waterworks is the result of a long process, involving a number of decisions at various stages of the project. At the same time, these decisions are not taken by one decision-maker. Rather, they emerge as the only possible results of negotiations conducted between the various group interests (e.g. local, regional, national, or landlords, workers, farmers, etc.) involved in the project.

4.   In such a context, the promoter of the project is given a crucial role: the promoter could be a politician, a civil servant, or anybody else. He is convinced that "something must be done" with a water resource. He has to convince some people to support the project (because he is not in a position to undertake it on his own), and others to remain neutral (often, only one determined opposition may prevent the project being undertaken). In doing so, the promoter must answer three basic questions:

    i) What is the project?
   ii) What will be its main effects?
  iii) How can it be financed? (And, therefore, how much does it cost?)

5.   The answers to these questions vary through time. At the beginning, the project is only a vague preliminary idea. If some of the major beneficial effects are in general contemplated (and often, overestimated), most of the possible adverse effects are ignored. The cost estimates are very rough, and the financing plan is rather a list of possible contributors. Later on, the plans are more and more precise, until the completion of the "feasibility study". In addition, these plans are not only more precise, but also different. At each step, the content of the project is redefined, in order to take account of, and overcome, all the difficulties which appeared in the preceding steps; a new industry is added to the project here, a dam is excluded there. Even after, the building of most of the water works, plans have to be updated, in order to take account of new economic, social, or environmental conditions, in the light of the discrepancies between the assumptions made in the feasibility study and the actual course of events in those parts of the project which are already completed.

6.   During this process, decisions are intermixed with information processing. In principle, this is not desirable. The persons involved in designing and evaluating water projects should not be the decision-makers, the former however should serve to generate information to be used by the decision-makers in making the final project selection.

7.   The reason for this is that decision-making is a political process involving the weighting of various national (or regional) objectives which are fulfilled by water projects. The assignment of these weights is a political step for it involves balancing the interests of different groups in society. Further, water development and management decisions are not politically independent of decisions being made in other sectors such as transport, agriculture and industry. For example, the decision to build a water project in one region may not be based primarily on maximum national economic advantage but upon equity among regions, perhaps following from earlier decisions that the region should be excluded from other developments.

8.   In practice, however, the authors of the studies have an idea about the utility function of the decision-maker. They never present the whole range of possible alternatives to him. This would be impossible for very practical reasons. In many countries, only the variant best suited to his goals is presented to the decision maker for approval. In other countries, where the law requests a formal choice, only a very small number of variants are presented, and, often, everybody knows, beforehand, what the choice will be.

9.   In that context, the "report presented to the decision maker" is not a collection of information upon which some decision has to be based. Rather, it is the result of the decision itself -- a kind of contract between all the parties interested in the decision (including the decision maker himself) and reflecting the consensus which has been reached under the current state of knowledge about the possible consequences of the project.

10.   What precedes does not imply that the role of the decision maker is purely formal and limited to the approval of choices made by others. On the contrary, the necessity for producing plans which have to be approved imposes a real strain on the choices made at all stages of the planning process. Thus, simply by stating his preferences in general terms, the decision maker influences the work of the designer. In this respect, it must be noticed that present as well as possible future decision makers may have a deep influence

over a project: because of the length of time between the first studies and
the completion of the project, plans must usually be satisfactory for several
successive generations of decision makers.

11.   The indepthness with which the studies have to be conducted also varies
widely through time, from casual discussions, to heavy surveys and computer
models.   In this respect, it is important to notice that (contrary to a common
creed) the crucial step for a hydraulic project is seldom the feasibility
study.   Most often, it is the time at which a permanent team is recruited to
proceed with detailed studies.   Before that stage, it is always possible to
abandon the project.   After, the problem is not so much whether the project
should be done than how and when it can be done in the best way.   Thus, the
setting up of an hydraulic project is a complicated recursive process, as de-
picted in figure 1.

12.   In this figure, items in rectangles are actions.   Diamonds indicate decisions to be taken, and, therefore, that a report is needed at that stage.
These reports must provide the proof that, given the current state of knowledge, the project should be supported because of its advantages, and is not
objectionable because of its drawbacks.   Bringing these proofs out requires
expertises in various fields.   The first and most important one is obviously
the science of the engineer.   At the same time, this aspect of project justification has been the object of so many books and treatise that it has not
been judged necessary to include it within the scope of the present document.
However, the economic, social and environmental sciences are almost as important as civil engineering for securing the success of a water resource planning activity.   Their applications in the field, however, are far less frequently taught or conscienciously used.   This is the reason for having restricted the scope of this document to these three last fields.

13.   Even with these restrictions, this document is not intended to be a
treatise in the sciences just mentioned.   Such documents exist already, and it
would be ridiculous to summarise them in some 250 pages.   The purpose of this
work is more specific, and, perhaps, more ambitious.   Two major problems arise
whenever expertise in a particular field is needed for a definite purpose,
such as preparing a multipurpose hydraulic project:

    i) The customer (in the present case, the promoter of the project, or
       the leader of the team of experts), although not himself a specia-
       list of the discipline, must have a knowledge of it sufficient to
       be able to specify the terms of reference of the desired study, as
       well as to appraise the quality of the result.
   ii) The expert in charge of the study must not be confined within his
       own discipline.   It is essential that he be able to communicate
       with his colleague of other disciplines, and therefore, that he has
       at least a good command of their vocabulary.   Above all, it is
       necessary that he be able to have a good picture of the insertion
       of the study, of which he is in charge, within the whole set of
       studies which, at each step of the design process, are necessary to
       bring answers to the three basic questions referred to in para-
       graph 4.

14.   The purpose of this book is to provide potential or actual promoters,
as well as the experts of various disciplines, with the information which is
needed to solve these two problems, at least for what concerns economics,

Figure 1 **A MASTER TIME SEQUEN**

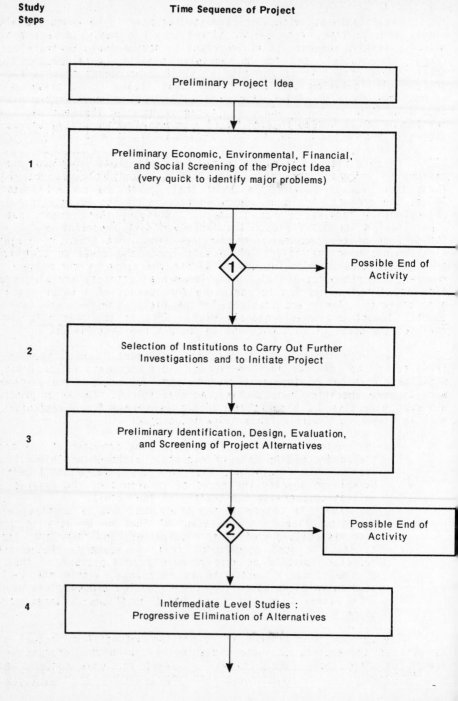

Figure 1 A MASTER TIME SEQUENCE

**Study
Steps**

Time Sequence of Project

Preliminary Project Idea

1   Preliminary Economic, Environmental, Financial,
and Social Screening of the Project Idea
(very quick to identify major problems)

① → Possible End of
Activity

2   Selection of Institutions to Carry Out Further
Investigations and to Initiate Project

3   Preliminary Identification, Design, Evaluation,
and Screening of Project Alternatives

② → Possible End of
Activity

4   Intermediate Level Studies :
Progressive Elimination of Alternatives

16

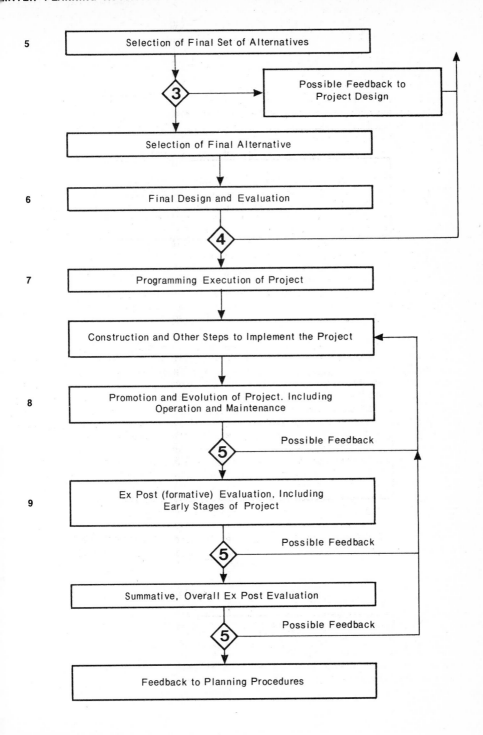

5   Selection of Final Set of Alternatives

3   →   Possible Feedback to Project Design

Selection of Final Alternative

6   Final Design and Evaluation

4

7   Programming Execution of Project

Construction and Other Steps to Implement the Project

8   Promotion and Evolution of Project. Including Operation and Maintenance

5   Possible Feedback

9   Ex Post (formative) Evaluation, Including Early Stages of Project

5   Possible Feedback

Summative, Overall Ex Post Evaluation

5   Possible Feedback

Feedback to Planning Procedures

social science, and environmental sciences. The best viewpoint for this is probably to look at the agenda of the economic, environmental and social activities at each stage of the planning process. The definitions of the technical terms used in that table will be presented later on.

15.   It is not possible, however, to give account of the various topics in the order in which they appear in this table. The process of problem definition, consideration of alternative solutions, projects design, evaluation and ranking does not usually proceed step by step as in the chapters of a book. Some steps may be performed concurrently and others may need to be repeated. Thus, the steps described represent necessary parts of the planning process, but the order of execution may differ from that presented in this document. The adopted plan is described in the following paragraphs.

16.   Part I is devoted to the general framework within which the studies in various disciplines take place. Chapter II sets out the whole set of studies which lead to the completion of a water project. Chapter III defines the basic vocabulary and principles which will be used throughout the document. Chapter IV describes the desirable institutional framework for achieving the task of building up a project. Chapter V considers the integration of the project into national and regional plans. Finally, Chapter VI deals with risk and uncertainty, as these aspects are too often neglected in water project planning by considering only "average" or "most likely" values of all parameters. Nevertheless, risk is a basic component of long-term planning and should be considered as such, especially as many well-established techniques now exist in this respect.

17.   Parts II, III and IV deal respectively with economics, social and environmental aspects, and adopt a similar structure as in Part I: a first chapter states the basic questions in the field considered. The chapters which follow indicate possible technical solutions for solving these problems. Some variations occur, however, because of differences between the disciplines. In economics, after Chapter VII, which pertains to general problems of benefit cost analysis, and Chapter VIII, which deals more extensively with the specificity of benefit costs analysis as applied to water projects, it was felt necessary to insert Chapter IX, on the measurement of the distribution of benefits and costs, and Chapter X, on Financing and Pricing. Similarly, special chapters in Part II are concerned with specific topics in the social fields, such as resettlement policies and the health consequences of the water projects. It goes without saying that every project does not necessarily need special attention given to resettlement and health problems.

18.   In Annex I, the reader will find, for illustrative purposes, a sketch of the basic reports which are necessary at each crucial stage of the planning process (1).

NOTE

1.   Examples of such reports have been completed by the experts of the Steering Committee in charge of the supervision of the present work, cf. Annex II.

Part I

BASIC CONSIDERATIONS

Chapter II

AGENDA FOR STUDIES IN WATER PROJECT DESIGN

19.   Before entering into the detail of the studies which have to be undertaken, it is necessary to have a broad picture of their timing and organisation. This topic is dealt with in the first part of this chapter. Accor-
dingly, the second part describes the various reports which present the results of the studies.

A. AN INTEGRATED ACTION PLAN FOR PROJECT DESIGN

20.   According to Figure 1 and the preceding discussion, the design evaluation and building process of a multipurpose hydraulic project is divided into
9 major steps, running from the "initial idea of the project", to the "summative evaluation".

21.   Step 1: Preliminary Screening of Project Ideas

Economic actions to be taken:

    1. Make quick calculations of net benefits of the "most obvious" alter-
       native, using market prices;
    2. Attempt to detect any adverse distribution of benefits and costs;
    3. Identify major sources of increased risk and their possible conse-
       quences;
    4. Recommend continuation or termination of studies.

Financial actions to be taken:

    1. Preliminary investigation of financial needs and sources, in ap-
       proximate figures;
    2. Identify major obstacles to the financing of the project;
    3. Recommend continuation or termination of studies.

Environmental actions to be taken:

    1. Determine likelihood of major negative environmental effects;
    2. Identify geographical scope of likely impacts;

3. Estimate possibility of mitigating negative effects;
4. Identify beneficial effects;
5. Recommend continuation or termination of studies.

Social actions to be taken;

1. Identify general social issues which may be important for the project and try to relate these issues to the project idea;
2. Sample public opinion on project idea (snapshot survey);
3. Set up a list of general social issues and analyse these issues on
   scope and time span;
4. Write report on these issues and recommend continuation or termination of studies.

22. Step 2: Selection of Institutions

Economic actions:

1. Determine the special economic skills needed on the team;
2. Establish a first contact with co-operating agencies regarding data
   and personnel.

Financial actions:

1. Nominate financial and accounting expert(s) for the team;
2. Establish contacts with potential sources of finance;
3. Establish initial political contacts regarding funding.

Environmental actions:

1. Nominate environmental expert(s) for team;
2. Establish first contacts with co-operating agencies regarding data
   base.

Social actions:

1. Select institutional arrangements most appropriate for overall planning task;
2. Initiate and differentiate public participation process.

23. Step 3: Preliminary Identification, Design, Evaluation and Screening
of Project Alternatives.

Economic actions:

1. Establish a data base and forecasting models:
   a) National and regional data and projections;
   b) Review of prior studies and available models.
2. Identify economics-related project design components: pricing,
   taxes, rules, repayment procedures, constraints on technology, etc.;
3. Estimate if necessary of shadow prices as needed for project inputs
   and outputs;

4. Assist design engineering team in designing the "benchmark variant" project design (which maximises economic net benefits subject to minimal environmental and social constraints);
5. Carry out direct benefit-cost screening (using present value of direct net benefits only) of project alternatives;
6. Carry out a preliminary distributional analysis of benefits and costs based on preliminary financial plan;
7. Carry out a preliminary risk screening in co-operation with the engineering-hydrology team;
8. Eliminate "dominated" project alternatives, i.e. those which are worse than others in all (economic, environmental, social) dimensions.
9. Conduct a rough analysis of the profitability from the client's point of view.

Financial actions:

1. Identify upper bounds on available financing;
2. Establish a preliminary financial plan for the "benchmark variant";
3. Eliminate or modify financially unfeasible project alternatives.

Environmental actions:

1. Set up criteria for initial screening;
2. Establish a data base:
   a) List existing sources and find gaps;
   b) Establish baseline conditions from available data and/or initial monitoring;
   c) Design continuing monitoring systems and their time grid;
   d) Identify likely irreversibilities.

Social actions:

1. Work out inventory of the social topics to be covered in the social monitoring process;
2. Collect and make an inventory of existing data-resources;
3. Identify and formulate the important social objectives;
4. Compile an initial list of evaluation variables;
5. Make an initial identification of population segments;
6. Meet with the public and political leaders concerning 3, 4 and 5; at the same time trying to get some complementary information on point 1 of this step;
7. Formulate initial forecasts on a number of identified evaluation variables;
8. Suggest ideas on additional and more detailed sociological studies;
9. Formulate screening-criteria for an initial evaluation of the project alternatives.

24.   Step 4: Progressive Elimination of Project Alternatives through Intermediate Level Studies

Economic actions:

1. Carry out needed field studies and surveys;

2. Calculate indirect benefits and costs;
3. Calculate distribution of benefits and costs using the detailed financial plans;
4. Make recommendations regarding elimination of alternatives with un-favourable net benefit and distributional characteristics.

Financial actions:

Draw up the detailed financial plans for remaining alternatives, inclu-ding the financial requirements for project-related activities.

Environmental actions:

Start initial environmental evaluations, including:
a. Intensification of monitoring;
b. Consideration of the role of formal computer models in further ana-lyses;
c. Apply extended checklist of environmental factors;
d. Analysis of the possibility of eutrophication and its prevention;
e. Consider visual and other aesthetic features;
f. Further public participation on environmental issues.

Social actions:

1. Start social monitoring process; bring in as many of the social topics (mentioned under step 3, point 1) as possible. Give also attention to the monitoring of the project-related participation ac-tivities;
2. Carry out additional and detailed sociological investigations (step 3, point 8); write reports;
3. Extract new evaluation variables for the screening of project alter-natives from both the social monitoring process and the additional investigations;
4. Construct scenarios to integrate the various social aspects and to work towards the final set of project alternatives.

25.   Step 5: Selection of Final Set of Alternatives for presentation to the Decision-Makers

Economic actions:

1. Determine the short term business cycle, trade balance, and infla-tionary implications of the timing of project construction;
2. Design of legislation required for the economic and financial imple-mentation of these alternatives.

Financial actions:

1. Obtain conditional statements of commitment from financing sources for each alternative;
2. Complete final financial plans;
3. Draw up proposed price schedule for project outputs for early public promulgation;
4. Further elaboration of funding which may be required in project-related activities.

Environmental actions:

1. Complete full environmental impact analyses and elaboration of the environmental account, including utilisation of water quantity and quality simulation models;
2. Make a prediction and analysis of problems to be encountered during construction.

Social actions:

1. Work out a full social impact analysis, using the "social assessment structure";
2. Return to alternative scenarios (step 4, point 5) to formulate detailed forecasts; use all information available (from consultation -- from existing sources -- from the social monitoring process -- from additional investigations);
3. Consult with the public (public meetings, summaries of scenarios analysing public comments, comprehensive survey);
4. Use additional forecasting techniques to formulate detailed forecasts (cross-impact analysis, model building);
5. Present forecasts on the social impacts of the project alternatives to decision-makers and the public.

26.   Step 6: Final Design and Evaluation

Economic actions:

completion of final economic evaluation from national and regional points of view.

Financial actions:

1. Make contractual arrangements for project financing, including subventions and loans;
2. Promulgate proposed price schedules for project outputs, plus details of other cost repayment arrangements;
3. Complete contracts with client groups.

Environmental actions:

completion of environmental impact statement.

Social actions:

1. Set up the chosen project alternative into programmes of a plan;
2. Prepare detailed procedural reports on the topics covered by the studies undertaken, working closely with all impacted groups.

27.   Step 7: Programming the Execution of the Project and actual Implementation and Construction

Financial actions:

1. Set the timing of funds' availability;

2. Establish detailed systems for expenditure control, and construction, contract negotiations.

Environmental actions:

detailed monitoring of construction impacts and execution of needed
mitigating steps.

28.   Step 8: Operation, Promotion and Evaluation of the Project

Economic actions:

1. Establish a properly trained, responsible operating and maintenance
team in co-operation with the engineering team;
2. Carry out a benefit/cost evaluation of possible changes in operating
rules arising from changes in demand.

Financial actions:

1. Collect project revenues;
2. Carry out debt repayment and sinking-fund management;
3. Promote project services.

Environmental actions:

continued monitoring and feedback.

29.   Step 9: Ex Post Analyses and Feedback.

Economic actions:

1. Assist in designing appropriate ex post studies;
2. Compare direct and indirect benefit and cost between projections and
realisations.

Financial actions:

1. Redesign of price schedules if justified;
2. Detailed analyses of profitability from the client's viewpoint.

Environmental actions:

completion of analyses of long-term monitoring data.

Social actions:

1. Execute formative social evaluation studies and feed information
back to construction and operation stages;
2. Execute summative social evaluation studies as a final judgement of
the project.

B. PRESENTATION OF RESULTS

30.   Clearly, the structure and content of the evaluation reports vary according to each of the steps defined above. Five types of reports will be sketched here, the correspondence between the steps of the evaluation and types of reports being as indicated in Table 1.

31.   "The preliminary evaluation report" corresponds to the case of a completely new project, for which only a minimum of studies has been done, and a minimum of data has been gathered.

"The examination of variants report" corresponds to the stage where the decision to undertake the project has in fact been taken but no technical choice has been made. The problem is precisely to make the choice in the best possible way.

The report on "the selection of variants" has fundamentally the same purpose as the preceding report. But the studies are far more in depth and elaborated.

"The final ex ante report" corresponds to the stage of the "feasibility study". It describes the choices which have been made, and their expected consequences. It will be the basis of comparison for further ex post studies.

"The ex post evaluation report" has two purposes: first to examine all possible discrepancies between forecasts and observed trends, and analyse their sources and consequences. Second, to prepare proposals for any decision of changing the plan previously adapted, in order to adapt it to new circumstances.

32.   In Annex I, the reader will find sketches of such reports, as needed at the crucial steps of the project.

Table 1

CORRESPONDENCE BETWEEN TYPES OF REPORTS AND STEPS OF EVALUATION

Types of reports	Corresponding steps in Figure 1	Observations
Report type 1: Preliminary evaluation	1-2	Report necessary only for Step 1. Step 2 involves only action, without report.
Report type 2 Examination of variants	3-4	Report needed at the end of Step 3. Step 4 needs no report.
Report type 3: Selection of variants to be presented to the decision-maker	5	
Report type 4: Final ex ante report	6-7	Report normally needed at the end of Step 6
Report type 5: Ex post evaluation report	8-9	Several reports of this kind must be prepared during the life of the project -- in principle at the beginning of each major new set of works

Chapter III

BASIC FEATURES OF WATER PROJECT EVALUATION

A. THE WATER PROJECT

33.   The iterative planning process discussed previously finally converges
to a plan for a water project. Curiously, it is difficult to give a general
definition of a project, partly because of its imprecise use in the past. The
term has been used to describe a simple drainage ditch, and it has also been
used to describe a system of structures in large river basin developments, the
construction of which spans over decades.

Table 2

ECONOMIC ACTIVITIES THAT ARE USUALLY INCLUDED AS PART OF THE PROJECT

-- Building of main structures (dams, distribution system, flood walls, etc.)

-- Agriculture and forestry receiving water from the structures

-- Agriculture and forestry in areas benefiting from flood-control

-- Urban areas benefiting from flood-control, including industries

-- Generation of electricity for domestic consumption and industry

-- Creation of recreational areas

-- Supply of residential and industrial water

-- Creation of new transport facilities

-- Fisheries

-- Production of cooling water

-- Water storage for water quality management

-- Fire protection for urban and forested areas.

34. It is clear that nearly all water resource projects involve the building of physical structures such as dams, power plants, flood walls, and drainage systems. An equally important component of water projects is the set of operating rules and policies that govern the use of the physical structures and that often influence water user behaviour. Examples would be the set of operating curves used in managing a reservoir, rules for water releases to generate power, rules concerning the allocation of water during shortages, the pricing of project outputs, rules for the distribution of irrigation water, and concepts of property rights in the water provided by the project.

35. The geographical limits of a project should ideally be defined to include all areas physically affected by the project activities. For example, the reaches of a river downstream from a reservoir in which the flow regime is significantly affected should ideally be included in the project definition. Agricultural lands provided with irrigation water should be included, as well as other users of project outputs. The important point is that projects must be designed, evaluated, and managed in a systems context so that no important physical, economic, environmental, or social impacts are omitted. When all relevant impacts are taken into account, it is not important whether all the impacted areas are defined as being part of the project or not.

Table 3

ECONOMIC ACTIVITIES THAT MAY BE INCLUDED IN THE PROJECT
IF APPROPRIATE MARKET CONDITIONS DO NOT EXIST

Non-exhaustive list

-- Food industries using agricultural produce from the irrigated or flood-control areas

-- Electricity-using industries

-- Secondary developments using the recreational facilities, e.g. resorts

-- Industries using industrial water

-- Industries using waterway transport facilities

-- Industries using land-transport facilities arising from the construction of the project

-- Industries using cooling water

-- Transport, housing and social facilities needed for the workforce employed on the project

-- Transport, port or infrastructure facilities connected with the increase in activity induced by the project.

36. Another difficulty in defining the geographical limits of a project is that the impacted areas differ for economic, environmental, and social project effects. From an economic viewpoint, it is desirable to define the project in

such a way that there are well established prices for products and services flowing out of the project to the rest of the world and well established prices for the input resources flowing into the project. From this point of view, Tables 2 and 3 below suggest the kind of activities which could be included in a project.

37.   From the environmental and social viewpoints, it is desirable to include all significantly impacted areas, but these could include areas far downstream or areas physically disconnected from the main project structure which receive populations displaced by the project. Thus, practical limits dictated by the importance of impacts and by the jurisdiction of the project authority must be drawn.

B. MULTIPURPOSE PROJECTS: THEIR INCREASING IMPORTANCE

38.   Most modern water projects are multipurpose in nature, i.e. they serve several purposes or produce simultaneously several products or services. Table 4 lists most of the purposes found in various combinations in modern projects.

39.   The multipurpose nature of water projects results from four main factors:

   i) the nature of the demands by users for different combinations of water ouputs;
  ii) the economies of scale that result from building larger projects;
 iii) the technical complementarities that can exist between the processes for producing the different outputs;   and
  iv) the possibilities of risk pooling that are open by the existence of several outputs.

40.   As an example of the first factor, electric power may be needed along with irrigation water to pump and apply the water. Water for waste dilution may be needed along with industrial process water. The second factor is illustrated by the fact that adding a few more meters to the height of a dam may increase the storage capacity of the reservoir much more than proportionately, providing added storage capacity at relatively low cost. When the demand for one output is not sufficient to justify the higher dam, adding other purposes may do so. The third factor is illustrated by the seasonal provision of flood storage capacity in the reservoir which also serves to capture and store the water for later irrigation uses. Irrigation and hydro-electric power releases can be complementary where irrigation diversions take place below the dam and when the water and power peak demands coincide. Finally, in a quickly changing world, it must be recognised that the benefits and costs of different purposes are often negatively correlated. For instance, a forecasting error in the rate of growth of domestic water demand may be balanced by an error of the same magnitude, but of the opposite direction, on the agricultural water demand. This is an illustration of the fourth factor.

Table 4

TYPICAL PURPOSES (OUTPUTS) OF MULTIPURPOSE WATER PROJECTS

-- Irrigation water supply

-- Urban water supply, that is for industrial, residential and public uses

-- Management of flows for water quality control

-- Flood control

-- Hydro-electric generation

-- Inland navigation

-- Water related recreation

-- Fish and wildlife maintenance or enhancement

-- Fire protection.

C. MULTI-OBJECTIVE PLANNING: ITS INCREASING IMPORTANCE

41.   Collective actions are usually stimulated either through society's perception of a problem or through the identification of an opportunity to change the current state of affairs in a favourable way. Examples of common water problems are those of water shortages, floods, deteriorating of water quality, salinisation of soils through poor drainage, or unreliability of water supply. Opportunities for improvement through the development or improved management of water would include regional economic development, new or improved fisheries, the reclamation of lands for agricultural or other purposes from the sea or marshes, and the provision of recreational and aesthetic opportunities.

42.   While the distinction between problem and opportunity stimuli for water planning cannot be made with complete clarity, it does relate to the likely nature of the planning process. Problems are likely to be perceived first at the local level leading to a bottom-to-top sequence of planning activities. New opportunities are likely to be perceived at higher planning levels and are likely to lead to a top-to-bottom planning process.

43.   Regardless of the origins of planning activities, the resultant execution of plans will have impacts on society that can be classified into three categories: economic impacts, environmental impacts, and social impacts. The achievement of favourable effects in each of these categories are called society's objectives in undertaking water planning. That is, water plans will be evaluated in terms of their net effects on the economic, environmental, and social criteria held to be important to society. When plans are designed and evaluated in terms of more than one objective, we speak of multiple-objective planning.

44.   Regions in early stages of economic development tend to place primary emphasis on the maximisation of net economic benefits (i.e. benefits minus costs) as a criterion for the design and selection of projects. Assistance in overcoming national balance-of-payments problems may also be important. As regional incomes are raised, other criteria assume increasing importance: protection of the physical environment, health and safety, special benefits for poorer areas, etc. The application of multiple criteria to project identification, design, and evaluation is a practice of increasing importance and attention in nearly all countries. It raises many conceptual, empirical, and even political problems: What weights should be given to the various criteria? How are some criteria to be quantified? When there is no longer a single criterion for the value of a project, who should make the decisions about project selection and financing (1).

45.   It is important to keep in mind that multiple objective procedures are used because of our inability to place monetary values on all relevant impacts of water projects. Thus multiple-objective planning raises the problem of the tangibility of economic, environmental, and social impacts. For example, how can we compare an increase in regional income or other benefits expressed in monetary terms with a change in water quality, a change in river ecosystems, or the effects that forced migration will have on the population involved? Is it theoretically possible for a political process, whatever its form, to provide the planner with weights to use for the comparison of different impacts. However, it is assumed here that planning is an iterative process in which planners present alternatives to the political decision-makers who then feed alternatives to the political decision-makers who then feed back opinions to the planners for the elimination of some alternatives and the revision of others. This process emphasizes the importance of a continuing dialogue between the planners and the decision-makers during the entire planning process.

46.   During the course of this process, the role of the technical team consists in providing the necessary data. It is clear that responsible decision-making requires unbiased and highly competent analyses from the technical team since the decision-makers will seldom be able to check the data presented by the technical team. This emphasizes the need to establish the credibility of the technical team which can only be accomplished by unquestionably objective work over time.

D. DIFFERENT INTERESTS TO BE SERVED BY THE PROJECT

47.   There are several directly affected groups whose interests must be given special attention if the success of the project is to be assured:

    1. the users of water;
    2. the organisation distributing the water;
    3. secondary industries which provide vital inputs or services for the water users;
    4. users of the outputs produced by the direct water users;
    5. the state or province where the project is to be located.

48.   Let us illustrate the problems which can arise from insufficient attention to these groups. Regarding the first, numerous irrigation projects

around the world are underutilised because farmers have found it privately un-profitable to settle on project lands and to use project water. This can occur because farm budgets have not been accurately judged or because neces-sary services such as marketing and credit are not provided. Such failures are not limited to irrigation. The Owen falls hydro-electric project in Uganda failed to attract the industrial customers for which it was construc-ted, because the profitability of such private undertakings was not sufficient to attract private capital in spite of low power costs. The Mexican River basin development experiments in the Grijalvas and Papaloapan Basins failed to "take off" because private investment did not occur, leaving the large water projects underutilised.

49.   Organisations for distributing water or power from large water projects can be organised in different ways. In some cases they are created and con-trolled by the direct water users. In other cases, they are independent pri-vate organisations. Then, the organisations must be able to make a reasonable profit on their operations but must be prevented from exploiting their mono-poly position.

50.   The attractiveness of the project area to secondary activities which provide vital inputs or services must be carefully considered, for in their absence the direct water users may not be able to survive: irrigation pro-jects stand idle because farmers cannot get seed and fertilizers and because they cannot market their crops. Families have abandoned new irrigation areas because services and amenities have not been provided by either the private sector or government.

51.   Finally, the state (in Federal Countries) or provincial government must be convinced that the project will yield net benefits to their region. In terms of economic benefits, this will almost always be the case if the project passes the benefit cost test from a national point of view, for most of the benefit will accrue to the project area while some costs will be spread over the nation. However, the state or province might perceive large environmental or social costs associated with the project, such as the loss of a beautiful river valley or the displacement of many people.

52.   Each of these groups must have a part in the planning and execution of the project if the project is to proceed smoothly. This may require some spe-cific inducements such as the pricing of water somewhat below cost, provided the effects of such inducements do not have strongly unfavourable effects on income distribution, total project benefits and that the financial disparity suffered by some groups as a result can be compensated in the framework of these inducements.

E. TWO PRINCIPLES FOR EVALUATION

a) The "with-without" principle

53.   The basic principle of any type of project evaluation is the "with-without" principle: Puting this principle in operation implies that, we attempt to estimate the state of the world from the time of project construc-tion into the indefinite future as it will exist with the project in

existence, contrasting that state of the world with that which would have existed in the absence of the project. To state the principle makes clear the complexity of project evaluation, for we must attempt to foresee into the future, with and without the project, in all its relevant dimensions. While this simple statement conceals many complexities which the technical team must face, it still is a very useful concept to keep in mind to direct one's thinking. The decision-maker, when presented with parts of a project evaluation, by the technical team, can always ask himself or herself whether or not the data describe well the "with and without" situation.

54. To illustrate the principle (and to check our understanding of it), it is clear that a project evaluation is not simply a comparison of "before project conditions" with "after project conditions". Such a comparison would attribute the continuation of all pre-existing trends to the project itself. We now proceed to the basic questions which should be asked by the decision-maker about any proposed project.

b) The "natural units" principle

55. Evaluating a project implies handling a vast amount of data. It is impossible to list all the data in the evaluation report. Therefore, it must be consistently aggregated, in order to get only a few significant figures. The way in which these aggregations are performed, and the level of aggregation required, raises a serious problem. It has often been proposed to associate only one figure with a given variant of a project -- for instance, an internal rate of return, computed in such a way that it reflects the utility of this variant from the point of view of the decision-maker. Although such an exercise may be useful, in giving a very concise summary of all the works done during the evaluation process, it is never sufficient, and can be very misleading if these various aggregated quantities are not properly weighted. For this reason, it is necessary that, in the evaluation reports, main characteristic quantities be given in their natural unit, i.e. tons or m^3 of water, or number of people in such and such a place, etc. This point holds for the economic part of the evaluation report, but it is of particular importance for the social and environmental part, because of the absence of an indisputable method to attribute a price to the untangible effects of a project.

NOTE

1. These questions are referred to, especially, by the Water Resources Council, 1974.

Chapter IV

INSTITUTIONAL FRAMEWORK FOR THE
PLANNING AND MANAGEMENT OF WATER PROJECTS

56.   One of the most crucial sets of decisions to be made regarding water
planning is the establishment of an institutional framework within which water
planning and the management of ongoing projects are to take place. The institutional framework is understood to be composed of three major sets of elements:

     i) the "rules of the game":
       - national laws relating to water ownership;
       - national laws and regulations concerning authority for water
         planning and management.
    ii) the agency structure, including what agencies exist, their mis-
        sions, and the structure of authority (who can tell whom to do
        what);
   iii) the channels for communication with non-water agency groups inclu-
        ding decision-makers, parties directly affected by water develop-
        ment and management, and the general public.

57.   Once the institutional framework is determined, the quality and nature
of the planning effort is largely determined too. Naturally, the choice of
individual team members and team leadership will still be crucial, but the
setting in which they work can do much to encourage or discourage innovative
planning and efficient operations management.

A. PLANNING AS A LEARNING PROCESS FOR THE TECHNICAL TEAM, THE
DECISION-MAKERS, AND THE PUBLIC

58.   Whatever the institutional framework, it must be flexible enough to
accommodate for the learning process which will be developed further on. In
respect to this, it is important to take note that, if the technical team of
planners has been mentioned but not described in detail. The interests of
this document dictate that we concentrate on the team members representing
economics, environmental science, and sociology or its related disciplines, it
should be remembered that these specialists are in addition to the traditional
engineer and hydrologist team members who have been responsible for project
design in the past. Naturally, their inputs remain crucial and it is vital to

successful planning that the more recent team members learn to communicate and work with those colleagues.

59.   At the beginning of the learning process which is part of every planning task, the team members become conscious of each others' viewpoints and
learn how to work together. The essential part of this document is intended
to help all the team members understand the roles of the economists, environmental scientists and sociologists whose functions in the planning team are
still relatively new.

60.   But, the learning process does not stop there. As project alternatives
are planned in greater detail, new problems or obstacles may be discovered.
Indeed, just as the engineers carefully monitor the first works to verify
their estimates of the physical setting within which they work and to change
designs if necessary, the other team members must monitor all reactions to the
project proposal from the very beginning. These are economic, environmental,
and social reactions to the project concept, and, later, to the start of works
and operation. To adjust to such new information, the planning process must
remain flexible and must anticipate the need to change the plan right through
the construction stage.

61.   A major source of new information comes through public participation in
the planning process. The traditional engineering approach to planning assumed that the relevant expertise was found almost exclusively on the planning
team, and that the affected public should be educated to accept the proposals
of the planners. This approach has become much more flexible and planning in
all democratic societies is understood as an open process in which inputs from
the affected public are an important part. Recognition of this fact has made
the life of the planner more complex and less comfortable, but public acceptance is better because the projects are more clearly understood and better
adapted, even though some of their initial technical perfection may be lost in
the process.

62.   Public participation must begin at the problem definition stage, which
is very likely before water is even decided upon as a solution. We cannot
overemphasize the importance of the problem definition stage, for a misunder-
standing of the nature of the problem can turn the entire planning effort in
an inefficient or even damaging direction. Here, both planners' creativity
and public inputs are both necessary. For example, a situation first perceived as a drought may be more a matter of inappropriate cultivation of the
land or poor location of activities and population. The planning team must be
alert to these possibilities, and be capable not only of interpreting public
opinion but also of helping objectively to educate the public.

63.   Public participation educates the planning team as regards to both public values and public misunderstandings. It permits a two-way flow of information. It also allows the planners to engage tne public in partial responsibility for the project's success. Experience has shown this factor to be crucial and sensitive, but this is no reason why the experiment has to be given
up.

64.   A second continuing dialogue with two-way educational value must be
that between the technical team and the decision-makers (or their representa-
tive) (1). The two-way flow of weights for the several objectives and of information about project alternatives is a vital part of the learning process.

65.   The learning process discussed above continues all through the project's construction and operating life. Monitoring during the operating life
alerts project managers to needed adjustments in operating rules and, eventually, helps to improve planning procedures. This important process is called
ex post analysis and should always be allowed for: this implies that quantifiable indicators should be established as well, at the implementation stage
of the project and this is of capital importance, the possibility of measuring
human and equipment resources.

B. CHOOSING THE INSTITUTIONS

66.   The optimum institutional framework will obviously differ from country
to country, depending on the culture, history, and level of development, it
may also differ from region to region. While there is no uniquely optimal
framework to be recommended, it is possible to give some general guidelines or
criteria for the selection of appropriate institutional frameworks. These are
listed below in Table 5.

Table 5

GUIDELINES FOR CHOOSING THE INSTITUTIONAL FRAMEWORK

1. Does the institutional framework permit the consideration of a wide range
   of alternatives, once it has been decided that water can efficiently contribute to problem solution?

2. Will the planning agency (or agencies) involved have the expertise needed
   for multiple objective design and evaluation procedures, especially in the
   economic, social and environmental fields?

3. Does the institutional framework permit and stimulate adaptation of plans
   to changing national and local priorities?

4. Does the institutional framework permit and stimulate the representation of
   the interests of all parties affected by water development and management?

5. Does the institutional framework reward initiative and innovation among the
   members of the technical team and within co-operating agencies?

6. Is the technical team sufficiently free from day-to-day responsibilities
   that they can concentrate on long range planning and anticipation of future
   problems?

7. Do the institutions have the capacity for learning and improving the project over time, including sufficient continuity over time and the utilisation of ex post project analyses?

8. Is there sufficient authority within the institutional framework to enforce
   conformity with construction and operating plans once they are made?

9. Is the institutional framework capable of guaranteeing an acceptable minimum level of professional performance by the technical team?

67.   Most of these guidelines are self-explanatory and have evolved from the experience of water planners in various countries (2). Point 4 re-emphasized the important role of public inputs. Point 6 emphasizes the need for planners to be sufficiently free from daily tasks to give extended consideration to long-term problems, an obvious but often neglected point.

68.   Point 7 raises the complex issue of improving planning and management over time through feedback from monitoring and ex post studies. A central issue here is the continuity of the planning efforts and the technical team. There are definite advantages in establishing long-service teams whose members accumulate experience and learn to work smoothly together. However, planning of large projects may only occur from time to time so that it may not be prac- tical to maintain the team after completion of the project. In such cases, definite allowance should be made for the recording and analysis of all as- pects of monitoring and of all ex post evaluations in a form readily available for planning personnel and future training seminars.

69.   Point 9 arises from the fact that it is not always possible to obtain the best personnel, the most capable and energetic for work on technical teams. Even the more energetic team members may find it difficult to work effectively together. Thus, the selected team leader and other oversight arrangements must be capable of monitoring the planning effort, getting out- side evaluations if needed, and enforcing a competent level of planning in more specific cases.

70.   The technical team is best recruited from the project region, although this depends on the availability of qualified personnel and the importance of experience within the region. The planning of large projects is often a co- operative venture among national, provincial, and local authorities, so ex- perts from national agencies may be loaned to the technical team for various periods of time.

71.   Experience has shown that it is useful to establish various advisory groups which can monitor and assist the technical planning team. Especially useful are the following:

    -- "an advisory team" of experts;
    -- a "steering committee" primarily from the national level; and
    -- a "political linking committee".

The "advisory team" provides periodic outside review of the planning effort and can act in a consulting capacity to the technical team. Its membership may include highly qualified and experienced persons who cannot take the time to serve as permanent technical team members. The existence of such a group often adds credibility to the technical team's work and the project. The function of the "steering committee", appointed primarily from the national level, is to judge whether or not the proposed regional developments are in keeping with national priorities and objectives, particularly in terms of the major functional areas such as agriculture, transport, health, etc. Finally, helpful linkage to the decision-makers can be provided by a committee of mem- bers of the relevant legislative committees at the national level and regional or provincial political officials. This provides the technical team with in- formation on the weights likely to be given to the various objectives in the evaluation of alternatives by the political process, and permits the technical team to inform the decision-makers of the range of available alternatives (Figure 2).

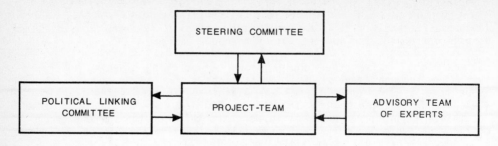

Figure 2. **RELATIONSHIP BETWEEN VARIOUS CELLS IN PROJECT ORGANISATION**

Figure 3 **POSSIBLE MATRIX STRUCTURE OF A MULTIPURPOSE HYDRAULIC PROJECT**

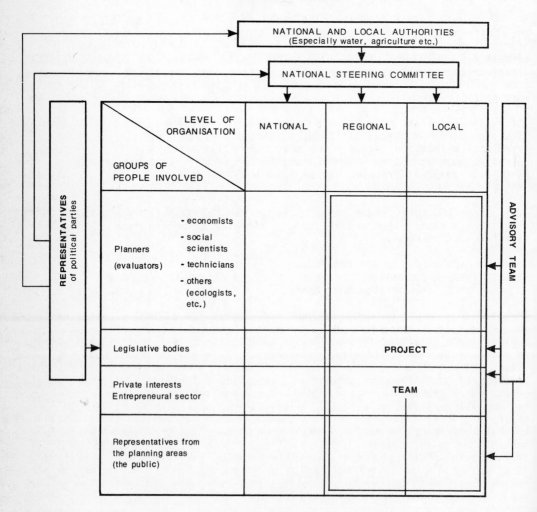

72.   Social scientists can translate these rules into the form of an organisation matrix that might have the following schematic appearance (Figure 3). The kind of relationships between groups or individuals described are likely to evolve through time: Depending on the planning stage different persons or groups of people will gain power, enter the project or have to play a dominant role for some time; in this respect this organisation can be called semi-permanent.

73.   The questions discussed above are concerned with the internal organisation of the project. In addition, care must be taken with regard to the insertion of this structure (and of the project itself) within the existing institutional framework. In this respect, Table 6 provides a list of guidelines, which are self-explanatory.

Table 6

INFORMATION AREAS TO BE COVERED FOR INSTITUTIONAL
ARRANGEMENT PURPOSES

Socio-economic structure

General structure of private and public enterprise in the region
System of land tenure
Credit institutions
Possibilities of land redistribution
Income distribution
Services provided in relation to beneficiaries of the project (frequency,
    payments by the users, maintenance responsibilities)
Agricultural extension services

Political structure

The planning structure of the region in which the water-planning has
    to be done
Water laws and regulation
Tax systems

Socio-cultural structure

What are the attitudes of people to water? Meaning of water from a
    hygiene point of view (in particular, are health problems linked with water,
    such as Malaria, recognised?); significance of water in relation to its use
    and to its physical allocation (e.g.: a well is often a social gathering
    place for women)
Patterns of leadership, authority and time budgets of the people in
    the planning area

Planning structure

What are the planning officers already operating in the planning
    area?
What are the planning approaches of main legislative bodies
    (e.g. centralised or indicative planning, etc.?)

C. SELECTING THE MEMBERS OF THE TECHNICAL TEAM

74.   Devising an imaginative yet relevant range of alternatives, designing these alternatives, and evaluating them as accurately as time and resources allow requires creativity, hard work and objectivity. Maintaining good communications and relations with the relevant decision-makers and the public is even more difficult. Hence, the selection of the team is a critical step in any project.

75.   It is difficult to give general guidelines for the personal qualifications of the technical team members. It is clear that persons with recent training in the techniques of micro and regional economic analysis, financial management, the environmental sciences, and sociology or its closely related disciplines must be present on the team, in addition to the traditional engineering and hydrologic skills. These skills are not enough, however, for experience in water planning within the particular cultural and political milieu is equally essential. These characteristics can rarely be found contained in the individual, and it is therefore necessary to unite several.

76.   The theories and methods of analysis in the environmental and social fields, especially, have been advancing so rapidly in the past few years that recent training must be emphasized. Naturally, this need not mean formal degree programmes but could consist of short courses, part-time studies, or even self-education. It is usually not sufficient that a person has gained a bureaucratic title of economist or environmental specialist by virtue of time in service, although such persons may be valuable members of the team in terms of practical applied knowledge.

77.   In establishing water planning teams, attention must be paid to the opportunity costs of team personnel, i.e. their importance to their present agencies and the costs that will be imposed on those agencies when skilled personnel are pulled away. Especially when interest in water planning has been created by a water crisis of some type, it is tempting to establish some type of "super agency" outside of the usual governmental constraints on personnel, salaries, etc., which can operate more freely and quickly and can attract exceptional personnel from other agencies. While this can work well indeed for the water sector, it can impose excessively high costs on other agencies.

D. MAKING USE OF FOREIGN EXPERTISE AND PRIVATE ORGANISATIONS

78.   For some countries, there remains the question of international participation in the planning of water development. If domestic expertise is lacking, it may be desirable to obtain assistance from one of the international organisations or on a bilateral basis. If international financial sources are to be used, the financial institutions may insist on providing some inputs into and review of the planning process.

79.   Such aid in advancing planning capacities can be valuable, but its use should be considered as part of a longer term training process and not simply for the drawing-up of one isolated plan. It is important that the external

experts work closely in a training capacity with the domestic technical team so as to guarantee an effective transfer of skills. Many bilateral and international planning projects have resulted in the domestic team being pushed aside, with the result that little expertise is transferred, little understanding of the plan is locally available, and that the experience gained is drained once the external experts leave.

80.   Finally, consideration should be given to the role of the private sector in water planning, development and management. In the early stages of the economic development of well-watered regions, most water development may be by private actions, and the resultant systems and structures may continue to be privately managed. However, most water development today is undertaken by public agencies because of the expense of the development and the high degree of interdependence with other projects. However, private agencies are able to play very useful roles as consultants in specialised areas such as computer model building, the design of data management systems, and other specialised parts of the economic, financial, environmental, and social analyses.

81.   Private organisations are very often the major purchasers of project water and power and very often take responsibility for the distribution of these outputs. Private irrigation districts, municipal water companies, and electric power companies are often already in existence and can efficiently handle distribution and its funding, taking a large burden from the public sector water agencies. Such organisations must not be allowed to profit unduly from monopoly positions, but they are frequently organised as co-operatives owned by their customers or are regulated by local government authorities, which minimise the above mentioned expenses.

NOTES

1.   For example, the team may not be able to meet with the parliamentary committee responsible for public works, but it surely can have continuing contact with the professional staff of that committee. In such cases, it is essential that no distortion should occur in the transmission of ideas and concepts. For important projects, however, the use of intermediaries is out of the question.

2.   This set of guidelines was developed by an international conference of water planners held in Vancouver, British Columbia, Canada in 1975.

Chapter V

THE INTEGRATION OF MULTIPURPOSE HYDRAULIC PROJECTS
INTO NATIONAL AND REGIONAL PLANS

82.   Water project planning always takes place in a larger setting in which plans are being made for different sectors (e.g. education, health, transport, agriculture) at different levels (e.g. local, river basin, provincial, regional and national). The evaluation of such projects should fit into existing planning schemes and, by a two-way dialogue, fit in with the objectives of such plans. Water projects should be physically consistent with the other sectors, and, in most cases, should reflect similar objectives.

83.   Water project planning also takes place within existing institutions and planning procedures. The idea of a technical team of the type recommended here may be totally new. Once the team has been established, it will have to work with the existing water agencies and other planning groups from other sectors and at higher levels. Thus the team seldom starts with a carte blanche to proceed just as it likes. It may have to try to change the surroundings within which it works, and it will always have to work hard at establishing its credibility with other agencies, the decision-makers, and the public. In the long run, this will be established by establishing an open and unbiased planning process.

84.   Several preliminary steps which are vital to the integration of water project planning must be taken before technical planning begins. These are discussed below.

A. PROBLEM DEFINITION

85.   Problem definition has typically been ignored or faced too late in water project planning, often with disastrous results. Too often, the planning process has started with the material means (specific resource systems) and procedures for harnessing those means, followed by an after-the-fact definition of problems which those means and procedures might help to solve. For example, the massive Mekong Basin programme once planned for Southeast Asia had as its goal the development of the water resources of the basin, under the assumption that the peoples' problems which might be ameliorated by water development would become obvious. This traditional approach offers little opportunity for an efficient approach to problem solving and increases the

44

probability that unpredicted harmful impacts will be experienced since the real nature of the social problems has not been analysed.

86.   The initial definition of problems should not be confined to or even biased towards problems with water. Rather, the real problems which people are encountering should be defined: rural poverty, inequitable access to land or other resources, heavy migration, unemployment, excessive dependence on other regions or countries, low productivity, political tensions, environment-ally related health problems, etc. Water planners cannot solve most of these problems, but they can propose projects that would help. In some cases it may be that water projects are an efficient, least cost way of achieving the desired result. In other cases, they will be ruled out.

87.   Once the problem has been defined, a wide range of alternative solu-tions must be considered, some to do with water development. It is clear that traditional water resource agencies do not have the capabilities or the moti-vation to undertake such broad investigations of problems and solutions. It is crucial, therefore, that provisions be made for such broad planning activi-ties at a higher level, and that the water development programme be required to follow the priorities and opportunities identified in this way. At this level, problem evaluation and national planning are concepts which are closely linked even though different.

B. INTEGRATION OF WATER RESOURCES PLANNING WITH NATIONAL AND REGIONAL PLANS

88.   It is obvious that water resource planning does not take place in a vacuum. In part, it must respond to the needs of the other sectors of the economy and, in part, it will initiate original projects intended to promote regional improvement. In both of these functions, water development and the operation of existing systems must be consistent with activity levels of other sectors, with the development plans of other sectors, and with the availabi-lity of capital at the national level.

89.   The natural geographical area for detailed water planning and manage-ment is the river basin because of the hydrologic interdependence of all acti-vities taking place in such a basin. Planning for other sectors (e.g. trans-port, industry) may more naturally relate to other regions corresponding to traditional political sub-divisions, areas sharing common problems, or econo-mically highly integrated areas. Thus, water planners, while utilising the river basin as the basic planning area, will have to co-ordinate their activi-ties with planners and managers at various levels of government and from dif-ferent geographical areas. A schema for the required interactions is shown in Figure 4.

90.   At the macro economic level, the first problem is the determination of total capital availability for development and replacement purposes. These calculations must be based not only on the national level of saving and avail-able international resources but on the acceptable values for inflation and business cycle activity. All these considerations are usually translated into capital and recurrent budgets transmitted in draft to the ministries or de-partments in charge of sector plans.

91.   Sector plans (e.g. agriculture, the various major industries, transport, education, etc.) are formulated in keeping with the national objectives,
consistency among target output levels and required inputs, and with the in-
corporation of new activities proposed by the ministries themselves. At the
same time, these sector plans are being broken down into regional sector plans
which must be checked for consistency within each region. Regional proposals
for new undertakings are added in draft form, and interactions continue among
these three levels until consistent regional plans have emerged, usually expressed in terms of sectoral operating and capital budgets.

92.   At the river basin level, the first task is to make the various projects compatible: for instance, a project which consumes irrigation water at
the origin of a river may be damaging for already existing irrigation systems
downstream simply because it will increase the salinity of water. But, of
course, at any time, the selected projects must also be compatible with the
limits fixed by national and regional plans for the total amount of investments and for the demand for water. This can be done by making an inventory
of proposed projects, from which those which do not meet the requirements thus
defined are progressively eliminated. This raises the question of identifying
alternatives at the river basin level.

C. IDENTIFYING PROJECT ALTERNATIVES AT THE RIVER BASIN LEVEL (1)

93.   The most important point in project identification is to consider initially the broadest possible range of alternative ways of achieving the goal.
It is essential not to be bound by traditional ways of doing things. For
example, if water is to be supplied to a town, the alternatives will include
surface water, ground-water from shallow wells or boreholes, construction of
home cisterns for catchment of rainwater, trucking in water, and so on. A
good study of the alternatives may indeed show that some agency other than
your own should undertake the job. The best design work and most careful
selection of projects from among the alternatives considered can still be bad
planning if an imaginative range of alternatives has not been carefully considered. A very good example is provided by Davis in connection with plans for
water quality management in the Potomac Estuary (DAVIS, 1968). The United
States Army Corps of Engineers had carefully designed an extensive system of
mainstream and tributary reservoirs for low flow augmentation as a means of
controlling water quality during low flow periods. A great deal of effort had
been made to optimising the features of the reservoir system: locating and
sizing dams, developing operating rules, and so on. Yet many alternative or
complementary technologies that might have been incorporated in the system
were not considered: higher degrees of treatment, use of high-operating/
low-capital cost treatment plants, bypass piping to transport wastes to points
where the assimilative capacity of the estuary is greater, in-stream reaeration, and so on. By considering these alternatives, Davis was able to design
alternative systems for meeting the dissolved oxygen (DO) targets at costs far
below that that was first envisaged. Naturally, the range of alternatives to
be considered tends to be restricted by two considerations:

    a) The definition of responsibility or competence of the agency within
       which the planner is located, and
    b) The nature of the problem that has led to the planning activity.

The first point is one that must be overcome if we are to have good public planning. If a water agency planner is led to consider solutions to a problem and if in the course of his investigation he concludes that schools, health programmes, or agricultural programmes would be more efficient ways of solving the problem, he ought to be rewarded for saying so, even if his recommendation may mean a lower budget for his own agency. Unfortunately, the reward structure seldom operates in this way.

94. What methods for generating alternatives are available? Clearly, no mechanical procedure can substitute for imagination and human creativity. One approach which has proved useful is that of creating a benchmark project design, typically a design which maximises quantifiable economic benefits subject to minimal environmental and social constraints. Alternative designs are then constructed as variants from this benchmark design, each variant placing greater weight on some criterion other than net economic benefits, conceptually by redesigning under tighter environmental or social constraints. Nonetheless, the consideration of a wide and imaginative range of alternatives is considerably stimulated if an independent evaluation and review function has been established.

95. One type of alternative that is frequently overlooked is the possibility of the joint management of surface water and groundwater. There are many opportunities for using the natural filtration and storage capabilities of the soil and underlying aquifers as part of a larger system. Aquifers can be used for seasonal storage either through natural or artificial recharge. Recharge areas can be flooded during periods of excess stream flow, groundwater then being pumped during the dry season instead of building more dams. This saves evaporation losses and can greatly reduce costs. Canals are purposefully left unlined in some areas so that canal losses recharge the aquifers. Water quality can also benefit from joint management, as in the case of sewage disposal through irrigation of field crops and forests.

96. As a further example, the alternatives for residential water might include additional surface development; ground-water development; desalination; importations from another basin; buying up agricultural water rights; better system maintenance; raising the price of water to reduce existing uses; circulation of cooling water; encouraging lawn and garden styles that require little watering; requiring water-saving types of appliances (toilets, washing machines, and so on) in new or renovated buildings; reclamation of waste water; dual water systems providing both low and high quality waters. A flood control plan that failed to consider flood proofing of buildings, floodplain zoning, improved warning and evacuation systems, and the possible use of flood insurance would very likely fall far short of the best possible plan.

97. Non-structural measures are likely to be part of any project alternatives. Zoning can play a role in such varied problems as flood damage control, water quality management, and the control of water demand. The price of water always influences its use more or less strongly according to its quality but it can only be adjusted over longer time intervals to influence demand. Requiring particular technologies in industry, residential and agricultural water uses can be used to affect demand and water-borne waste loads. Care must be taken, however, that such steps are used in economically efficient ways so that costs are not simply transferred from the water sector to other sectors.

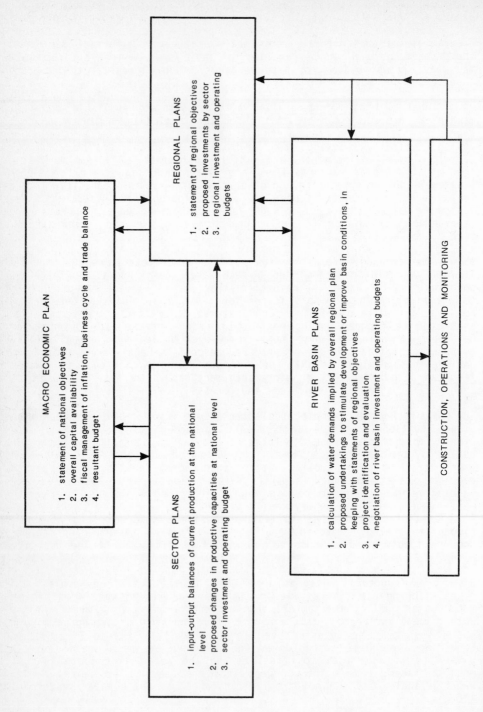

Figure 4 **DIFFERENT PLANNING LEVELS AND THEIR RELATIONSHIPS**

MACRO ECONOMIC PLAN

1. statement of national objectives
2. overall capital availability
3. fiscal management of inflation, business cycle and trade balance
4. resultant budget

SECTOR PLANS

1. input-output balances of current production at the national level
2. proposed changes in productive capacities at national level
3. sector investment and operating budget

REGIONAL PLANS

1. statement of regional objectives
2. proposed investments by sector
3. regional investment and operating budgets

RIVER BASIN PLANS

1. calculation of water demands implied by overall regional plan
2. proposed undertakings to stimulate development or improve basin conditions, in keeping with statements of regional objectives
3. project identification and evaluation
4. negotiation of river basin investment and operating budgets

CONSTRUCTION, OPERATIONS AND MONITORING

98.   _Local people and organisations may have many ideas about productive_
project possibilities. Some will know the area and its geology and hydrology
well. Others will be aware of existing water related problems and unmet water
demands. Thus opportunities for public suggestions may have a high payoff for
the planner. Care must be taken, however, to screen out narrow special interest projects which may be highly undesirable from a broader point of view.

D. SCREENING OF ALTERNATIVES: A NON-TRIVIAL TASK

99.   Let us suppose that we are starting to plan an undeveloped river which
has 20 potential reservoir sites of two possible sizes each (2). Ignoring all
the design variables whose values are needed to define operating rules and
targets for water supply, recreation and power, there would be 3^{20}-that is
3.5 x 10^9 possible configurations of the fully developed system. Even if
professional judgement could eliminate 99.9 per cent of these alternatives
(leaving 3.5 x 10^6), an analysis of the remaining system configurations requiring one minute of computer time per alternative would require 6.6 years of
computer time! Thus it is clear that the screening process by which bad
alternatives are eliminated and reasonable ones are identified is not a trivial task.

100.   Screening can be approached in two ways: through informal application
of engineering and economic judgment, or through the construction and application of highly simplified analytical optimisation models (3). Such models
must be computationally feasible and capable of screening out all but a few
system alternatives which then must be studied further. It is not possible to
include in such models many potentially relevant features of a basin and its
hydrology, so that solution of such models cannot be guaranteed to be the optimal design for the system. Experience has shown, however, that models can
be formulated which are adequate to screen out the majority of inefficient
storage projects, leaving detailed project and operating design to more accurate analytical models and simulations (4).

101.   On some occasions, it is possible and convenient to present the various
alternatives in the form of a matrix structure. This matrix structure can be
represented by considering a cube with intervals marked along each of the 3
axes. Let the x-axis denote the different purposes (or outputs) of the project, the y-axis the various social objectives served by the project, and the
z-axis the various social groups of interest which support project costs or
benefits. This is pictured in Figure 5. Such an evaluation matrix would contain both quantitative and qualitative data, e.g. monetary benefits accruing
to local farmers, indexes of water quality, and statements such as "In the
best judgment of our ecologists, migratory wildlife will be injured by this
reservoir". Naturally, each country will determine for itself the categories
that are important on each axis, but the mode of presentation is quite general. Each project or project alternative will have its evaluation matrix and
it is the decision-makers' task to associate a social utility value with each
matrix so the projects can be ranked.

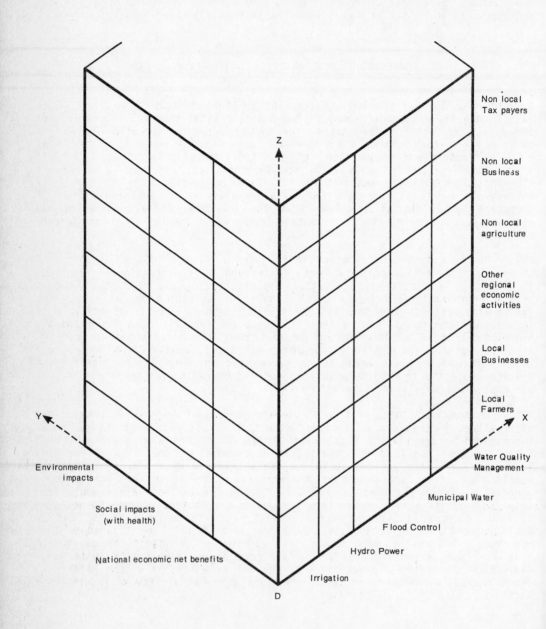

Figure 5 **MATRIX STRUCTURE FOR SCREENING OF ALTERNATIVES**

Non local
Tax payers

Non local
Business

Non local
agriculture

Other
regional
economic
activities

Local
Businesses

Local
Farmers

Z

Y

X

Environmental
impacts

Water Quality
Management

Social impacts
(with health)

Municipal Water

National economic net benefits

Flood Control

Hydro Power

D

Irrigation

NOTES

1. The word "alternative" as used here means a variant or another way of accomplishing the project objectives. It <u>does not</u> imply mutually exclusive variants.

2. Thus each reservoir could be omitted from the plan, constructed to size 1, or constructed to size 2.

3. See Jacoby and Loucks (1972) or Marks and De Neufville (1974).

4. See Acres (1972) or Loucks <u>et al</u>., (1969) or also Börlin (1971).

Chapter VI

RISK AND UNCERTAINTY CONSIDERATIONS IN   WATER RESOURCES PLANNING

102.   The planning horizon of any multipurpose project is long. This fact
implies that many unexpected events will occur between the time at which the
project is designed, and the time at which it is put in operation. In fact,
the only thing the project designer can take for certain is that his plans
will never be realised exactly as they were designed. The planner of a project cannot avoid considering this point. But how is he to cope with it?

Two ways are possible:

103.   i) When choosing between different projects, or different variants of a
project, it is not sufficient to consider only the expected outcome of each
project, or of each variant. In order to reach a sound decision, the risk,
associated with each alternative must be taken into account as well. This implies that a tradeoff must be established between the utility of the expected
outcome of each alternative and the degree of risk associated with them. Obviously, in such an approach the measurement of the "degree of the risk"
raises a problem as well as the determination of the tradeoff.

104.   ii) When designing each alternative, it must be recognised that, as
time will pass, some fresh information will be available, making it possible
to modify the initial plans so as to increase the benefit of the project.
This approach also raises several problems: how to keep the project flexible
enough to take advantage of these possibilities of modifications? How to take
account of these possibilities in the ex ante evaluation of the project?

A. MEASURING RISK AND UNCERTAINTY

105.   Setting up an index of risk or of uncertainty is not a trivial task.
In fact, even from a theoretical point of view, this problem is not solved in
the present state of the social and mathematical sciences. In principle, one
should at least distinguish between risk situations, for which a probability
law can be associated with each uncertainty variable, thus making the use of
probability calculus possible, and uncertainty situations, where the available
information is so poor that even a probability law is not available. The discussion of this distinction, and of its consequences are outside the scope of
this manual. In practice, the only convenient way of representing an

uncertain numerical result is to give together with the <u>expected</u> value of the result, the <u>range</u> within which the true value will stay under any reasonable assumption. This range is not necessarily an "absolute range", in the sense that it is not <u>absolutely</u> sure that the benefit of the project will stay within the range in <u>any case</u>. Obviously, such an absolute range would be meaningless -- often virtually infinite on each side. It is more convenient to evaluate the range within which the benefit of the project will stay with a high degree of likelihood -- say with a probability of 90 per cent, if the degree of likelihood can be expressed in terms of probability.

106. The determination of this range is difficult. The problem arises because it is necessary to start from the ranges of each basic data, and compound them so as to evaluate the range of the final outcome. Whenever probability distributions will be available for each basic data, it will be possible, at least in theory, to make use of probability calculus to estimate the range of the outcome at the project level. It is common knowledge, however, that, in many cases, even a probability distribution of the basic data is not available, so that the estimated ranges of the final outcome will rely upon a large amount of judgement and subjective impressions.

107. It is nevertheless important to point out an essential feature of multipurpose projects, as opposed to single purpose projects, in this respect: the range of the outcome of a multipurpose project is normally smaller than the corresponding figure in a monopurpose project, all other things being equal. This is explained by considering the values of benefits for each purpose of a multipurpose hydraulic project. Usually, their range will be relatively large. For instance, let us imagine that they are 20 per cent around the expected value. If the causes which are likely to produce a deviation from the expected values were common to all purposes, it is clear that the range of the total benefit of the project would have the same relative magnitude, that is, for our example, 20 per cent around the expected value. In general, however, these causes are not the same for all purposes. They will often be <u>independent</u>, in the sense that the occurrence of an event unfavourable to one purpose has no reason to be tied to the occurrence of another event unfavourable to another purpose. The range of the total benefit is therefore normally smaller in relative value to the corresponding range of the benefit for each purpose. In fact, the causes may be <u>negatively correlated</u>: for instance, a cause of failure for irrigation projects may be an unexpected rapid urbanisation of the irrigated area, which will convert the agricultural land into dwelling and recreational areas. But if the project is designed to supply domestic water as well as irrigation water, unforeseen urbanisation will result in an unforeseen increase of domestic water needs, thus raising the benefits from this latter purpose. The total benefit of the project may therefore remain unchanged, even though the agricultural purpose benefit will reach the lowest bound of its range, because the domestic water purpose will be correspondingly at its highest value. It is extremely important to take account of this process in evaluating the range within which the total benefit of a multipurpose project is likely to stay.

108. In this respect, it is essential to note that a mere <u>sensitivity analysis</u> will not suffice to provide a good account of the degree of uncertainty associated with a given project. A sensitivity analysis consists in computing the change in the outcome of the project which is produced by a given change in one of the basic data: Suppose for instance that the expected rate of return of a project is 15 per cent. If we consider that it will be lowered to

12 per cent by a 20 per cent increase of the cost of the manpower, and to 10 per cent by a 10 per cent decrease in the price of corn. Then, the sensitivity analysis of such a project may be presented as in Table 7 below:

Table 7

EXAMPLE OF SENSITIVITY ANALYSIS
In percentages

Nature of data producing the change	Percentage change	Corresponding change in the rate of return	Value of the rate of return associated with the change in the basic data
Cost of manpower	+ 10	- 3	12
Price of corn	- 10	- 5	10

109.   Such a table enables readers to identify the "key variables" upon which the rate of return relies. Obviously, in the example above, the rate of return is more sensitive to the price of corn than to the cost of manpower. But this table is by no means an indicator of the risk associated with the project. If the price of corn and the cost of manpower are negatively correlated, (i.e. if the cost of manpower is low, then the price of corn is probably high), it is likely that if the cost of manpower is near its upper bound, the price of corn will probably be near its lower bound and the rate of return of the project will probably be closer to 8 per cent than to 12 per cent. Conversely, if the two variables are positively correlated, when the price of corn is at its lowest value, the cost of manpower will also be at its lowest value and it is very probable that the rate of return will be above 12 per cent. Sensitivity analysis does not provide a sufficient ground for estimating the range of variation associated with the expected outcome of a project. It is therefore recommended that the more sophisticated techniques be used in evaluating the degree of uncertainty of a project. The "Monte-Carlo" method (using correlation between variables), or the building of a general simulation model of the project can be envisaged for this purpose (1).

110.   It should be noted that the notion of expected value itself is not so clear as it might seem. There are at least, two possible ways to define it, either:

  i) The mathematical expectation, i.e. the sum of each possible actual value, weighted by the probability of occurrence of each of these values, or
  ii) The "Most likely values" i.e., the value with the highest probability of occurrence.

111.   The two concepts are not identical (2). In practice most of the computations are performed using the most likely values of the data. Moreover, as it has been already said, estimates of the probability laws of most of the basic data are not available, so that it is not, in general, even feasible to

perform full mathematical expectation computations. For these reasons, it is recommended that the various outcomes of a project be estimated in terms of "most likely values" -- it being understood that this "most likely value" is often smaller than the "expected value" owing to the dissymmetry of the probability distributions.

B. THE COST OF REDUCING RISK

112.   From a general view point a highly predictable situation is preferred to one in which the outcome can vary according to chance. If two investments each had most likely rates of return of 20 per cent per year but the first had a range of possible variation from 15 per cent to 25 per cent while the second had a range of 18 per cent to 22 per cent, the second would be chosen by most investors, but not necessarily by all. In the context of some situations, the first investment might be more attractive. For example, if the 25 per cent rate of return is in fact achieved, the profits might make it possible to finance other desirable undertakings which would otherwise be impossible.

Figure 6 **COST OF A DAM AS A FUNCTION OF THE PROBABILITY OF MEETING A GIVEN ANNUAL DEMAND FOR WATER**

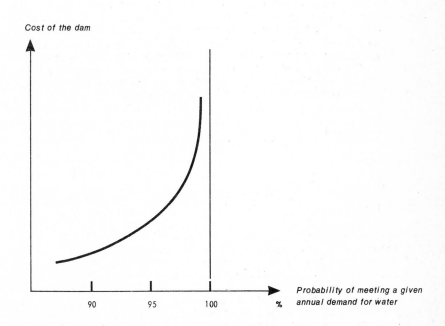

Cost of the dam

90   95   100

% *Probability of meeting a given annual demand for water*

55

113.   As another illustration of this problem, let us consider the question of designing a reservoir from which it is planned to withdraw each year a uniform quantity of water.   Since the inflows into either a surface or underground reservoir are random variables (3) the outputs of the reservoir, although modified in pattern so as to be of greater utility to society, are still random variables.   We must describe the water supplies, the hydroelectric power output, the recreational services of the reservoir pool, and the flood flows below the dam in probability terms, i.e. we must attach a level of reliability to them.   Usual engineering practice identifies some highly reliable level of output as the design capacity of the project, e.g. the rate of water withdrawal which we can expect to be met or exceeded in 95 years out of 100 years.   These practices may be too conservative for some purposes.   It can sometimes therefore be necessary, at an additional cost, to provide the reservoir with an over capacity.   But the cost of this over capacity rises very quickly as the degree of reliability increases, as shown in Figure 6.

114.   This analysis of hydrologic risk shows that the incremental costs of water supply from a specified river increases very sharply after some annual rate of withdrawal is reached, and that the costs increase with the level of reliability desired.   While hydrologic risks are usually taken into account, other sources of uncertainty which are equally important to the success of the project are often ignored or insufficiently analysed.   These are economic, demographic, social, and perhaps environmental uncertainties.   For example, when the demand for water is a forecast, the result is not just a number for a future date, but a range of possible values.   If demand for water is much lower than expected, the expected benefits will not be generated and the project will fail just as surely as if the dam fails to produce the expected water supply because of low inflows.   Many irrigation projects around the world sit unused not because of poor physical design or faulty hydrologic analysis, but because population failed to move into the area, or because social unrest and disease kept people from farming efficiently, because unanticipated plant diseases appeared, or because agricultural credit was not provided. Some of these problems occur because of bad planning and inadequate pre-project studies, but these variables will remain subject to some uncertainty even under the best planning.   This uncertainty must be acknowledged because unanticipated events can be very costly to the project (4).

C. STRATEGIES FOR REDUCING RISK

115.   What strategies are available to planners to reduce uncertainty and to deal with the remaining uncertainty?   The following steps or strategies have proved to be important.

116.   Risk pooling as described above (paragraph 40), is the most frequently recommended method.   At the level of a particular project, it is relatively easy to work with.   In such a case, however, it will only reduce risk, without eliminating it, because it is impossible to rely upon the law of large numbers.

117.   It has been suggested that this method be used at a national level.   In fact, if there are a large number of projects, for which the risks are independent, and if, benefits and costs are shared over the whole population,   in

such a way that no individual can suffer from the failure of one particular
project, then, it can be shown (Arrow and Lind, 1970) that the social disuti-
lity of risk tends towards zero. Assuming that these conditions are true,
decisions concerning projects should be made only on the basis of the mathematical expectations of benefits and costs, without considering their varia-
bility. This proposition is not likely to be fulfilled in practice. Firstly,
many uncertain parameters in a given project are highly correlated with those
of other projects. For instance, the cost of energy. Second, some individual
may suffer from the failure of a given project, without being compensated by
the success of another one.

118. One of the best ways to cope with the kind of risks faced by water project designers, is to keep the project and its operation flexible so that
beneficial responses can be made to new information about the project and its
setting. (See Walters, 1975.) This fact is illustrated by a simple example:
Suppose the expected discounted benefit of a project is 100, but may be reduced to 50 if the economic development is slower than expected. Two variants
are envisaged: Variant A consists of building one large dam, the cost of
which is 60, and which will have an excess capacity during the first 10 years
of the project. Variant B consists of building a first small dam at the beginning of the project, the cost of which is 40, and then, to build an additional dam after 10 years, when the capacity of the first one will be insufficient. The discounted cost of this second dam is 30. Clearly, if the demand
reaches its expected value, the benefit cost ratio of

variant A, $\frac{100}{60}$ = 1.666 is better than the ratio of

variant B, $\frac{100}{40+30}$ = 1.429.

This is due to the economies of scales associated with the big dam, despite
the fact it will remain underutilised during the first 10 years. But suppose
the demand reaches only its lowest possible value of 50. Then, the production
of the first dam of variant B will be sufficient to meet the demand, so that
the building of the second dam, is not necessary. Therefore, under this
assumption, the benefit cost ratio of variant B is $\frac{50}{40}$ = 1.25 whereas that of

variant A is $\frac{50}{60}$ = 0.833. The comparison of the two variants can be summarised

in Table 8 which shows clearly that variant B is safer than variant A.

Table 8

COMPARISON OF TWO VARIANTS OF A SAMPLE PROJECT

	Expect. benefit/ cost ratio	Minimum benefit/ cost ratio
Variant A	1.666	0.833
Variant B	1.429	1.125

119.   This over-simplified example captures nevertheless an essential feature of what is termed as "sequential decision-making": By delaying a decision until the necessary information can be available, it is possible to reduce risk, often (but not necessarily) at the expense of a reduction in expected value.

120.   How can this general idea be applicated to the design of multipurpose hydraulic projects? To answer this question, it is necessary to bear in mind the actual timing of any river basin project. The planning process is a step by step procedure, involving a preliminary project idea, a first set of decisions, a formative evaluation, a second set of decisions, etc., as shown in Chapter 1.

121.   The total process may last several decades, so that it is very probable that the "state of the world" at the end of this period will be quite different to that which could have been expected at the beginning. However, at each stage, a lot of options will be foreclosed: once a big dam has been built on a river, several small dams are no longer feasible. Conversely, if several small dams have been built, the construction of one large dam is still feasible but at a higher cost. The manner in which options progressively disappear is pictured in Figure 7.

122.   In estimating the "most likely" benefits from the decision taken at a particular step, it is obviously assumed that the future development of the whole hydraulic system will be undertaken according to "the most likely" on the basis of the information available at the time the decision is taken. But in estimating the lower limits of the range within which this benefit will stay in almost every case, it is necessary to take into account the fact that the actual sequence of events (procedure) will probably be different from the "most likely one".

Figure 7 **FORECLOSURE OF OPTIONS IN A SEQUENTIAL DECISION PROCESS**

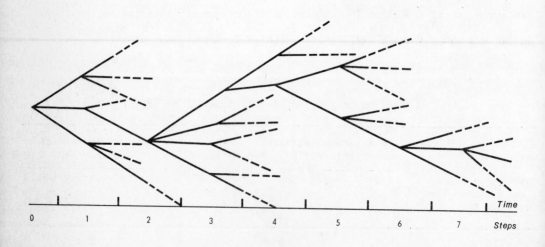

123. Very often, as was the case in the rough example which was given at the beginning of the present section, the solution which optimise the most likely benefit will not, at the same time, maximise the range of this benefit. On the contrary, it may happen that some of the solutions which are slightly sub-optimal from the point of view of the maximisation of the expected benefit, because of their increased flexibility, will have a much narrower range of possible benefits, and will thus be very much safer. As far as possible, it is preferable to consider such solutions as opposed to those which simply maximise expected benefits.

124. How can the preceding principles be implemented? First of all, they can be applied in an informal manner: pooling risks and keeping the project flexible may be done without formal computations, by mere common sense. For this is sufficient to keep the preceding developments in mind at each step of the designing process. These principles readily lend themselves however to econometric models and computer aided reasonings. The trouble, in this case, is that such models would be necessarily somewhat complicated. This is an un-fortunate feature of any reasoning involving probability calculus. To re-course to this powerful tool implies making use of notions such as conditional probabilities, integrals of functions, standard deviations, etc., which can be handled only by specialists. These aspects are outside the scope of this book and will therefore not be developed here (5).

NOTES

1. See Pouliquen (1970) or Reutlinger (1970).

2. Let us assume that the internal rate of return of a project is 10 per cent, 12 per cent and 15 per cent with probability, 0.5 0.2 and 0.3 respectively. The mathematical expectation of the rate of return is $10 \times 0.5 + 12 \times 0.2 + 15 \times 0.3 = 11.9$ per cent. The most likely value is 10 per cent.

3. That is to say variables whose values occur according to a probability law.

4. Examples of such studies (although not directly connected with water projects) can be found in Rasmussen (1974) (reprint in Zeckhauser, 1975). See also Kendall and Moglewer (1975).

5. However, it must be noticed that an article, published in Econometrica (Roberts and Weitzman, 1981) provides the same basic and useful guide-lines in this respect.

Part II

ECONOMIC CONSIDERATIONS AND FINANCING

Chapter VII

THE BASIC ECONOMIC QUESTIONS IN WATER PROJECT PLANNING

A. BASIC PRINCIPLES

125.   The decision-maker wants to ask the following fundamental economic questions about the project:

-- What is the net economic value of the project to the nation?
-- How does the project compare from an economic point of view with other projects which might be undertaken by the public sector?
-- How will the benefits and costs of the project be distributed among the various relevant sub-groups of the nation, i.e. who will enjoy the benefits and who will pay the costs?

126.   It is up to the economists on the technical team to answer these questions for the decision-makers, making clear the levels of uncertainty involved in their responses.   In doing so, it will be necessary to multiply quantities by prices.   Errors and uncertainties in both terms of the multiplication will result in errors and uncertainties in the final results.   It is therefore just as important to forecast the quantities as to multiply them by the relevant prices.   Unfortunately, it is difficult to give general rules for the estimation of the streams of input and output quantities flowing in and out of a project.   The only general principle in the field is the "with -- without" principle already stated (See paragraph 53).

127.   A part of the data (mainly, those concerning the inputs) will be supplied by the technical team of the project.   The remaining part will have to be estimated with the classical tools of economic forecasting and will therefore not be dealt with in this text.   The determination of prices raises however, specific problems which will be examined here.   The general framework for which are the general principles of benefit cost analysis.   Two of them are of special importance.

a) The Discounting Principle

128.   Since the utility of any quantity of any good is not the same when this quantity is available immediately or in a more or less remote future, a time decreasing weight must be applied to quantities obtained at different dates. It is usually assumed that the weights decrease exponentially with time, e.g.,

the benefit (cost) B obtained during year t is equivalent to the benefit (cost) $B(1+r)^{-t}$ obtained just now, r is called the discount rate.

From that principle, one can derive the expression of the Present Value of Net Benefits:

$$PVNB = (B_o - C_o) + \frac{(B_1 - C_1)}{(1 + r)} + \ldots + \frac{(B_n - C_n)}{(1 + r)^n}$$

where B_t and C_t are the benefits and costs in year t.

129.   Two or more projects can be compared in terms of the present value of their net benefits given in the preceding expression. It is often useful, however, to be able to rank projects in order of their rates of return for purposes of selecting the most productive ones to be undertaken within a limited investment budget. For this purpose, two indexes are used: the internal rate of return, ρ , and the benefit-cost ratio. The first is a percentage rate like 12 per cent while the latter gives the present value of net operating benefits per unit of capital in the initial investment. It is, therefore, a number like 1.1, 3.2 or 0.9, usually not very different from 1.

130.   To calculate ρ , one must simply solve the earlier PVNB expression for the r value which makes PVNB = 0. There may be several positive real solutions. This represents a conceptual difficulty associated with the notion of ρ . (In practice however there is seldom more than one practical solution.) The benefit-cost ratio, B/C, requires knowledge of the discount rate to be used and is usually given by:

$$B/C = \frac{\displaystyle\sum_{t = 1}^{n} (B_t - C_t)/(1 + r)^t}{C_o}$$

where C_o is the construction and start-up cost.

131.   There exists an extensive literature on appropriate choice of the discount rate (e.g. Little and Mirrlees, Marglin, Haveman, etc.), but it is sufficient to note here that each country has established some procedure for calculating an acceptable discount rate. Many countries today are using between 6 per cent and 8 per cent per annum, at constant prices.

b) The Shadow Pricing Principle

132.   Since the economic evaluation of a project has to be conducted from the point of view of the national community, market prices (either observed or predicted) do not always, reflect the social utility of inputs and outputs, as it would have been the case if the evaluation had been conducted from the point of view of a private firm. It must be stressed that shadow pricing is not mandatory. On most occasions, particularly in developed or semi-developed countries, and for certain commodities, markets are functioning well enough for these. For such countries and for these commodities, shadow prices are

simply identical with market prices. Thus <u>one attempts to estimate shadow prices and insert them in project evaluation only where market prices are strongly suspected of being inaccurate value measures.</u> The situations most frequently requiring the calculation of shadow prices are listed in Table 9:

Table 9

SITUATONS REQUIRING THE COMPUTATION OF SHADOW PRICES

Price	Situation
1. Wage rates	Where long-term unemployment exists
2. Imported and exported goods	Where exchange rates are in long-term disequilibrium
3. Farm commodities	Where tariffs and price support programmes maintain artificially high prices
4. Manufactured goods	Where monopoly restrictions on output keep prices artificially high
5. Pollution damages	Usually not counted as a cost beyond the costs of abatement equipment, but residual damages should be counted as a cost
6. Natural resources for which no market prices exist	Water in the stream often has no price even when being fully used downstream; recreation on water bodies often has no price
7. Discount rate	See text on paragraph 155
8. Any project output	When the change in output is large relative to the market, so that market price is significantly affected

B. RESULTS FROM THE ECONOMIC STUDIES

133.   According to the principles just stated, the computation of benefits and costs implies the following steps:

   i) Delimiting the extent of the project.
  ii) Estimating the physical quantities of inputs and outputs which flow out from and into the project, for each year within the planning horizon.
 iii) Multiplying these quantities by their prices, or eventually shadow prices.

iv) Summing up the discounted value of benefits (i.e. the value of commodities which flow out of the project) and of costs (i.e. the value of the commodities which flow in the project).

v) Computing the economic indicators associated with the project (i.e. the benefit cost ratio, the internal rate of return, or the net present value of the project).

134.   The results of these calculations can be presented for the whole project or they can be broken down according to suitable rules in order to show the main sources of costs and of benefits. Tables 10 to 15 can be filled in in this respect.

135.   Table 10 shows where the benefits come from. Headings of rows correspond to the purposes of the projects. The columns distinguish between the benefits arising from sales, both at nominal prices and at shadow prices, and the other benefits. The latter correspond in part to estimated consumer surplus and other benefits not having market price. Obviously, they have no nominal value, and cannot be estimated but at shadow prices value. Undiscounted values are shown, mainly because the decision maker needs to have an idea of the magnitude of the project, without being misled by the conventions associated with economic calculations. Discounted values are obviously necessary to perform the benefit-cost ratio computation. The residual value of equipment, the life of which is longer than the planning horizon, and the value of water downstream of the project (if any) have been added in the table, because they constitute the counterpart of costs included in Table 11.

136.   Table 11 shows how the costs are broken down by nature of works. Labour costs and purchase cost of commodities are distinguished, in order to make possible a comparison of several technical variants of the project, differing by the relative importance of the cost of labour and of other commodities. Costs from natural resources are included in the total cost.

137.   Table 12 indicates at what time costs and benefits occur. It is necessary for the computation of discounted values.

138.   Table 13 needs not to be filled in every case. It is necessary only if a detailed evaluation of induced benefits and costs prove to be useful. In that case, the headings of the various columns up to n must correspond to the definition of the activities or regional input/output table used to perform the analysis. Row totals must correspond to the corresponding figures in Table 12.

139.   Table 14 will be useful in comparing the benefits described in Table 10 to the corresponding costs of each project. It will have to be filled up during project design calculations since optimum project capacities require marginal benefits to equal marginal costs.

140.   Table 15 is to provide information about the physical quantities (expressed in tons, or cubic meters, or any other convenient unit) produced by the project at different stages of its development. During the initial stage (when the water works are not completed), during the development stage (before the full production is reached) and during the steady production stage. The time span of each of these stages is quite variable from project to project, and must be indicated in the headings. The productions are evaluated under the two hypothesis "with" and "without project". A percentage of increase

(ratio of the figure "with project" over the figure "without project") is computed. It is eventually infinite, if the quantity "without project" is zero. The list of commodities to be incorporated in this table depends obviously upon the nature of the project. Only the main commodities involved in the project need to be mentioned.

141. The data for filling in these tables is described throughout this chapter. In fact, each of them must result from a careful discussion of many data, and from numerous auxiliary calculations. Auxiliary tables, to be completed if necessary, are described in the remaining part of this chapter. Although net benefits of a multiple-purpose project normally exceed the total net benefits of several single-purpose projects, the work of evaluation must be completed for each purpose separately, since each of them raises special problems. After indicating the general principle for evaluating shadow prices, we shall review each purpose and the sources of difficulties associated with each of them specifically.

142. The preceding considerations apply to the evaluation of <u>direct</u> economic costs and benefits. It has been argued that, in addition, <u>induced</u> costs and benefits should be taken into account when deciding upon a project. In fact, with a small project and correct shadow prices, this should not in general be necessary. With a large project, or when the shadow prices are not correctly evaluated, evaluating induced costs and benefits may be desirable. But it is always a very difficult task. The problem is discussed at length in the OECD Guide for irrigation projects (Bergmann and Boussard, 1976).

C. PROJECT TIMING

143. A project yields benefits only insofar as it is used. If the demand for project outputs is growing over time, the more a project is deferred, the more quickly it is likely to be used to capacity, and the greater the benefits generated per time period of project life will be. Tending to offset this situation, however, is the simple fact that the present value of benefits diminishes as we push the project further into the future.

Thus there will be an optimum point in time to construct the project, it often pays to defer project construction. The nature of the problem can be examined by looking at Figure 8 and Figure 9. Figure 8 gives a pictorial representation of the effective degree of project capacity use if the project, the life of which is L years, were to be built at two different points in time, t_o or t_1. It shows that if the project is started at date t_o, it will be underutilised during most of its life, whereas if it is built at date t_1, it will be saturated at the very beginning of its existence.

144. Figure 9 has been drawn in the same way, except that the starting date varies continuously from t_o to t_1, and that the vertical axis represents the net present value of the whole project if it is started at the time indicated on the horizontal axis. The optimal starting date t^* can therefore be easily seen. This type of analysis should be carried out in principle for any project that will not be used automatically to full capacity from the start. The only exception, which can be important, concerns the situations in which the demand for the project output depends upon the completion of the same

Table 10

BENEFITS BROKEN DOWN BY NATURE OF OUTPUT
OVER THE PLANNING HORIZON

	Undiscounted nominal benefit from sales		Undiscounted benefits from sales at shadow prices		Undiscounted other benefits at shadow prices		Undiscounted benefits at shadow prices		Discounted benefits at shadow prices	
	Value	%(*)	Value	%(*)	Value	%	Value	%	Value	%
	(1)	(2)	(3)	(4)	(5)	(6)	(7)	(8)	(9)	(10)
A. Water										
a) Irrigation										
b) Domestic supply										
c) Industrial supply										
d) Cooling water										
e) Residual value of water downstream the project										
B. Electricity										
a) Domestic supply										
b) Industrial supply										
c) Energy value of water sold to electric producers										
C. Flood control										
a) Protected activities										
b) Expected decrease in losses from floods										
D. Transport										
a) Waterways										
b) Other transport facilities										
E. Recreation										
F. Other										
a)										
b)										
....										
G. Benefits from residual values at the end of the planning horizon										
TOTAL		100		100		100		100		

* Whenever shadow prices differ from nominal prices.

68

Table 11

COSTS BROKEN DOWN BY NATURE OF WORKS *
OVER THE PLANNING HORIZON

	Commodities bought from outside the project			Direct labour costs			Total	
	Undiscounted at nominal prices	Undiscounted at shadow price **	Discounted at shadow price **	Undiscounted at nominal price **	Undiscounted at shadow price **	Discounted at shadow price **	Undiscounted at nominal price	Discounted at shadow price **
	(1)	(2)	(3)	(4)	(5)	(6)	(7)	(8)
-- Investment costs								
-- Main civil works: Water works a b								
-- other a b								

-- Mechanical plants   a
  b
  .
  .								

-- Farms								

-- Industries within the project   a
  b
  .
  .								

-- Operating costs								
-- Main civil works								

-- Mechanical plants   a
  b
  .
  .								

-- Farms								

-- Industries within the project   a
  b
  .
  .								

Cost from natural resources								
TOTAL								

*   Rate of discount ...%.
** Whenever shadow prices differ from nominal prices.

Table 12

BENEFITS AND COSTS BROKEN DOWN BY YEAR OF OCCURRENCE

Years	Undiscounted				Discounted *	
	Value at nominal prices		Value at shadow prices **		Value at shadow prices	
	Costs	Benefits	Costs	Benefits	Costs	Benefits
Columns	(1)	(2)	(3)	(4)	(5)	(6)
1						
2						
3						
4						
5						
6						
7						
8						
9						
10						
11 to 15						
16 to 20						
25 to 30						
up to 30						
TOTAL						

* Rate of discount ..%.
** Whenever shadow prices differ from nominal prices.

70

Table 13

COSTS OF PURCHASED COMMODITIES BROKEN DOWN BY SUPPLYING INDUSTRIES (NOMINAL PRICES)

Columns	Purchased from				Labour		Total
	Branch 1	Branch 2	....	Branch n	Type 1	Type 2 ..	
	(1)	(2)		(n)	(n+1)	(n+2)	(m+1)
I -- Investment Costs Year 1 2 3 4 5 ...							
II -- Operating Costs Year 1 2 . . n							

71

Table 14

COSTS BROKEN DOWN BY PURPOSE OF THE PROJECT

	Nominal value undiscounted (1)			Nominal value discounted (2)			Discounted value at shadow prices * (3)		
	Investment	Operation	Total	Investment	Operation	Total	Investment	Operation	Total
A. Water									
Irrigation									
Domestic supply									
Industrial supply									
Cooling water									
B. Electricity									
Domestic supply									
Industrial supply									
Energetic value of water sold to electricity producers									
C. Flood control									
Agricultural area									
Industrial and urban area									
D. Transport									
Waterways									
Other transport facilities									
E. Recreation									
F. Other benefits a)									
b)									
TOTAL									

* Whenever shadow prices differ from nominal prices.

Table 15

MAIN PRODUCTIONS OF THE PROJECT
Average physical quantities per year

Commodities	Development stage of the project						
	Initial stage (years from: to:)			Development stage (years from: to:)			Steady state stage (years from: to:)	
	With project	Without project	% of increment	With	Without	%	With	Without	%

73

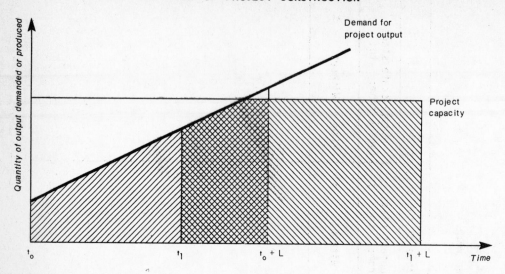

Figure 8 **THE DEGREE OF CAPACITY UTILISATION AS A FUNCTION OF TIME OF PROJECT CONSTRUCTION**

project: this is the case, for instance, for irrigation, because no one will pay for the various equipment linked with irrigation without being sure of the availability of water. In such cases, the project is unavoidably underutilised during the first few years of its life.

D. STAGING OF PROJECTS

145. In addition, one may notice that frequently, each project is one of a sequence of projects that will be built over time, and we have an option concerning how large (in terms of, say, the annual output capacity of the project) the projects in the sequence are to be built. An example would be building additions to the basic source of water supply for a growing city.

146. In determining how large to make each increment or project (and the timing of that increment), three basic facts are nearly always in conflict:

a) it pays to build large increments to the system because there usually are cost savings (economies of scale) involved in increasing project size;

b) the commitment of resources to a capacity that will not be used for a long time is costly. It pays to defer investment as long as possible since future costs are more heavily discounted than present costs;

c) maintenance of flexibility is important.

147. Thus a very small plant might not be optimal since small plants are likely to be high cost plants (in terms of cost per unit of capacity); but a huge plant, which has a low cost per unit of capacity, involves a huge

74

expenditure today and the carrying of substantial excess capacity for a long time (until demand catches up with capacity). The huge plant also locks us into a fixed technology for a long period of time.

148. The problem can be illustrated (1) by Figure 10. The size of the additions is specified as X_1 (smaller additions) or X_2 (larger additions). The growth of demand over time is shown. Thus two larger additions would provide the required capacity for about the same time period as three smaller additions. It has been assumed in the illustration that no shortage is permitted to occur, a policy that may make little sense in practice since occasional shortages during unusual drought may be much cheaper than carrying great excess capacity. (In water systems, the concept of shortage itself involves some very complex issues.)

149. What is desired is the timing and sizes of additions to the system that will meet the demands at a minimum present value of all costs. In some problems, permitting shortages to occur but attaching a penalty to any shortage makes sense. In general, an optimum solution to these sequencing problems is difficult to determine. Their solution usually involves the mathematical representation of the entire sequence of costs appropriately discounted, the solution being arrived at by methods of calculus or numerically on any digital computer.

150. Short of using the methods of modern operations research, the systems designer can attempt by trial and error to find a sequence of additions sized to minimise the present value of costs over some fairly short (10 to 20 years) time horizon. Clearly, if he is to find that sequence, the designer must have good estimates of:

    i) The growth path of demand;
    ii) The cost of additions as a function of the size of the additions; and
    iii) The appropriate discount rate with the appropriate risk allowances.

With these data at hand, approximately optimum solutions can be derived by trial and error methods.

E. CONSEQUENCES OF UNCERTAINTY IN DEMAND FORECASTS

151. The preceding considerations apply when future demand is known. Obviously, this is never the case: uncertainty about demand is usually the major source of uncertainty in project appraisal. What are the consequences of this fact for what has just been said?

152. A first approach would be to reason only on the expected demand, therefore, maximising, as indicated above, the expected benefit. But this course of action would be misleading whenever the failure of the project to meet actual demand would be catastrophic. This is the case, for instance, with domestic water supply: a shortage of domestic water in an urban area would entail dramatic social and often political consequences. How can the fact of avoiding these consequences be valued in a benefit/cost analysis?

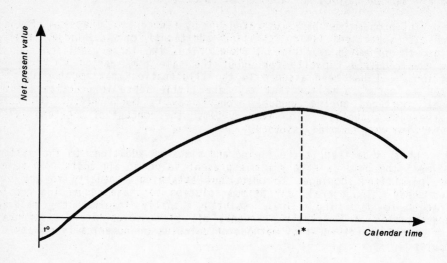

Figure 9 **PROJECT NET PRESENT VALUE AS A FUNCTION OF TIME OF CONSTRUCTION**

Figure 10 **THE SEQUENCING OF ADDITIONS TO A SYSTEM**

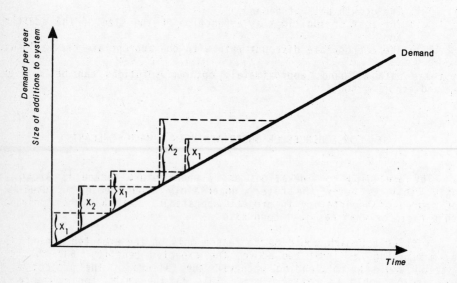

153.   The best way to cope with this problem is a special case of sequencial decision rule (see §119-124 above).   Instead of building one plan for the project in any circumstances, build a set of at least two plans: one for the case where the demand takes its most likely value, and one for the case where it takes its upper range value (eventually, some intermediate cases could also be considered).   The next step is to design the combination of alternative plans so as to maximise the expected benefit (2).

NOTES

1.   See Riordan (1971 a, b) for a particularly clear presentation of the sequencing problem in urban water supply.

2.   A real life example is provided in Howe and Cochrane (1976).   See also Hufschmidt and Fiering (1966, pp.77-82).

Chapter VIII

GENERAL TECHNIQUES FOR THE EVALUATION OF BENEFITS AND COSTS

A. GENERAL PRINCIPLES FOR COMPUTING SHADOW PRICES

154.   The general methods to be used for the computation of shadow prices are
described by various authors, among which Little and Mirrlees (1974),
Dasgupta, Marglin and Sen (1973), Lal (1975), Squire and van der Tack (1976),
Bruce (1976) and others. They need not be rediscussed here. Let us however
recall the main results:

a) The Discount Rate

155.   The discount rate used to compute the present value of the benefits and
costs may be thought of as either a shadow price -- the price of the capital
invested on the project -- or as a coefficient reflecting society's preference
for the present compared with the future. In both cases, it may be different
from the market rate of interest, and from the "opportunity cost of capital"
used for the public sector, which is determined by the rate of return of the
least profitable public project using up the available funds. In fact, it
should be fixed for the whole country by financial authorities, such as the
Ministry of Finance.

b) The Cost of Labour

156.   The employment of an additional worker for the project leads to various
consequences:

    i) Another segment of the economy is deprived of the corresponding
        labour force, so that some production (or at least, some leisure
        time) is lost for the Society;
   ii) If the income of the new employee is larger than what it would
        have been without the project, his consumption level will be in-
        creased. Hence additional commodities must be produced, which
        means an extra burden for the society;
  iii) One more job, and a larger income for one individual is a benefit
        for the society;
   iv) If a share of the additional income is saved, the net withdrawal
        project from the stock of available savings is reduced by the same
        amount.

The various formulae which have been proposed for evaluating the labour shadow price generally consist in an attempt to compute a weighted sum of these elements. In practice, however, the opportunity cost -- i.e., the loss of production which is associated elsewhere with the recruitment of one worker by the project -- remains the most frequent and the most reliable basis for reasoning. And, within a normal and well managed economy, this cost is simply equal to the nominal wage rate. Whatever formula is ultimately used, it should be noted that:

   i) Results for an engineer should be different when compared to those for an unskilled worker: It is therefore very misleading to make use of only one shadow wage rate. This is the reason for having mentioned several manpower categories in Table 13;

  ii) Because of the business cycle, results should be different for each year. In particular, if the economy of a given country is deeply depressed, so that the problem of the shadow wage rate is acute at the time the project is undertaken, an improvement in the situation may be hoped for a few years later. Consequently, in such a case, the shadow price of labour should progressively become identical to the nominal wage rate, as it is in the normal case. Thus although the adoption of a relatively low shadow price of labour may be justified for the investment phase of the project, the gap between the shadow price and the nominal price should disappear after a few years.

c) The Cost of Imported and Exported Commodities

157.   Whenever the exchange market is not free, the shadow exchange rate is obtained by dividing the value of exports, in national money, by the value of imports, in international currency. This gives the national cost of acquiring one dollar (1). However, there are complications due to the fact that international prices are not stable. Agricultural products prices in particular are determined in narrow markets subject to wide fluctuations. This is also true for products such as oil, whose price depends on both politics and on the discovery of new deposits. Yet the assumptions made about the prices of oil and agricultural products may have an absolutely decisive influence on the profitability of a multi-purpose hydraulic project. It is therefore essential to take account of price fluctuations in evaluating the benefits and costs of such projects and in particular not to regard the average market price recorded in the last few months before the project study as a definitive price which will remain stable for the next 50 years.

158.   Recommendations for taking account of probable price changes are:

   i) One should try to take fairly high values for the prices of the goods entering into the costs of the project and rather low prices for the goods which enter into its benefits;

  ii) One can go by the domestic production cost of substitution products. In particular, it may be desirable to evaluate energy on the basis, not of the price of the oil, but of the price of energy produced in the country, depending on the source of marginal supplies;

 iii) Foreseeable long-term trends rather than prices observed in the short-term should be taken as a basis. It can never be repeated

79

often enough that the lack of imagination of project evaluators can often lead to mistakes. It is rare to find an evaluation report which foresees prices diverging by more than 10 or 20 per cent from the prices ruling when the report was written, yet in practice if often happens that prices change in real terms, [i.e. after correction for the effects of inflation] by 50 or 100 per cent in a few years. Indeed the success or failure of a project often depends on correct long-term forecast of product prices. Such a forecast can only be made by carefully studying trends in the markets concerned, as well as the outlook for consumption and the probable reactions of competing producers.

d) The Cost of Commodities Produced in the Country

159.   Theoretically, it would be necessary to break down the inputs for the product concerned into labour, capital and imports. In practice, this is hardly feasible. It is only possible to correct market prices from obvious distortion, for instance, when the shadow price of the labour used in an activity is very small, and when the labour is the essential input of this activity.

e) The Utility of the Commodities Produced by the Project for Consumption by the Domestic Market

160.   Outputs should be determined by the prices which consumers are prepared to pay for the outputs. There may be difficulty if the quantity produced by the project is such that the market price is liable to fall below the marginal cost of production. It will then be necessary to use the system of evaluation indicated in paragraph 161 below. In the case where a new product is being produced the consumers' "readiness to pay" must be directly evaluated from the demand curve for the new output, established by econometric techniques. Fortunately, this extremely difficult case is not often relevant to water projects.

f) Changes in Prices

161.   The possible consequences of a multi-purpose hydraulic project include changes in prices. For example, the provision of a navigable waterway should bring down the cost of transporting some commodities, or the introduction of irrigation might lead to such a production of a particular crop that its price should fall. The introduction of irrigation by sprinkling, while economising water might increase total production costs and force prices upward. As shown for example by Howe and Easter (1970), such effects can be large and may deeply modify income distribution among the beneficiaries of a project. The correct way of proceeding in the case of domestic water is indicated below. It can be applied mutatis mutandis to other commodities. In most cases, as shown by Turvey (1974) the shadow price to be used can be calculated as $\frac{P_1 + P_2}{2}$ where P_1 represents the price "with" the project and P_2 the price "without" it.

g) The Price of Natural Resources

The opportunity cost of natural resources (and especially water) can only be established by studying the other uses of water including possible alternative and genuinely feasible projects.

h) The Problem of Inflation

162.   There is no difference between calculating the rate of return in constant values or in nominal values provided tha. in the latter case, the discount rate (assumed to be r in the case "without inflation") is increased by I + rI where I is the rate of inflation. Moroever, if the inflation rate I is low, the quantity rI is very low and can be left out (2). However, since it is impossible to make predictions on the inflation rate over a horizon of more than a few months, there is a strong argument for keeping "constant prices" in order to eliminate the difficulty. Moreover, it is often difficult to separate when considering the evolution of a given price, what is due to the "general price evolution" and what is due to the change of a particular price in relation to the others. To avoid this difficulty, it is often useful to make a projection of each price in nominal value and then divide these evaluations by an estimation of the general future price index through which we obtain again an evaluation in "constant prices". This method, although approximate, is probably the one with the minimum error.

B. THE ALLOCATION OF PROJECT COSTS TO THE VARIOUS PROJECT PURPOSES

163.   In the optimum design of a multiple-purpose project, all that is required is the comparison of incremental costs to incremental benefits as new purposes are added or as project size is increased. There is no need, then, from a design or economic evaluation viewpoint to allocate joint costs to particular purposes. However, government regulations (3) or lenders may require that all project costs, capital and operating, be allocated to particular purposes, even though the allocation of joint costs is arbitrary. For example, a dam and its reservoir may provide for irrigation and hydro-electric power. While canal costs are clearly attributable to irrigation and power-house costs to power, the allocation of the other costs of the dam and land among the two purposes is arbitrary. Even if, say, 40 per cent of the active storage is to be used for irrigation and 60 per cent for power, the allocation of costs will depend on which purpose is considered central and which is marginal.

164.   A frequently used procedure for allocating costs is called the "separable cost-remaining benefits" method which will be described here. Another is the "alternative justified expenditure" method. All such procedures are based on some arbitrary assumptions, but they are generally accepted as an equitable basis for calculating cost repayment requirements.

165.   A logical start on allocating costs can be made by computing the "separable costs" associated with each purpose. Separable costs of a particular purpose are those clearly identified with that purpose, i.e. costs which would clearly be escaped if the purpose were dropped from the project design. Following separable cost determination, joint costs are allocated by some

process. The crudest way of proceeding is to allocate joint costs proportionally to separable costs: Let C_1 and C_2, be the separable costs associated with purposes 1 and 2, J_1 and J_2 the amount of joint costs. Then J_1 and J_2 are chosen such that:

$$\frac{J_1}{J_1 + J_2} = \frac{C_1}{C_1 + C_2} \quad \text{and} \quad \frac{J_2}{J_1 + J_2} = \frac{C_2}{C_1 + C_2}$$

Thus, in general:

$$J_i = \left(\sum J_i \right) \frac{C_i}{\sum\limits_i C_i}$$

Of course, this process is totally arbitrary and may seriously bias the analysis against certain purposes having large separable costs. Some purposes may be found to have a negative net benefit, even if their separable costs are smaller than their gross benefits. This is why another method called "SCRB" (separable-cost-remaining-benefits), has been proposed.

166. While the SCRB procedure is widely used, it too is basically arbitrary. It may not be considered as equitable in some cases, because the "weakest" purposes (those with justifiable costs only slightly in excess of separable costs) get assigned the smallest portion of joint costs. Table 16 provides an example of the SCRB method (4) for a two purpose project. An optimum design for the project is assumed, the total (annualised) costs being 180 and the benefits 140 and 100. Separable costs (line 4) have been arrived at either through the optimal design of two single purpose projects, comparing them to the joint project costs or, more likely in practice by simply

Table 16

EXAMPLE OF THE APPLICATION OF THE SCRB METHOD TO A TWO-PURPOSE PROJECT
All figures on an annualised basis

	Purpose		Total
	1	2	
0. Total project costs	–	–	180
1. Benefits	140	100	240
2. Alternative costs	100	120	220
3. "Justifiable costs" (smaller of 1 or 2)	100	100	200
4. Separable costs	80	50	130
5. "Remaining benefits" (3-4)	20	50	70
6. Allocated joint costs	14	36	50*

* Total joint costs are first found by substracting separable costs from total project costs.

82

identifying those project components which are clearly associated with only one purpose (e.g. pumping stations and canals for irrigation, penstocks for hydro-electric generators, pipelines for municipal supply, etc.). Alternative costs (line 2) refer to the cost of the optimised single purpose alternatives. "Justifiable costs" (line 3) represent the largest sum that one could economically justify spending on a particular purpose in this joint project. "Remaining benefits" (a misleading name, line 5) represents the maximum amount of joint costs which can be "absorbed" by each purpose, keeping total costs less than or equal to justifiable costs. Joint costs (50) are then allocated to purposes 1 and 2 in the ratios of 20/70 and 50/70.

C. INDUCED BENEFITS AND COSTS

167.   While the direct inputs and outputs of the project are usually obvious, there may also be indirect project effects which create indirect benefits and costs further removed from the project itself. This is a complex issue, both in theory and in practice, so that most economists prefer to treat indirect benefits and costs in the manner recommended for shadow prices above, i.e. to attempt their estimation only when their existence is obvious and their magnitude substantial. There are two major reasons for taking this position. The first is that already existing secondary activities which provide water project inputs or use water project outputs often move closer to the project when they expand or renew their physical plant. Such a move may result in some real cost savings but the appearance of these activities in the project area may be interpreted as the creation of a new industry attributable to the project. This can lead to great overstatements of indirect benefits, as has often been the case in the analysis of industries moving alongside a newly navigable waterway. This is really a problem of understanding what the real "without project" situation would be, but anticipated locations changes often have led to confusion in defining project benefits appropriately.

168.   The second reason is that all public investments will have some indirect effects. Since they are difficult to trace and subject to wide errors of estimation, it seems prudent to omit their estimation for all project alternatives unless unusual conditions exist which indicate that indirect benefits or costs for one alternative will be significantly higher than for the other alternatives. In addition, it must be stressed that when a project induces an increase in activity in sectors outside it, this increase in activity is not necessarily a benefit. To achieve the increase in production concerned certain costs have to be borne. It is vital to be aware of this aspect before going further in the discussion because too many of the advocates of a systematic study of indirect effects imagine that the latter will increase benefits without any change in costs (5). Thus, the evaluators must be careful of evaluating both induced costs and induced benefits, and not induced benefits only (6).

169.   The procedure for evaluating induced effects starts with evaluating the extent of the increases in activity that the project may induce in the industrial activities outside it. For this, the simplest kind of empirical model is the input/output table. These are square tables of coefficients in which each row and each column corresponds to one of the sectors of the economy, such as agriculture, engineering industries, banks etc. At the intersection

of column i with row j is to be found the quantity of products of sector i. Using such a table, it is possible to work out the increases in activity for all the sectors necessary to produce the total quantity of input consumed by the project or to absorb the total quantity of output that it produces, or to satisfy the demand induced by the income distributed by the project (7). Using this information, and if the magnitude of the underemployment of the capacity of the economies of scale, external economies or monopoly effects in this or that sector is known, it is possible to work out an induced bene-fit/costs ratio for the whole of the economy.

170. The results of calculations of this type need to be interpreted with care, the following comments being called for.

i) Results depend on the quality of the initial input-output table used to establish the technical coefficients. Now, although it is relatively easy to construct fairly detailed and more or less reliable tables at the national level, they are extremely rare at the regional level. Thus, if the induced effects of a project are to be studied at the regional level, the computations have to be based on a "made-to-measure" regional input-output table. Build-ing up such a table from nothing is a difficult task, generally beyond the capacity of a project evaluation team and this greatly reduces the interest of the method unless consideratiom is con-fined to the induced effects on the national economy;

ii) In all these calculations, it is assumed that there are mechanical and linear links between all sectors of the economy. Clearly, this assumption is debatable. Not only does it rule out any study of economies of scale and external economies but it also assumes that there are no cases of reducing productivity or changes in price. Such phenomena do exist. Adjustments by changes in price in particular are extremely frequent(1). What is more, the tech-nical coefficients obtained are average values. Marginal be-haviour in the economy concerned may be very different from the average behaviour which is all that an input-output table reflects;

iii) With the reservations we have just made, input-output tables en-able the volume of induced effects to be measured but in no way indicate the corresponding benefits and costs. The results of the calculation may be expressed in terms of an increase in value added. It is also possible to work out the increases in interme-diate consumption. The increases obtained in value added may be split between the additional labour and capital necessary to allow the various sectors of the economy to increase their activity. Generally speaking, it is difficult to quantify either of these two quantities. The necessary data are lacking in most cases, particularly those concerning capital.

171. For all these reasons, estimating the induced effects by means of input-output tables is a difficult task which produces results which need to be interpreted with great caution and which does not seem to be a priority re-quirement for cost/benefit studies. Such estimates could however be carried out if it is wished to fit a project into the framework of an overall planning study, to analyse its effects on the balance of payments, or to compare the scale of the induced effects of two very different projects showing similar rates of return. Unfortunately, there are few other econometric instruments enabling the same kind of analysis to be carried out with greater accuracy.

NOTES

1. Dasgupta, Marglin and Sen (UNIDO Guide 1973) suggest one single shadow rate of exchange which balances all exports and imports of consumer goods disregarding customs regulations. Little and Mirrlees (1974) and the OECD manual suggest as many shadow rates of exchange as there are types of products and allows for both external prices and costs of producing substitutes domestically. The UNIDO method is obviously simpler, but the OECD method is more accurate. In practice, the UNIDO method can be recommended each time the problem of external payments are not crucial in appraising the project, and the OECD method otherwise. Bussey (1976) compares both methods and Chervel and Legall provide an overview of the problem.

2. See Hanke, Carver and Bugg (1974).

3. They are developed in detail by H.E. Marshall (1970).

4. An excellent description of the SCRB procedure is found in Loughlin (1977), on whose work the present discussion draws heavily.

5. The same reasoning holds, obviously, with the IRR, or with the Present Value of Net Benefits. Except, perhaps, that this latter criterion will take greater values -- either positive or negative -- when taking account of the induced effects.

6. Bergmann and Boussard (1976) discuss these questions at length, and provide a precise terminology on the matter.

7. A very careful and complete description of the process is given by Roessler, Lamphear and Beveridge, (1968). See also Bergmann and Boussard (1976, Chap. 6), and Bell and Hazell (1980).

8. From this standpoint, there is far greater justification for using input-output tables at the national level than at the regional level to the extent that it is far easier to assume the marginal nature of the project at the national level than at the regional level.

Chapter IX

EVALUATION OF BENEFITS AND COSTS FOR EACH PURPOSE

A. BENEFITS FROM WATER PRODUCTION

172.   Water is a perfect example of a commodity the shadow price of which is extremely different from its market price, if the latter does indeed exist. Whenever the elasticity of water demand with respect to price is low, the existence of important consumers' rents in the estimation of the social utility of water must be accounted for. On the other hand, water suppliers are usually in a monopoly position. It is therefore often difficult to take any competitive price as a basis of estimation. Two possibilities exist for tackling the difficulty:

i) If water is needed as an intermediate commodity for the production of other goods, for which a competitive market price does exist, then the easiest way of estimating the utility of water is to extend the limits of the project to include the producing activities which make use of water. So far as the relevant data are available, this solution is certainly the better one. It is the usual rule whenever irrigation is concerned. It can be employed in a similar way to industrial firms each time water is used to foster economic development in a newly served area.

ii) If water is used by the final consumer, or if the water using industries have alternative ways of providing water to themselves (so that the project is not the only way of developing these industries) then the limits of the project must be put at the end of the distribution network. Then, a shadow price for water must be estimated from surveys or econometric analyses of "willingness to pay".

a) Irrigation, and Industries Included in the Project

173.   Estimation of benefits from irrigation have been extensively described in the OECD guide for irrigation projects(1). The latter therefore, only need be briefly summarised here. Benefits from industries included in the project are estimated in exactly the same way as for agriculture. Therefore, they do not need to be treated separately. Two sets of provisional budgets must be built up for different points of time in the future, and for each firm in the project: one for the situation "without project" and one for the situation "with project". If the number of firms is great, as it is the case with

irrigation projects, it is possible to build up the budgets only for a few typical firms or farms, assuming that the input/output coefficients are the same for all the firms or farms belonging to a given type. These budgets must show the investment costs and the current costs of the firms in each situation, so as to compute the net costs by subtracting the costs "without irrigation" from the costs "with irrigation", and to report them on Tables 10 to 15. They must be computed at nominal prices and at shadow prices. It is necessary to check that using water at nominal cost is profitable, under the assumption made for water pricing in the project.

174. Table 17 shows how the results of these computations can be summarised. This table must be completed for each firm or type of firm, and for each year budgets have been computed. The breakdown of costs and benefits is a matter of convenience, but it is recommended that it be the same as for the columns of Table 10. Table 18 summarises the results of Table 17 with respect to the year of occurrence of the net benefits. Notice that the year 1 of the project from the point of view of the firm need not be the same as the year 1 of the project. For instance, if the building of the main water works lasts 5 years, the year 1 of investments for the irrigating farms is the year 6 of the project.

b) Direct Shadow Pricing for Water

175. This method will be used mainly for domestic water supply. But it can be used also for irrigation water when irrigation is not a main purpose of the project, and for industrial water, whenever the analyst has reasons to think that including the water using industries is not convenient.

176. The first problem which will be encountered in this task is the definition of the quantity of water. This problem is the same as for water pricing, and is discussed at this occasion (see §218 below). A shadow price must be estimated for each of the various dimensions associated with the "quantity of water" produced by the project. Once these dimensions have been defined, their shadow prices can be estimated in two ways. The first is from the standpoint of the project itself. Then, the "needs" for water are supposed to be equal to the water production of the project. For serving these needs in the absence of the project it would be necessary to increase the level of other activities -- "alternative activities" -- whose costs we are in a position to know. Clearly, the cost of these alternative activities has to be higher than that of the project, otherwise there would be no point in proceeding with it, and the aternative activities would always be preferable. There are then two possibilities:

i) It is assumed that there is no way the population can do without the quantity of water considered. This means that its value is at least equal to the costs of the alternative activities which therefore provide an evaluation by default of the benefits of the project; or

ii) Conversely, it is assumed that if the project were not feasible, it would certainly not be worth proceeding with the alternative activities and that it would be better to do without the water that they could provide. Then it is clear that the water must implicitly be valued at a lower price than the unit cost of the alternative activities. This cost represents an upper limit for the shadow price. This method of working out shadow prices by reference

Table 17

SUMMARY OF THE ANNUAL BUDGET OF A FIRM INCLUDED IN THE PROJECT
Typical budget from year ... to year ...*

	Benefits & costs without irrigation at nominal prices	Benefits & costs with irrigation at nominal prices	Net benefits and costs at nominal prices
	(1)	(2)	(3) = (2) - (1)
I. Investment and renewal costs a b c . . labour			
II. Operating costs a water b ..... c ..... labour			
III. Benefits a b c			

* The same tables can be used with shadow prices.

88

Table 18

NET BENEFITS AND COSTS BY YEAR OF OCCURRENCE, FOR A TYPICAL FIRM INCLUDED IN THE PROJECT*

Year from the beginning of the project	Year from the beginning of invest. for the firm	Net benefit at nominal prices	Net cost at nominal prices	Net benefit at shadow prices	Net cost at shadow prices
(1)	(2)	(3)	(4)	(5)	(6)
	1				
	2				
	3				
	4				
	5				
	6 to 10				
	11 to 15				
	16 to 20				
	21 to 30				
	31 to 40**				
	41 to 50**				

*   The same table may eventually be completed using shadow values.
**   If necessary.

to "alternative production cost" is therefore relatively easy to use. But the values it gives are only approximate, either more or less than the true shadow price. This is why the second method for calculating shadow prices is used whenever possible -- remembering that the results must be compatible with the upper and lower limits from the first method.

177. Unlike the first method, the second analyses the entire economy. To maximise its utility function, the "rest of the economy" is prepared to pay a certain price for each category of water. These prices correspond exactly to the utility to be attributed, in the project, to the production of the corresponding water categories. This we shall call the "willingness to pay" method. The results that it gives are, in theory, more satisfactory than those from the "cost of alternative production" method. Unfortunately, it is also more difficult to use. Even in this case, it may happen that the utility of water for the national community can be evaluated by measuring the increase in utility to the users concerned. But how can the utility of the water for the user be evaluated?

178. One way is by comparison: if the population in a neighbouring town is similar to that to be served by the project, and if, there, the price of drinking water is accepted without too much protest, then this price must be a reliable lower limit to future users' readiness to pay. Similarly, if industries similar to those that it is planned to supply are already paying a given rate for the use of water of equivalent quality to that which "we" shall be supplying, that rate is also a lower limit for "our" industries' readiness to pay. This comparison method is of limited use, partly because old tariffs are often very low. Therefore, the utility of water is underestimated by an amount which corresponds to the value of the "consumer surplus". In fact the problem is how to find out whether future readiness to pay is higher than its present level and by how much. Therefore, other ways need to be found to measure readiness to pay for water.

179. A direct survey would not be of much use in this respect, for at least two reasons:

     i) Potential water users are not likely to be sincere in answering what price they would be willing to pay for the water they will consume.

     ii) It is necessary to take account of foreseeable changes in the economic situation that could affect users' readiness to pay for drinking water. For instance, in a poor country with a bad distribution of income, one can suspect it will be low (2). But it might also be hoped that future economic growth would increase this readiness to pay. Thus, calculations based on present readiness to pay do not have much significance.

180. Therefore, it is necessary, when the comparison method does not seem sufficient, to make use of econometric studies for estimating a water demand function. Such a study will be useful not only for determining the shadow price of water, but also in estimating the quantity of water which will be demanded from the project under various pricing policies at various points in time. Therefore, knowledge of the demand curve may be necessary to the project design itself, and not only to project evaluation. A water demand function is a relation between the quantity of water consumed and the factors affecting that consumption. The quantity is expressed in volume, flow or energy potential. It relates to water of a certain quality, supplied to a given

point to fit specific hourly and seasonal requirements. For drinking water, the energy potential is expressed in terms of pressure X volume. For technical reasons, this pressure varies within relatively narrow limits from one project to another so that consumption in terms of energy potential is very much the same as consumption in terms of volume. Similarly, flow is proportional in most cases to volume, so that volume is the only quantitative characteristic for drinking water.

181. Many factors could affect the consumption of drinking water, price obviously being one, particularly if we want to estimate readiness to pay. However, demand elasticity for domestic water in relation to price, though not negligible is low. For a precise forecast the following factors need to be taken into account:

 -- users' income per head,
 -- distribution of this income,
 -- number of users,
 -- climate,
 -- season,
 -- the life-style of these users (living in flats or houses with gardens, cultural level, sanitary equipment, swimming pool, etc.),
 -- distribution losses.

This last factor depends on the project's technical characteristics. There is hardly any way of measuring the effect of the others except by least squares regression or variance analysis (3). An important note here is that the domestic demand for water is linked to the demand for sewage disposal, which needs to be studied at the same time.

182. Once a demand curve has been estimated for domestic water, it is necessary to evaluate readiness to pay to obtain the shadow price. The simplest solution would be to find the intersection between the demand curve and the quantity of water it is planned to supply by the project (Figure 11). If this quantity is Q_1, the reference price will then be price P_1 shown on Figure 11. In fact, P_1 represents the price at which it will, in practice, be possible to sell this water to general consumers. Because of the generally steep slope of the water demand curve, many would readily pay a very much higher price for their water.

183. One way to account for this factor is to compute a shadow price as follows:

Assume that P_1 is the market price corresponding to quantity Q_1 (situation "with project"). If the quantity had been Q_2 (in the situation "without project") $Q_2 \leqslant Q_1$), the market price would have been P_2 ($p_2 \geqslant P_1$). Marginal consumers at price P_2 enjoy an advantage of $P_2 - P_1$ because the effective price is P_1. The total advantage that these consumers derive from the fact that the price is P_1 can be shown as the hatched surface area A in Figure 12. A is called the consumer's surplus. The shadow price to use is $P_1 - A/(Q_1-Q_2)$. (See Figure 12). (If the demand curve is linear, it is simply $(P_1 + P_2)/2$ as noticed previously in paragraph 161). Quantity A clearly depends on all the other factors affecting water demand (consumers' incomes, life-style, etc.). To avoid making a fresh calculation each year, it is reasonable to suppose that these parameters vary in stages, for example, every 10 years during the project life-time. The value for these parameters at each stage will naturally depend on assumptions about regional development. These calculations can be used to give the shadow price of water at each period of the life-time of the project and for each quantity of water consumed.

184.   The method just proposed is difficult to apply, and requires the collaboration of a skilled econometrician. Therefore, it must not be used in the earliest stages of the project design and evaluation. At these stages, the comparison method is usually sufficient. Nor is it recommended when domestic water supply is only a minor purpose of the project. The gain in accuracy would not compensate for the increased cost of studies. But it is the only precise method available when domestic water supply is an important part of the benefits of the project, and when the demand for water, as well as its shadow price, must be estimated accurately, during the final stages of the project planning. Whatever the method retained for estimating shadow prices, the results can be summarised in Table 17, which must be completed for each water quantity definition used in the computation. Totals from these computations are indicated in Table 19, and reported into Table 10. Notice that the results of the comparison method do not make use of the consumer's surplus concept, so that they should be reported in columns 3 and 4 of Table 10, whereas results from the demand function method have to be put in columns 5 and 6 of this table.

B. BENEFITS AND COSTS ASSOCIATED WITH ENERGY PRODUCED
OR CONSUMED BY THE PROJECT

185.   Since transmission costs for electrical energy are relatively low, energy sources -- even when separated by large distances can -- substitute for each other, in contrast to the situation with water. Estimating demand and calculating shadow prices are put in rather different terms than for water. It is often difficult to speak of the demand for the energy produced by a given project. It is more a question of satisfying growing demands which may be met by different technical resources. For this reason the problem is not to determine whether the project is warranted by the existence of a specific demand but that of knowing whether it can make a useful contribution towards the entire system's operations.

186.   The utility of the electricity produced by the project will normally be evaluated by the cost of producing the given quantity of electricity by another method. This "alternative cost" principle should not be used mechanically. If alternative cost is to be calculated correctly, it should be based on foreseeable trends in overall demand and technological progress, particularly in nuclear or solar energy production. In short, it should be based on overall energy resource planning. Such a calculation can be only approximate. On the other hand, precisely because of its general nature, the calculation does not need to be repeated for each project. It is conceivable, and even to be recommended, that a national energy agency should publish at intervals the shadow price to be used for energy production projects. It is important to notice that a distinction has to be drawn between the total volume of energy supplied and the power available at any given instant. In addition, as for water, energy storage is costly. Structures have to be provided for storing appropriate quantities of water with high energy potential. Energy can

Figure 11 **WATER DEMAND CURVE**

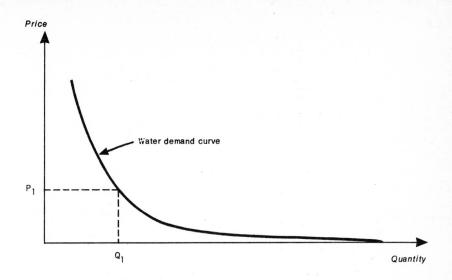

Figure 12. **CONSUMER SURPLUS**

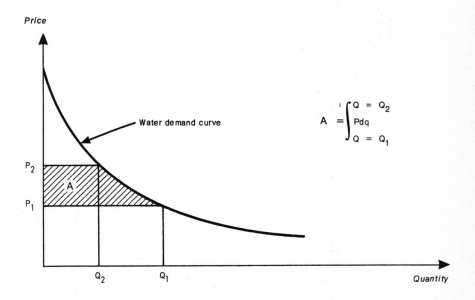

$$A = \int_{Q = Q_1}^{Q = Q_2} P dq$$

Table 19

BENEFITS FROM WATER PRODUCTION
Quantity of water defined as: ...

Years	Quantity consumed by project's users 1	Nominal price 2	Nominal value 3 = (1) x (2)	Shadow price 4	Shadow value 5 = (1) x (4)
1					
2					
3					
4					
5					
6 to 10					
11 to 15					
16 to 20					
21 to 30					
31 to 40					
41 to 50					
Total undiscounted					
Total discounted					

also be stored by the final user -- for example in storage heaters. Consumers have to be given the incentive of a special tariff to bear the cost of purchasing such appliances. As a result, the quantities of energy produced at different times of the day and at different periods of the year will need to be regarded as different products. Lastly, although moving electricity is comparably cheaper than moving water, it still has a cost. Quantities of electricity will therefore need to be differentiated in relation to their point of consumption. In other words different products or outputs should be taken into account when evaluating a project.

187. In practice, it will be necessary to make evaluation calculations for two or three different periods of daily production, two or three monthly periods of production in the year, and a few dozen points of supply (which already totals a hundred different products). Table 19 may be used to summarise the results of these computations. It is only necessary to replace the words "quantity of water" by the words "quantity of electricity".

C. DIRECT BENEFITS FROM FLOOD CONTROL (AND FIRE CONTROL)

188. Three sets of consequences may be expected from a flood control programme. (The same developments apply, mutatis mutandis, to fire control benefits.)

    i) Damages to existing activities in the previously flooded area will
       be reduced;
   ii) New activities will be developed in this area;
  iii) As a result of (i) and (ii) the price of land in the protected
       area will increase.

Two methods are available for measuring the benefits from these effects. The first one estimates directly the benefits from the inventory of effects (i) and (ii) in the protected area. It is somewhat tedious to work with, but is fairly easy to implement with the research resources available to a project design office. The second estimates the benefits from the changes in the price of land. This method is theoretically attractive. But it requires the collaboration of a skilled econometrician. Thus, it cannot be recommended on a routine basis.

a) The Traditional Approach

189. We have already seen, for irrigation, how project benefits are most frequently evaluated not on a shadow price for irrigation water but on the value of the agricultural produce obtained as a result of irrigation. Similarly, instead of estimating a shadow price for flooding, an attempt can be made to estimate the value of the additional output that will be obtained in the zone concerned because of the flood control project.

The new activities that may be introduced to the flood control areas will have to be guessed. Those activities will use inputs whose value at shadow prices will be added to the costs of the project. They will produce outputs, whose value at shadow prices will be added to the project's benefits.

95

The production of activities that are possible in flood zones "without pro-ject" are deducted from the benefits. Similarly, the cost of these activities "without project" has to be deducted from the cost of the project. Tables 17 and 18 can be used for these computations. Then, results are to be reported in col. 1 to 4 of Table 20. However, though thanks to the project, the proba-bility of water damage may be very low, it is never zero. Though the setting up of new activities in the zone protected against "ordinary" flooding implies that an "extra-ordinary" flood can have more damaging consequences than would be caused by the same flood if there were no project. This will need to be taken into account in evaluating benefits. The general practice is to calcu-late the expected loss from such an extraordinary flood and to deduct this loss from the benefits. The corresponding figures should be reported into Table 20, columns 9 to 12.

190.   This reasoning applies whenever the activities contemplated in the pro-tected area cannot be developed elsewhere. This is mainly the case with agri-cultural production. In the case of industrial activities, on the contrary, the location outside the protected area is usually possible, although at a higher cost. Whenever this occurs, only the difference in cost between the location inside and the location outside the project must be accounted for among the benefits of the project. This difference is computed, and reported on Table 20, col. 6 to 8.

b) The Econometric Approach Using Land Values

191.   The risk of flooding is an intrinsic characteristic of a plot of land as is its fertility or the distance separating it from the nearest main road. In other words, the purchaser of a plot of land acquires the associated risk of flooding as well as agricultural potential. The price therefore depends on the flood risk. Any change in that risk, for whatever reason, must cause a change in the value of the land. If the land market is sufficiently competi-tive, these changes in values are a fair reflection of the utility to the owner of the plot of the project development that alters the flood risk. If b_i is the difference between the price of "floodable" plot i and that of another plot, identical under all respects to the former, except that it is flood protected, and if the change in the flood risk occurs in project year t, the benefits from the project in year t have to be increased by quantity $\sum_i b_i$, aggregated for all plots affected by the project.

192.   This method has three difficulties. There has to be a relatively com-petitive land market and while this is generally true in the countries of the West, and particularly in the OECD Member countries, it is not in the Socia-list and many developing countries. Secondly, changes in land value represent solely the opinion of transactors of the land market in relation to future de-velopment potential in the flood-protected area. That opinion is based on consideration of many individual forecasts arrived at by persons who are very likely to be better informed than even the best research scientist aided by computer and econometric models. Nevertheless, the fact remains that these are only opinions and they could, in the long run, prove unfounded. Lastly, and above all, it has to be possible to find out the price difference between two plots that are identical except for the risk of flooding. Obviously this is not feasible. The difficulty can be overcome using regression techniques or variance analysis (5).

Table 20

COMPUTATION OF BENEFITS FROM FLOOD AND FIRE PREVENTION -- TRADITIONAL APPROACH

Years	Activities which could not be located outside the protected area					Activities which could be located outside the protected area, but at a higher cost			Expected losses from flood and fire		Total benefit	
	With project		Without project		Net	Cost outside (6)	Cost inside (7)	Benefit (8)	Without project (9)	With project (10)	Undiscounted (11)	Discounted (12)
	Cost (1)	Benefit (2)	Cost (3)	Benefit (4)	Benefit (5)							
1												
2												
3												
4												
5												
6 to 10												
11 to 15												
16 to 20												
21 to 30												
31 to 40												
41 to 50												

(5) = (2) - (4) - (1) - (3)
(8) = (6) - (7) + (9) - (10)
(11) = (5) + (8) + (9) - (10)

To be reported in Table 9.

193.   Unfortunately, results given by multiple regression using least squares or variance analysis are increasingly imprecise, the closer the so-called explanatory variables (here the C_{ij}) are inter-linked through other relationships external to the model being used.   It is evident that for land prices, the explanatory variables, such as the earnings of the local population, the demographic situation and even the fertility of the land itself are cross-linked in many different ways.   Therefore, estimates drawn from this method must be used carefully, and under the supervision of an econometrician.   Moreover, the data are not easy to get.   In many countries, the prices at which land transactions occur are not sincerely declared to lawyers or to the administration, so that these data must be carefully checked.   The result of this approach can be directly reported in Tables 10 to 15.

D. DIRECT ECONOMIC BENEFITS FROM WATERWAYS OR OTHER TRANSPORT FACILITIES

194.   The construction or improvement of an inland waterway has two kinds of effect:

i) certain transport operations carried out by other modes before the project will now be switched to the new mode. The benefit of the new mode is then represented by the difference in the cost of shipment by the old and new systems;

ii) new trades, not possible with the old system, will be feasible with the new one. This allows new economic activities whose costs and benefits have to be added to those of the project.

Conceptually, therefore, establishing the costs and benefits of a new waterway presents no problem but in practice it is extremely difficult to estimate correctly the amount of business that will be switched and even more difficult to quantify the effects in terms of new trade.

a) Estimation of the Reduction in Existing Transport Costs

195.   It would seem relatively easy to study the various transport services in an area between the points served by the projected waterway. The transport tariffs are known and so are the rates at which waterway craft operators could carry, based on their own costs, the charges foreseen in the project and port costs (trans-shipment costs in particular). If the cost of shipment of waterway is lower than existing transport tariffs, it seems logical to suppose that the goods concerned will be sent via the waterway. In reality, it is less simple because transport tariffs (6) often distort the cost of the transport system to the community. The reason is that transport operators, and particularly railways, have fixed costs amounting sometimes to as much as 80 per cent of their total costs. This gives them plenty of manoeuvering room to operate discriminatory tariffs tailored to meet competition from other transport systems. A new waterway, therefore, may have no other effect than to lower railway tariffs for certain of their "products" and to raise them for others, perhaps creating a change in income distribution to the benefit of waterway craft operators and their customers and to the detriment of say railway users. Since the marginal cost of existing transport is generally very low,

the lower transport cost -- even though the cost of waterway transport is itself very low -- will rarely be sufficient to justify the project. The real
justification for a new waterway is the likelihood that it will create new
trade.

b) Estimation of New Trade Brought about by New Transport Facilities

196.   Here, the difficulty arises because development of new trade is bound
up with economic growth in the region concerned; therefore complete development models for the regions are required. First, these models should be run
"without project" and then, after modifying them to allow for the facilities
provided by the project, re-run. In practice this is hardly feasible. Once
again, it will be necessary to approximate, and this generally means modelling
the industries expected to use the waterway. In the process, the tendency
will be to underestimate the utility of the project because it is likely that
other industries not taken into account in the calculation may well benefit
from the project. The simplest case will be of the kind still encountered in
certain developing countries where the waterway will be used in opening up of
a new mineral deposit. The waterway development is only one part of the opening up of the new ore field, and both would need to be part of the same
study. Another extreme is when the rail services between points that could be
served by waterway are saturated, and the question is whether it is better to
build an additional railway line or switch part of the traffic to the waterway
to enable the railway to increase its capacity for other commodities. The
benefit of the waterway is then equal to the cost of the additional railway
line.

197.   The situation is generally intermediate. The new waterway will mean
that new activities can be developed in the areas it serves, and much of the
traffic carried by water could, if necessary, be transported by other modes;
this being so, there is no universal method of analysis. The following calculation, however, gives an approximate, generally adequate, evaluation of the
benefits of a waterway.

      i) First, make an inventory of the goods presently going by waterway
        or those which go by rail but could be shipped by competitive
        waterway.
     ii) Forecast growth for the industries using these commodities, based
        on foreseeable growth rates in the demand the industries have to
        meet. To calculate the growth for a particular firm, based on
        final demand, an inter-industry trade table can be used. Final
        demand is calculated on past growth rates and any information
        about trends in income (and the impact of the increase in income
        on the demand for the products of certain industries such as
        building, using heavy materials) and international trade pros-
        pects (particularly for fuel and agricultural products such as
        grain).
    iii) Study such special cases (e.g. new mineral deposits, new firms to
        be set up, etc.) as may justify an increase in tonnage shipped.
        This calculation has, of course, to be made on a probable assump-
        tion of transport costs derived from the cost of the project and
        an estimate of the tonnage shipped. Since there is no way of
        arriving at tonnage shipped before completing the calculations
        (i) and (ii), the successive approximations method is used.

iv) From the above, deduce a provisional estimate of the tonnage to be carried by waterway at various future dates. Let Q_1 be the result (Q_1 is a vector whose elements Q_{1t} correspond to the various dates for which the forecast has been carried out).

v) Calculate the cost of the infrastructure necessary for this traffic and, from it, work out the unit transport cost with project P_1.

vi) Calculate the cost price P'_1 to destination of the same material using an alternative route (for instance rail) for the "without project" situation

vii) Consider whether in the light of this, the transport forecasting should not be revised; then arrive at the quantity Q_2 to be carried out by rail in the "without project" case at the price P_2 (P_2 is different from P_1 because the average cost of transporting Q_2 is probably different from that of transporting Q_1).

viii) It is then possible to calculate the next benefit of the project by the following formula:

$$A = (P_2 - P'_1) Q_2 + \frac{(P_1 + P_2) (Q_1 - Q_2)}{2}$$

The first term is the benefit obtained for quantity Q_2 and the second term is equivalent to the value of the extra quantity carried, assessed somewhere between the costs by waterway and by rail.

c) Benefits from Other Transport Facilities Brought about by the Project

198.   A multi-purpose project should obviously not include in its main purposes the production of transport facilities by rail and roads. It may happen however, that roads, railways, or harbour must be built for the completion of the project, either because they are necessary for transporting the materials necessary for the construction of the water works, or because the realisation of its purpose imply the existence of these facilities (for instance, if the project aims at developing agricultural production, it may be necessary to increase the capacity of the harbour through which this agricultural production must be transported to final consumers). The costs of building these facilities must be included into the cost of the project. Therefore, the benefits must not be neglected, and must be included into the benefits as well. The way these inclusions must be done is similar to what has been described for the waterways. The same tables and procedure of evaluation can be used.

d) Presentation of Results

199.   The results of these computations can be presented in Tables 21 and 22 which must be completed for each category of commodity transported -- these categories are established in such a manner that each one represents all the commodities defined by the same units and for which the unit cost of transportation is the same.

E. ECONOMIC BENEFITS AND COSTS CONNECTED WITH RECREATIONAL AREAS

200.   All the above kinds of benefit concern production of quantifiable goods or services. There is however generally no simple physical measurement for the utility of recreational areas. For a park with an entrance fee, it is easy to calculate the number of people who go in but often multi-purpose hydraulic projects "produce" (or possibly "consume" e.g. when fishing areas are submerged by the impounded water) recreational facilities for which no entrance fee is paid and which, therefore, never appear in any system of accounts. What is more, the number of visitors to a park is only a very approximate measure of real utility. The entrance fee may be a purely token amount, and many visitors would be prepared to pay more. Conversely, the very fact that people visit a park could, reduce its value, if there were too many. Therefore, providing a second park nearby might not necessarily alter the total number of visitors but it could reduce their density in the previous park and thus have a high social utility. The difficult arises because the value of a given recreational facility depends on its location in relation to its users as well as on its intrinsic qualities. A swimming pool in an urban area is of very high value because it costs swimmers little time and money to reach it. Conversely, a bigger bathing facility but remote and difficult to get to would, in practice, interest only a limited number of users, even if free of charge. The preceding considerations make it clear that evaluations of economic benefits or costs associated with the creation or the disappearance of recreational areas are always questionable. This is why they should be isolated in columns 5-6 in Table 10. Two methods are available for their estimation. The "transport cost method" is somewhat sophisticated, and should be employed only if the benefits and costs in question are large compared with the other benefits and costs of the project, and if skilled professional economists are available in the project planning team. Otherwise, the more simple, and more crude method of "recreational days" must be recommended.

a) The Transport Cost Method

201.   The data are obtained from a survey among the users of a recreational area similar to that which it is intended to provide. This survey must give the following information about each individual in the sample:

    i) The distance he has travelled to reach the facility (expressed in
       terms of distance and time) and the costs related to the trip;
   ii) His socio-economic status (sex, age, job, income, etc.);
  iii) The "quantity" of recreational services he has consumed during the
       past year (measured in man-days for example).

    From such data, it is possible to derive a curve, for each socio-economic status, such as T_0C_0 in Figure 13, relating the cost of travelling with the demand for recreation, expressed in terms of "recreation days". Assuming that each user will respond to an entrance fee just as he would to an equal increase in travel cost, the institution of various levels of fees will result in corresponding leftward shifts of the curve. These are represented by T_1C_1, T_2C_2, etc., each one corresponding to the entrance fee P_1, P_2, etc. Then, knowing the social characteristics of the population of the potential users of the new planned facility, as well as the corresponding travel costs, it is possible to compute the total demand in terms of

Table 21

BENEFITS FROM TRANSPORT FACILITIES BROUGHT ABOUT BY THE PROJECT REDUCTION IN TRANSPORT COSTS

Years	Quantity transported (1)	Without project				With project				Difference in transport values at:	
		Nominal price (2)	Nominal value (3)=(1)x(2)	Shadow price (4)	Shadow value (5) =(1)x(4)	Nominal price (6)	Nominal value (7)=(1)x(6)	Shadow price (8)	Shadow value (9)	Nominal price (10) = (7)-(3)	Shadow price (11) = (9)-(5)
1											
2											
3											
4											
5											
6 to 10											
11 to 15											
16 to 20											
21 to 30											
31 to 40											
41 to 50											
Total undiscounted											
Total discounted											

Discount rate = %

102

Table 22

BENEFITS FROM TRANSPORT FACILITIES BROUGHT ABOUT BY THE PROJECT -- NEW TRADE

Year	Quantity transported without project O_2 (1)	Price of transportation without project P_2 (2)	Quantity transported with project Q^1 (3)	Price of transportation with project P_1 (4)	Cost of transporting the quantity Q_1 without project $P*_1$ (5)	Benefit from the project $(P_2-P*_1)Q_2+\frac{(P_1+P_2)Q_1-Q_2}{2}$ (6)
1						
2						
3						
4						
5						
6 to 10						
11 to 15						
16 to 20						
21 to 30						
31 to 40						
41 to 50						
Total undiscounted						
Total discounted						

Discount rate = %

recreation days, of this population for different levels of entrance fee. This is actually sufficient to draw a demand curve for the facility (Note that this demand curve is <u>not</u> the curve T_oC_o represented in Figure 13). This demand curve is then used just as a demand curve for water (cf. above, para. 182).

Figure 13. **DERIVING THE DEMAND CURVE FOR RECREATION FROM THE COST OF TRAVELLING**

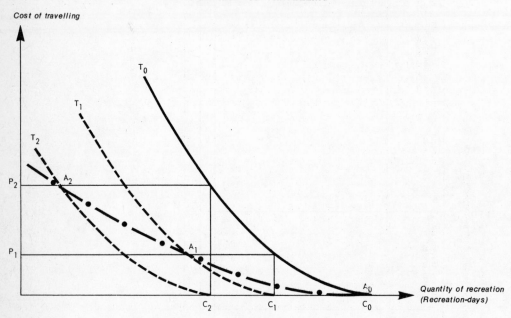

Especially, if it is not intended to levy an entrance fee, the benefit is equal to the whole consumer rent, i.e., the whole area under the demand curve. If the later is linear, the area is obtained as shown in Table 23: the number of recreation-days forecasted is multiplied by half the maximum theoretical entrance fee, i.e., half the entrance fee for which the number of recreation-days would be zero.

202.   Three remarks must be stated about its application.

    i) Transport cost has two components: the marginal cost of the mode of transport used (e.g. a car) and the time lost when travelling. Unfortunately, it is difficult to correctly measure the opportunity cost of travelling time (8).

    ii) The "transport cost method" requires the contruction of a full-scale model of the demand for recreational services. This serious analysis of the problem is an advantage. But if the model is to be reliable, it has to be constructed with great care. The above rough description can be supplemented by reference to the given bibliography. It should be pointed out that the demand curve to be estimated depends on many parameters, the most important of which are probably personal incomes and the other recreational opportunities in the region. Each of these parameters is likely to change considerably during the life of the project and it is essential to bear this point in mind in the analysis.

iii) This still leaves the question of whether the benefits estimated in this way should simply be added to the other benefits of the project such as those from irrigation or electricity generation. While the method just described may be used to compare two alternative recreational projects, it may be questioned whether "utilities" measured in this way are really comparable with those, for example, from an increase in electricity production.

These results can be presented in Table 23, which must be completed for each major recreational area involved in the project, and each kind of service provided by the given area. Such tables can be used either for estimating cost associated with the elimination of an area, or for estimating benefits produced by a new area created by the project.

b) The "Recreation Day" Method

203. This method requires the grouping of the recreational services provided by the project into main categories, such as "general" or "special" (9). "General" cover the vast majority of recreational services such as swimming, sailing, ordinary fishing, etc. "Special" services relate to more specific activities such as big game hunting or salmon fishing. Next the potential of the project is estimated in number of days of each type of service. An all-in price, worked out at national or at least regional level, on the average cost of other similar facilities in the country or area is then attributed to these "days". The result of multiplying the price by the quantity is then a measure of the benefit of the project, and can be reported in Table 24. In practice, this procedure does not differ greatly from the preceding one for participation rates must be predicted from the same type of model, linking usage rates to socio-economic characteristics. The unit value is then assigned by judgment rather than being inferred from response to travel costs.

Table 23

SUMMARY OF RESULTS FROM THE TRANSPORT COST METHOD FOR EVALUATING BENEFITS AND COSTS FOR RECREATION
The demand curve is assumed linear; the recreational service is free

Area: Recreational services:

Years	Number of Recreation-days without entrance fees	Maximum entrance fee (outside this value nobody will make use of the service)	Undiscounted value of the service	Discounted value
	(1)	(2)	(3) = (1)x(2)x0.5	(4)
1				
2				
3				
4				
5				
6 to 10				
11 to 15				
16 to 20				
21 to 30				
31 to 40				
41 to 50				
Total undiscounted				
Total discounted				

Discount rate:...%.

Table 24

BENEFITS AND COSTS ASSOCIATED WITH RECREATIONAL FACILITIES -- RECREATION DAY METHOD

	Expected number of recreation days in the region										Estimated prices		Estimated value	
	General services					Special services					General services	Special services	Cost (3)+(11) (8)+(12)	Benefit (2)+(11) (7)+(12)
	Without project (number)	Supplied by the project (number)	Eliminated by the project (number)	With project (1)+(2)-(3) (number)	Increment (4)-(1)/(1) %	Without project (number)	Supplied by the project (number)	Eliminated by the project (number)	With project (6)+(7)-(8) (number)	Increment (9)-(6)/(6) %				
	(1)	(2)	(3)	(4)	(5)	(6)	(7)	(8)	(9)	(10)	(11)	(12)	(13)	(14)
1														
2														
3														
4														
5														
6 to 10														
11 to 15														
16 to 20														
21 to 30														
31 to 40														
41 to 50														
Total undiscounted														
Total discounted														

NOTES

1. Cf. Bergman and Boussard (1976).

2. Or rather, it will be high for that part of the population with high incomes, and practically non-existent for the others.

3. The process is described in considerable detail by Howe and Lineaweawer (1967).

4. This increase in land value is a capital gain which should therefore be counted only once -- in the year when the flood control system becomes effective. It should not be confused with an income.

5. The price of plot i is P_i, which depends on a number of characteristics associated with it: fertility, geographical location, average income of potential buyers, population pressure nearby, etc. Let C_{ij} be the jth characteristic of plot i; C_{i1} is the risk of flooding specific to plot i. We then write:

   $$P_i = f(C_{ij}), \quad j = 1\ldots n$$

   The prices at which land has changed hands recently in the project area are observed. On the basis of these observations and using regression by least squares or variance analysis, the parameters of the most probable analytical specification of function f are estimated. P_i/C_{i1} can then be calculated, giving the increase in price due to

   a given reduction in the flood risk. This enables $\Sigma_i bi$ to be calculated for different project alternatives.

6. See Eckstein (1958), Chapter 6.

7. This method is described at length by Clawson and Knetsch, 1970; Knetsch, 1974; Gum and Martin, 1977; Knetsch (1977).

8. Bear in mind however, that the journey itself may be part of the recreation: many people travel only for the pleasure of travelling, the goal of the journey being only a pretext.

9. Water Resources Council, 1973, (p. 23804).

Chapter X

FINANCING AND PRICING

A. THE BASIC FINANCIAL QUESTIONS IN WATER PROJECT PLANNING

204. The four following major issues need to be dealt with in the financial planning of any project:

1. The need for and nature of a complete financial plan;
2. The pricing of project outputs and other methods of cost repayment;
3. The allocation of project costs to the various project purposes for determining repayment requirements;
4. Determination of the feasibility or profitability of the project from the water user's viewpoint.

The last two points having been discussed earlier, the attention in this chapter will be focused on the former two.

205. The financing of a project from the moment construction begins until the end of project life is vital to the functioning of a project. While benefits of all forms may fully justify the project, many types of benefits do not produce a flow of monetary receipts to the project agency. Compensatory measures will therefore have to be included in the financial plan. Examples would be the improvement of water quality, the improvement of fisheries, and perhaps the provision of flood protection. The type of products which produce earnings for the agency depends on the practices within each country and perhaps on the skill of the agency in imagining ways of getting the project beneficiaries to pay for project costs. It is also clear that some project costs do not take the form of money flows, e.g. environmental costs. Even if project beneficiaries always repaid all project costs, there would still be problems of financial timing, i.e. budgeting since most project receipts begin only after project outputs can be sold, while most costs are incurred during construction. The project beneficiaries are usually expected to repay part if not all of these costs, usually with interest on the outstanding balance.

206. The complete financial plan should map out the time paths of necessary expenditures for the entire project and the sources from which the needed funds will be obtained. All needs must be accounted for, including constructions, operations, replacements, special studies, taxes and other government charges, interest payment or debt and allowances for increases in prices. The complete financial plan relates closely to the project definition described

earlier. Clearly, the financing of all works to be undertaken by the agency itself must be included, but there may be major civil works such as roads, telecommunications, ports, health and administrative facilities which are an integral part of the project while being the responsibility of different agencies. The assignment of all financing responsibilities to responsible agencies should be clearly outlined in the plan, in keeping with accepted practices and the ability to enforce these assignments.

207.   The water planning agency, when drawing up the financial plan, may even be called upon to estimate the capital requirements of private investments which are needed or expected in relation to the project. Such information may be needed by government to answer questions about total capital availability. The inclusion of <u>allowances for inflation in financial plans</u> is vital. The measurement of benefits and costs discussed in preceding chapters is usually carried out in terms of monetary units of constant purchasing power, i.e. as if the general price level were constant. However, in laying financial plans, inflation must definitely be taken into account for at least the following reasons:

i) Operating, maintenance and replacement costs will rise in money terms over time, and funds must be available to meet these obligations;

ii) If it is desired to obtain repayment of capital costs in real terms (i.e. in dollars of constant purchasing power), then beneficiary charges must be increased over time.

Thus, in developing the financial plan for the project, it will be necessary to project rates of inflation over the project lifetime.

208.   What kinds of financing other than project revenues will be needed?

1. Long term investment capital:
   a) grants from different government units;
   b) "soft" loans at subsidised rates;
   c) "hard" loans at commercial rates.
2. Funds for interest payments required on borrowed money used during construction.
3. Funds to cover any operating deficits.
4. Funds for the replacement of major equipment parts.
5. Credit for the equipment of farms and other public works if this is the water agency's responsibility.

209.   The sources of financing are particular to each country, but in all cases <u>thorough practical knowledge of the formal and informal procedures for obtaining financing is essential</u>. In most cases, it will be advisable to have a financial expert on the technical team to formulate the financial plan and to set up the accounting system for the control of expenditures and receipts. This expert or others must maintain contact with the various possible sources of finance, including political contacts which may be helpful in finding funds. It must be remembered that the formally stated rules for project financing may differ considerably from actual practice and that it may be necessary to use a great amount of ingenuity in obtaining the required funding.

B. PRACTICAL IMPLEMENTATION

210.   The general principles just stated have to be implemented in a financing plan which should be included within the various reports issued at critical steps of the project design process.

a) The Financing Plan (1)

211.   Table 25 can be used for presenting the financing plan at various stages.   The table displays the various nominal costs, broken down by sources of financing.   Costs raise no problem, except that only investment costs should be indicated here.   Current costs should normally be financed by the current receipts.   But a provision must be made for financing current expenses before any receipt can occur.   Sources of financing must be broken down so as to make apparent the subsidies, the loans and their sources.   Once again, only those subsidies and loans designed to finance investment should appear here. Moreover, for projects of long duration, some benefits of the project may be reinvested in order to finance the last investments.   (This is the reason for having introduced the right most column "reinvestments from benefits").   It should be noticed that receipts from the sale of project's products should normally be affected first to the repayment of loans, and then, to the financing of current expenses.   Hence, only a very small part of these benefits can be used for the financing of the project itself.

212.   This table can be completed for the project as a whole, without consideration of the time at which receipt and expenses are likely to occur.   The same table can be completed year after year in order to show the evolution of the distribution of receipts and expenses through time.   However, this distribution will be displayed in a clearer way using table 25, which is self-explanatory (notice only that rows 13 and 8 should be equal).

b) Financing Reports at Each Stage of the Project Design

213.   In practice, there are five different fundamental stages each ending with the production of a financing report (see Table 1).
Problems of funding should be dealt with in all five reports, mentioned in Table 1, the first four being primarily concerned with their identification and the fifth with their consequences.

Preliminary Report

At this stage, it is necessary to plan firm and detailed arrangements for financing the studies, which fall into two broad categories:

1. General studies

i) "one-shot" studies
ii) recurrent studies (cycles or series to be repeated every year).

The first type includes geological and pedological studies, and the second studies relating to climatology and hydrology, as well as social and environmental monitoring and periodic economic assessments.

2. Technical studies designed to define the facilities to be built and their scale, and to provide initial rough estimates.

As a general rule, 100 per cent funding is required for these studies, as in their case no direct return can be assumed. The attention of Members of the design and appraisal team is drawn to the need to define the scale of funding necessary for investment projects in the region in question for whatever purpose, including social and ecological expenditure. Examples are financing for proposed housing, as well as schools, roads, and airports. Further analysis of the nature of the funding required by the investment project with particular reference to the double aspect of the grant element (and what percentage it should be) and the type of loans to be made (interest rate, term) is not necessary at this stage.

3. Report on the Examination of Project Alternatives

Apart from the monitoring of the funding for the studies, the feature of this phase is a preliminary rational and all-inclusive approximation of the cost of each project alternative. From an examination of these costs, including both the initial capital outlay and the annual operating costs, the neutrality of the funding arrangements has to be verified. The point here is that funding for technical facilities breaks down into a grant component and a loan component to make up the shortfall. These combinations of funding provide the basis for calculating rates of return and taking the appropriate decisions. The attention of members of the multi-disciplinary team is simply drawn to the effects that funding decisions may have on the technical choices. Some proposals on this score are set out below. It should also be remembered that the origin of the loans granted for the project will generally determine which government departments are responsible for overseeing the operation. At this stage and in the light of the foregoing, the proposed capital expenditure needs to be broken down by order of magnitude, e.g.:

Class A: Very heavy investment with long-deferred returns e.g. dams, breakwaters, main highways.
This class should be 100 per cent financed by grant.

Class B: Facilities with some direct return in the medium term for large users. Examples are large-scale water supply networks, main distribution systems, telephone exchanges, secondary roads.
Here there should be a large grant component, 60 to 80 per cent plus long-term loans with deferred redemption.
Loan repayments in such cases are often made by local authorities rather than by the State.

Class C: Facilities producing direct returns in the short term, e.g. water or electricity distribution networks, third-class roads, minor harbour developments.
In this case the grant component can be quite small; with medium-term loans, simple business return calculations will indicate the level of grant required to ensure a project's financial and economic equilibrium.

Table 25

FINANCING PLAN

| | General total | Subsidies from: | | | | | | | | | | | Loans | | | | | | Owned funds | | | |
| | | Government | | | | Local Communities | | | | Others | | | With rebate | | | | Without rebate | | | Private households Farmers | | | Reinvestment from benefits |
		Total	Ministry 1:	Ministry 2:	....	Total	Community 1:	Community 2:	....	Total	1:	2:	....	Total	Bank 1:	Bank 2:	......	Total	Bank 1:	Bank 2:	......	Total	Firm type 1:	Firm type 2:	....	
Studies and planning																										
Lot 1:																										
Lot 2:																										
....																										
Total																										
Public works																										
Lot 1:																										
Lot 2:																										
....																										
Total																										
Private investment																										
Agriculture																										
Power plants																										
Domestic water																										
Industrial water																										
Waterways																										
Ports and coastal defence																										
Servage disposal																										
Recreation																										
Total																										
Interim interests																										
Provision for inflation																										
Provision for unexpected expenses																										
Financing funds for current expenses																										
Total																										
General Total																										

Table 26

RECEIPTS AND EXPENSES THROUGH TIME

			Rows	1	Years 2...........50
Agency in charge of the project	Expenses	Investments	1		
		Current expenses	2		
		Loans repayment	3		
		Report of balance	4		
		Total	5		
	Receipts	Subsidies	6		
		Loans	7		
		Receipt from sales of project's products	8		
		Report of balance	9		
		Total	10		
Private operators	Expenses	Increases in investment	11		
		Increases in current expenses	12		
		Purchase of projects products	13		
		Loan repayment	14		
		Report of balance	15		
		Total	16		
	Receipts	Subsidies	17		
		Loans	18		
		Increases in sales	19		
		Report of balance	20		
		Total	21		

Class D: Investments with high short-term returns, largely private. This class covers investment projects by individuals or firms. Loan finance of varying kinds to suit the problem involved is sufficient in most cases; housing finance is one example.

4. Report on the selection of project alternatives

In this report the broad lines of the above funding schemes are simply developed and defined in greater detail. checks and audits are made to make sure that funding is comprehensive, neutral, equitable and not likely to dry up. This is also the stage for negotiations with the Ministry of Finance for the conclusion of any specific financing arrangements which may be necessary for the satisfactory implementation of the project. At the same time, the financial procedures must be finalised: special funding agreements for interest payments on borrowed money used during construction, funding channels tailored to the interministerial and multi-disciplinary nature of the loan.

5. Ex ante final report

In this report, the overall financial plan finalised in the previous step is simply applied to the selected technical variant. It is taken in the form that was finally agreed upon, and only a few simulations of the future are conducted to check that the funding system will lead to any harmful consequences. The latter point is the last check of all and is therefore all the more important.

C. BASIC PRINCIPLES FOR PRICING PROJECT OUTPUTS

214. It must be emphasized at the outset of any discussion of pricing of project outputs that a good pricing strategy has at least four major objectives:

1. It should help to induce the socially desired pattern of use of project outputs once the project is operational;
2. It should provide water cost information upon which water users can make rational long term investment decisions of their own;
3. It should warn the water agency of when new capacity is warranted;
4. It should contribute to project financing.

Unfortunately, it is usually impossible to meet all these objectives simultaneously. Consider a typical case of a project built to meet growing demands. At first there will be excess capacity, and finally demand will equal capacity and continue to grow (2). From the the point of view of pricing objectives (1) and (3) above, it would be desirable to start project operation with low prices just sufficient to cover short-run incremental costs. As the project reached capacity, prices could be raised so that no excess demand existed and guaranteeing that only the economically highest value users received the available water. When prices reached a level equal to the full unit cost of water corresponding to the next addition to capacity, it would be a signal to build that addition. Unfortunately, such a pricing scheme would make it very difficult for water users to forecast their costs and to choose appropriate technologies. Low prices in early project life and high prices later would add to the financing problems and would not guarantee full project cost repayment. Thus, all four objectives of pricing must be kept in mind and the final pricing plan must be a compromise between them.

215. A good, practical compromise for many cases is found in long-run marginal cost pricing, i.e. setting a product or service price equal to the full cost of a unit of output of the next addition to be made to the system. (Hence, it is greater than the average price.) This pricing rule will achieve pricing objectives (2) - (4) above, although it may somewhat delay full project utilisation when demand growth is slow. It also has two great practical advantages:

1. It avoids the troubles which always accompany and often prevent the raising of price in later project life;
2. It requires sufficient payment from the direct water users that it discourages political lobbying for unjustified projects.

216. Pricing project outputs in keeping with long run marginal costs is a relatively new practice and is not yet widely found in practice. Most governments have regulations or laws specifying the division of project costs among direct project beneficiaries, local government units, and the national government. Again, these cost sharing rules often interfere with the efficient pricing of water and water services, but they may reflect certain objectives other than economic efficiency (e.g. maintain the family farm, keep agriculture attractive, promote flood control).

217. In addition, a pricing system cannot be envisaged without any reference to the financial capacity of the customers will not be able to afford. From this point of view, the main shortcoming of the marginal cost pricing theory is that it seemingly ignores the demand aspect. In fact, this is not true. If customers are not able to pay the marginal price, this means that the project plan is inaccurate, given the present income distribution. Three alternatives are open in this case:

1. Abandon the project (or redesign it, in order to get a lower cost);
2. Redefine the way the marginal cost is computed: especially, discuss more thoroughly what is fixed (and consequently, should not be charged to the customers) and what is variable in the project design (this topic is discussed in the next paragraph);
3. Change income distribution among customers by subsidising them, either directly or through the agency in charge of the project.

D. PRACTICAL IMPLEMENTATION: MARGINAL COST PRICING

218. The general principle of marginal cost pricing may be applied in a great variety of ways depending upon the way the commodities produced by the project are defined. It has been seen previously, for example, that the "energy produced by the project" represented in fact a great variety of commodities, distinguished between instantaneous power and total annual volume and among the various locations of supply. The same kind of problem arises with

water. The "quantity of water" notion covers, in fact, several commodities which can be priced separately:

  i) Total volume supplied in the year (measured for instance in cubic meters);
 ii) Maximum available flow (measured in litres per second);
iii) Energy potential (measured by the pressure or by the altitude of point of supply);
 iv) Geographical location of supply (measured by the distance of transportation);
  v) Supply period and time (since water in peak hour, or in the hot season is more costly);
 vi) Water quality (which depends upon a great number of parameters, such as salinity, and upon the use of water, such as irrigation or drinking).

219.   A marginal cost, as well as an average cost, can be computed for each of these commodities, and the pricing can be set up in accordance with the results of these computations (3).   However, pricing a highly differentiated product is difficult because the user may find it hard to understand the logic of a highly complicated tariff and the measurement of quantities consumed is itself more costly. In particular, providing meters to distinguish different types of consumption as a function of the time of the day, etc., may be more costly than the advantage it brings in levelling out production peaks.   A distinction has to be drawn between the problem of project evaluation and that of the rates to be effectively charged. It may be useful, when the project is being evaluated to give different shadow prices to electricity or water produced at different times of the day without putting any obligation on the utility to provide a differentiated tariff with attendant costs.

NOTES

1.   Examples of complete financial plans are presented in the Guide to the Economic Evaluation of Irrigation Projects.   H. Bergmann and J.M. Boussard.

2.   The growth of demand must be interpreted in the economic sense of the demand curve shifting to the right.

3.   The OECD Guide to the Economic Evaluation of Irrigation Projects (see Bergmann and Boussard, 1976) provides detailed guidelines in this respect.

Chapter XI

ESTIMATION OF THE DISTRIBUTION OF BENEFITS AND COSTS

220.   Up to now we have been primarily concerned with aggregate benefits and costs, and not with who enjoys the one and bears the other. It would, however, be wrong to plan a project in which certain persons suffered serious disadvantage even though others derived considerable benefits and though total benefits exceeded total disbenefits. In such a situation it is theoretically possible to remove part of the benefits from those who stand to gain and switch them to those who stand to lose as a form of compensation, but this is not always feasible in practice, particularly because not every cost or benefit can be given a monetary value. In addition, if compensation is possible, then the project has to include the institutional machinery for applying the compensation system. The financing and pricing policy of the project is crucial in this respect for obvious reasons. Even on the assumption that a project is prepared in such a way that, with or without compensation, everyone stands to gain from it, the difficulty remains that some persons will do better than others. Different alternatives will, therefore, favour different persons. The decision-making authority cannot ignore this when making its choice. This is the reason for why the technical team must be ready to measure the distribution of benefits costs of various alternatives.

221.   The objective is to show which categories of people stand to gain or lose from the implementation of a project. The first step is to identify a small number of categories of people affected by the project and to establish the effects of the project on them. Next, a system of accounts is drawn up showing the gains and losses which correspond to the benefits and costs for the whole project.

A. CATEGORIES TO BE CONSIDERED

222.   There are few set rules for defining these categories, but the criteria will be primarily geographical (e.g. Plain of X, Mountain Y etc.), functional (consumers, agricultural producers, industrial firms, landowners, etc.) and social (rich or poor). Often, it will be useful to draw up two sets of accounts in which a number of different distribution scales are applied one after the other. A first set, for example, could be used for studying the distribution of costs and benefits by geographical areas (such as region I, region 2, etc.). The calculation is then repeated to give the distribution for each socio-economic category.

223.   On the other hand, if an account system is to be regarded as coherent, it will always be advisable to choose categories so that when recombined they reconstitute the project. The reader will then find aggregates for the project alongside the tables and will find this useful in helping him to follow the evaluation report (1).

B. ACCOUNTS TO BE PREPARED

224.   These accounts should be drawn up as follows: the effects of the project on each of the categories (region, socio-economic category, etc.) already defined are studied as if the boundary between what is inside and outside the project corresponded exactly with the boundary of the category itself.   In other words, everything will be studied which, because of the project, are "inputs" and "outputs" for the category concerned. All inputs are regarded as costs for the category and all outputs as benefits. Each category's inputs and outputs are evaluated in two different ways depending on their source or destination.

-- If the interchange is with another category in the project, the price to be used has to correspond to the rules specified in the project for the transaction. For example, if one of the categories is "farmers" and the other the "body managing the irrigation plant", the water purchased by the farmers from the irrigation operator must be valued at the price at which the operator actually sells it to farmers;
-- If the movement involves the outside of the project, the price to be used has to be the shadow price.

225.   There is therefore no basic difference between the calculations to be made for each category and those made at the level of the project as a whole. The most obvious difference is that transactions between categories will cancel out at the level of the overall accounts for the whole project. As an illustration, Table 27 shows in a simplified form how the benefits and costs of a hypothetical project are distributed between the company operating the irrigation plant, the State, farmers and other users (here, the people benefiting from the flood control system). The columns give the categories of users of the project among whom the benefits and costs are distributed. The rows relate to the various transactions. The figures shown are the values -- at the discount rate used for the calculations (2) for the various transactions spaced over time.

226.   For example, the value for drinking water from the project, measured at the shadow price for drinking water, is 1 500 units of account. This is put down to the company operating the plant which sells the drinking water. The value appears again at project level because the drinking water is not consumed by another category in the project (3). The same applies to the generation of electricity and to the sale of produce by farmers.

227.   Conversely, the activity induced by the project gives rise to additional taxes paid by all categories. These taxes are in the accounts at their nominal discounted value, but their aggregate is nil because all tax activities are assumed to be internal to the project. The same applies to the

Table 27

SIMPLIFIED EXAMPLE OF ACCOUNTS (DISCOUNTED SHADOW VALUES) BY SEGMENTS -- BREAKDOWN BY SOCIO-ECONOMIC FUNCTIONS

	Government		Management company		Farmers		Landowners		Other Transactors		Balance for project	
	Benefits	Costs	Benefits	Costs	Benefits	Costs	Benefits	Costs	Benefits	Costs	Benefits	Costs
Drinking water			1 500								1 500	
Electricity			1 000								1 000	
Irrigation water			500			500						
Taxes	1 233			333		100		300		500		
Grants		1 500	1 500									
Construction and maintenance of plant				4 000		100		50				4 150
Land rental						500	500					
Sale of agricultural products					2 000						2 000	
Total	1 233	1 500	4 500	4 333	2 000	1 200	500	350		500	4 500	4 450
Balance	-267		167		800		150		-500		350	

120

grants paid by the government to the managing company, the land-rental paid by farmers to land owners, the cost of irrigation water paid by farmers (at the nominal price laid down for the project) to the operating company.

228.   At the discount rate used, the whole project shows a benefit/cost ratio above 1 (4 500/4 150 = 1.084 to be precise). The various transactors do not all benefit equally; farmers and landowners benefit more than government and taxpayers.

229.   With such a table it is possible to study how to change an unsatisfactory distribution. For example, one could increase the charge for irrigation water. Inelastic demand will increase revenue of the management company, enable grants to be reduced and the government's benefit/cost ratio to be improved, or taxes to be cut and fiscal pressure reduced.

230.   These accounts on shadow prices show the distribution of economic benefits and costs among the categories of transactor. When the financial equilibrium of particular categories of transactors has to be studied, it is necessary to present the same accounts in nominal costs. Table 28 shows the accounts for one of the elements (the management company) of the project illustrated in Table 27. This shows that with nominal costs, the undertaking's accounts are balanced (as is vital for satisfactory financial administration) but not if shadow prices are used.

231.   The same project can be presented in a different way if the transactors in the project are defined differently, and the results for "urban/rural" are in Table 29. It will be noted that the figures for "taxes" is far smaller because taxes paid by urban transactors to the government (also "urban transactors") no longer appear. Similarly, "grants" no longer appear. Charges for irrigation water, on the other hand, are a transfer from "rural" to "urban". Lastly, the "Total for project" column is the same as in Table 27. Other analyses could be chosen depending largely on the dialogue there has to be between those responsible for the evaluation and the political authorities commissioning the study. The reason is that only the political authorities know the terms of the problem and the categories of users between which trade-offs are necessary. Finally, so far, the tables have been drawn up in terms of the value of economic benefits and costs. Similar tables can be in physical quantities for benefits and costs whose values cannot be quantified, as shown in Table 30.

C. PERSONAL INCOME DISTRIBUTION

232.   The effects of a multi-purpose hydraulic project differ greatly according to the purpose considered. It is hardly possible to measure the personal income effects of domestic water supply: This effect will in general manifest itself through an increase in the market value of the dwelling supplied with water, thus the correct way of studying it would be to estimate the capital distribution effects of the project. This is seldom feasible because data are usually lacking. The same consideration could be applied to electricity generation, cooling water production, supplying of water transport facilities, etc.

233.   However, whenever firms are included in the project, such as with

Table 28

EXAMPLE OF COMPARISON BETWEEN BY-SEGMENT ACCOUNTS BASED ON SHADOW AND NOMINAL COSTS --
Case of the management company in Table 27

	Quantity (1)	Nominal price	Shadow price	Nominal benefit	Nominal costs	Benefit at shadow price	Cost at shadow price
Drinking water	1 500	1.42	1.0	2 133		1 500	
Electricity	10 000	0.15	0.1	1 500		1 000	
Irrigation water	5 000	0.1	0.1	500		500	
Taxes	333	1.0	1.0		333		333
Grants	1 500	1.0	1.0	1 500		1 500	4 000
Construction and maintenance	4 000	1.2	1.0		4 800		
Expropriation	500	1.0	-		500		
Total				5 633	5 633	4 500	4 333

1. Discounted physical quantities.

122

Table 29

SIMPLIFIED EXAMPLE OF BY-CATEGORY ACCOUNTS -- (VALUES AT DISCOUNTED SHADOW PRICES) --
BREAKDOWN BY GEOGRAPHICAL LOCATION

	Urban transactor		Rural transactor		Ba project	
	Benefit	Cost	Benefit	Cost	Benefit	Cost
Drinking water	1 000		500		1 500	
Electricity	733		267		1 000	
Irrigation water	500			500		
Taxes	150			150		
Grants	0			0		
Construction and maintenance of plant		4 050		100		4 150
Land Rental	500			500		
Sale of agricultural produce			2 000		2 000	
Total	2 883	4 050	2 767	1 250	4 500	4 150
Balance	-1 167		1 517		350	

Table 30

SIMPLIFIED EXAMPLE OF BY-CATEGORY ACCOUNTS IN PHYSICAL QUANTITIES --
BREAKDOWN BY GEOGRAPHICAL LOCATION

	Urban areas		Rural areas		Project	
	Benefit	Cost	Benefit	Cost	Benefit	Cost
Environmental amenity	Disappearance of an exposed drain			Disappearance of a wooded valley under the impounded water	Disappearance of an exposed drain	Disappearance of a wooded valley under the impounded water
Recreational facilities			Creation of a 20 ha. fishing area		Creation of a 20 ha. fishing area	

irrigation, it is possible to measure the impact of the project on the incomes of people operating these firms. For instance, usually, an irrigation project deeply affects income distribution among farmers. It is then necessary to show the extent of this impact of the project. It is necessary, in principle, to use one of several indicators, corresponding to different income distribution characteristics. The most popular of them is the Gini index (4).

234. In practice, the computation of such indexes is seldom feasible because data are usually lacking. On most occasions, the distributional impacts of the project will be described by defining two or three levels of income categories (such as, "poor", "medium", "high"). A first possibility is to complete a table such as Table 31 where the per capita income of the beneficiaries of the project in each category is shown with and without project. In fact, this solution is difficult to work with.

235. More subtle information can be drawn from the building of tables such as 32, which analyses the project described in Table 27 in the following way:

-- The total "payments for drinking water, irrigation, electricity" is drawn from Table 27, multiplied by the nominal price in Table 28;
-- The total of the "taxpayers" now is the difference between the grants and the taxes;
-- The total of the row "additional cost incurred by farmers" is drawn from "construction and maintenance" in the columns "farmers" of Table 27, multiplied by 1.2 to account for the difference between nominal prices and shadow prices.
-- The total "increases of farmers income" is the difference between the benefit from the sales of agricultural products, and the increases in rentals. (Shadow and nominal prices are assumed to be identical here).
-- The total increase of land owners income is equal to the increase of rentals.
-- The benefits from electricity and potable water consumption evaluated at nominal cost.
-- The analysis of the totals by row is done according to the operating rules of the project. For instance, the "payments for irrigation" are obtained from the crop system of the high, medium, or low level of income farmers, and from the tariff applied to each of them. Similarly, the row "taxpayers" is analysed from the reading of statistical surveys showing the share of each income category in the total tax burden.

236. The following conclusions can be drawn from the next table:

i) The project interests mainly low and medium incomes (82 per cent of benefits, and 85 per cent of costs);
ii) The internal operating rules tend to favour higher incomes, the shares of which are only 14 per cent for costs, and 18 per cent for benefits.

237. Contrary to what happens with Table 31, or with Gini index computations, Table 32 can be completed for any purpose of the project, using the operating rules of the project (such as pricing policy) and the identification of the beneficiaries to compute the share of each category of beneficiaries in the total cost and benefits. The main advantage of this kind of analysis is that

it enables the project designer to evaluate the consequences of changing the planned operating rules in order to improve the distribution of costs and benefits between the various categories.

Table 31

PER CAPITA INCOMES OF THE BENEFICIARIES OF THE PROJECT, BY CATEGORY OF INCOME, "WITH AND WITHOUT" PROJECT

	Low incomes (less than:)	Medium incomes (between.. and)	High incomes (more than:)	Average
Without project				
With project				
Increment (%)				

NOTES

1. Additional remarks on the problem of defining population segments can be found in paragraphs 255 and 275.

2. Possibly at the internal rate of return.

3. The consumer of drinking water is regarded as being outside the project boundary.

4. Cf. Kendall and Stuart, Vol. 1, p. 47.

Table 32

EXAMPLE OF PERSONAL INCOME DISTRIBUTION ANALYSIS -- CASE OF THE PROJECT DESCRIBED IN TABLE 27
Values at Discounted Nominal Prices

	Low income (less than ....)		Medium incomes (between ...and ...)		High incomes (more than ... units)		Total	
	Benefits	Cost	Benefits	Cost	Benefits	Cost	Benefits	Cost
Payments for irrigation		250		100		150		500
Payments for drinking water		1 422		640		71		2 133
Payments for electricity		200		1 000		300		1 500
Taxpayers		67		100		100		267
Additional costs of farmers		20		50		50		120
Additional farmers' incomes	600		600		300		1 500	
Additional landowners' income	0		150		350		500	
Drinking water	1 422		640		71		2 133	
Electricity	200		1 000		300		1 500	
Total	2 222	1 959	2 390	1 890	1 021	671	5 633	4 520
% of total	39.45	43.34	42.43	41.81	18.12	14.85	100	100

127

Part III

<u>SOCIAL CONSIDERATIONS</u>

PART III

SOME CONSIDERATIONS

Chapter XII

BASIC SOCIAL CONSIDERATIONS

A. SOCIAL ISSUES IN WATER PROJECT PLANNING

238.   The analysis of the broad social impacts of public works is a more recent development in the area of water project planning. Naturally, the economic and environmental impacts have always been evaluated from the point of
view of human welfare, but it has long been felt that important benefits and
costs are not properly captured in these more traditional analyses.   The
earliest question was perhaps that of the value of human life and health: are
these sufficiently captured by measurements of earnings foregone or costs of
medical care? Many technicians and politicians feel that they are not.

239.   Sociologists and anthropologists have long been studying the behaviour
of social groups in all types of societies, but the results of social research
were seldom incorporated in development planning, nor was applied social research made a part of the planning process.   Traditional water planning assumed that society would adapt to the project and that social investigations
at best played the role of helping to solve problems which arose after the
project was in place. Some agencies hired social scientists to look at potential social problems, quickly dropping them when serious questions about the
efficiency of water development were raised.

240.   It is now quite clear that social investigations must be made an integral part of the planning and execution of large water projects. The need to
establish baseline data and the desirability of following the impacted population groups overtime imply the need to start the social investigations at the
inception of the project and not as an afterthought or only after problems already exist.

241.   It must also be borne in mind that social investigations will involve
significant expense and must be directed by persons of training and experience. The investigations can arouse suspicions and can become controver-
sial. At the same time, the limitations on social prediction and measurement
must be appreciated.

242.   The following list of questions illustrates the kinds of social issues
which may arise in relation to large water projects. The technical team
leader and the decision-maker can expect the social scientist to give aid and
advice on these matters.

1. What special social objectives should the project have, e.g. increasing the skills and incomes of the poorest groups; increasing geographical mobility; increasing rural skill level; improving health conditions? How is achievement to be measured and monitored for such objectives?
2. What social groups will be affected by the project, either intentionally or unintentionally, and how will each be affected? What is the implied geographical scope of the project?
3. What are the interests, values and likely attitudes towards the project of the groups identified in (2) above?
4. What arrangements for public participation and input should be made?
5. What employment and social opportunities will be provided for the resident population, and to what extent does their skill structure fit those opportunities?
6. What specific steps must be planned if a project objective is to benefit the poorest population groups?
7. What patterns of migration into and out of the project area are likely to be induced by the project?
8. What do migration patterns imply for resettlement programmes?
9. What direct or indirect health effects are likely to come from the project?
10. What are the net nutritional impacts of the project likely to be on the affected groups?
11. What instances of group and political conflict are likely to arise from project related changes?
12. What opportunities for project-related social benefits will exist and how can they be efficiently exploited? For example, training programmes, acceptance of education or health measures, improvement of communications.
13. What can be learned specifically about project performance and generally about planning procedures from ex post analyses of the project?

These are not necessarily the only questions and some of them may be impossible to answer. Firstly, it is important to take notice of few important observations, which will be put into perspective in the later sections.

243. The planning of public participation is vital and cannot be left to chance. Public inputs can be invaluable at every stage, from project definition to final design and operating rules. The various public groups can be tapped for ideas and for data, and their participation gives them an interest in the success of the project. Conflicts are uncovered early and can be minimised through mutual negotiation and education.

244. A major problem with the development of contacts has been that the resident population of the project area is often displaced by the project, either physically or by immigrants who stream to the area to take advantage of the new opportunities. Since aiding this population may be a major social objective, this possibility must be carefully analysed and, when appropriate, steps taken to prevent undesirable consequences of unsettlement. Training programmes are often needed. The issue of displacement and resettlement is so vast that it will be treated in detail in Chapter XVI. It should be noted again, however, that resettlement has generally been a much more difficult and expensive problem than anticipated. Ultimate resettlement costs have exceeded total project construction costs in several well known cases.

245.   Project related health effects rank with migration and resettlement as major issues which must not only be anticipated but which can be sufficiently negative to warrant stopping a project. At the Volta Project in Ghana, bilharzia not only spread around the edges of the huge reservoir, but "river blindness" transmitted by the simulium fly spread throughout the river delta because of the constancy of reservoir releases. The spread of bilharzia in Egypt due to the Aswan High Dam is well documented. While these diseases are not endemic to OECD countries, the planning team is obligated to be alert to possible problems. Naturally, health improvements can also occur as the result of drainage, improvements in water quality, better nutrition, and a qualitative and quantitative improvement in water supply.

B. DIFFICULTIES OF SOCIAL EVALUATION STUDIES

246.   Social evaluation studies are not easy. At least four categories of problems related to social evaluation study can be mentioned. These categories should be kept in mind when a decision to start a social evaluation is at issue.

    -- Social evaluations are usually expensive and time consuming. Funds may not be readily available. In general a weighing-up is necessary between the costs of the evaluation study and the expected increased project effects and decreased project costs;
    -- There exists some substantial limitations on what social impacts can be measured. We will usually have to be satisfied with indicators, the validity of which are not always known;
    -- Social evaluation of the different project objectives can be controversial. Project managers, citizen groups, and people affected tend to be defensive when their values and positions are at stake. When social evaluations bring controversial objectives to the surface, conflicts between different interests may be the result.
    -- The evaluation of social impacts of a project usually requires highly skilled experts, who are not always available. Special social evaluation staffs are expensive. The carrying out and elaboration of the evaluation results may call for very specialised social study knowledge.

247.   From these problem categories one can extract at least four related problem fields insofar as social evaluation is considered:

    a) The predictability of social events;
    b) The nature of social events: "good" or "bad";
    c) The identification of population segments;
    d) Data collection.

These problem fields will be discussed briefly.

a) Predictability of Social Events

248.   A first question is the extent to which social developments resulting from the project can be predicted. Social phenomena have a relatively low

degree of regularity, but existing regularities are best brought to light by the analysis of the data of some past interval of time, using relevant theories, and then testing predictive capabilities by predicting conditions in another past period. This process is called post-diction. If such post-dictions are acceptably close to observed conditions, some confidence can be felt in the predictive system. The system can then be extended to prediction of conditions in future periods. However, processes or events which have not occurred during the post-diction periods cannot be predicted by this process.

249. Sometimes, a social scientist has good reasons to believe that certain developments may take place, that have not occurred previously in the social system under consideration. In that case he has to make a list of the most important potential new events. Each entry on this list is supplemented with information about:

a) The relative chance of occurrence of the event;
b) The impact of the event in case of occurrence;
c) The direction of the impact (positive or negative with regard to the objectives of the development project) and
d) differences in (a), (b) and (c) to be expected as a result of the point in time the "new event" takes place, and
e) differences to be expected as a result of the occurrence of combinations of "new events".

250. The relative predictability of developments in social systems varies to quite an extent. If migration in a region is low, for instance, the development of the age structure of the population is highly predictable. If the cultural and the economic patterns are relatively stable, the number of children born and the number of people dying is highly predictable. Aspects like the emergence of protest groups, however, may prove to have a low predictability.

b) Are Social Events "Good" or "Bad"?

251. The desirability or undesirability of a social event cannot be judged without reference to the project objectives. The importance and the variety of such objectives has already been stressed (cf. Supra §41 and following). For this reason a water-project will certainly have (directly or indirectly) social objectives. Examples are provided in Table 33.

252. A special aspect which should be kept in mind when formulating project objectives, is that they should include the various social variables that the project is designed to affect. Not only the direct project-related objectives (for instance concerning fishery facilities, agricultural opportunities and recreational facilities) should be mentioned. Indirect objectives (like the changes in health and safety conditions and of the satisfaction of the people affected) should also be formulated. The unintended social consequences of a project should be considered too.

253. In formulating the evaluation variables the most crucial question is the choice of variables which will be measured. Here again the social conditions which the project will affect (health, safety, housing, people's satisfaction) come to mind. In general it is better to have too many variables than to eliminate some that might be important. In looking for evaluation

Table 33

EXAMPLES OF POSSIBLE SOCIAL OBJECTIVES

Development of the regional economy
Reduction of poverty level
Increasing the health level
Increasing the safety level
Increasing the income level
Reduction of unemployment level
Increasing soil-productivity level
Provision of educational facilities
Provision of transport facilities
Provision of communication facilities
Improving the housing quality
Improving the fishery facilities
Improving recreational facilities
Increasing the general satisfaction of the people affected

variables one should not be concerned with how and whether they can be measured, because some very interesting variables may fall out.

254.   The basic variables or <u>social indicators</u> used in social assessments are found at three levels of aggregation: the individual component (either a person or a household); the sub-system or institutional level component (e.g. the population of a town or river basin, the workers on a farm, members of an occupation, etc.); and the social system level component. Examples of frequently used indicators at these three levels are given in Table 34.

c) <u>Population Segments</u>

255.   The identification of the relevant <u>population segments</u> is also a basic element of a social evaluation study. Different groups may be affected by a project at different degrees.

256.   It is important to identify such groups and to formulate evaluation variables reflecting the project's impacts on them. In general each project will have some intended beneficiaries, and some groups that are not the direct clients, but which are nevertheless (detrimentally or beneficially) affected. A general clientele group classification scheme is shown in Table 35.

d) <u>Data Collection</u>

257.   The different components of the social evaluation study determine what kind of data will be necessary for a specific social evaluation. The objectives and the evaluation variables indicate what indicators can best be used to evaluate a project. The population segments give us an idea of the levels of aggregation. etc.

Table 34

SOCIAL INDICATORS AND THEIR UNITS OF MEASUREMENT

Categories	Indicators	Units of Measurement
a) At the individual level		
Nutrition	Caloric intake	Calories per day as per cent of norms
	Protein intake	Grams per day by type
Health	Level of parasitic or infectious disease	Per cent of population having the disease; probability of resultant death
Shelter	Housing per capita	m^2 per inhabitant
Personal satisfaction	Index	Ordinal index of perception of social, physical and cultural environment
b) At the sub-system level		
Demographic	Population	Size, density, age, sex, marital status, ethnic composition
Education	Average level	Enrolment, years per capita
	Literacy	Tested literacy rate
	Occupational training	Doctors, lawyers, teachers per 1 000 population
Government services	Police protection Fire protection	Policemen per capita Trucks per km^2
c) At the social system level		
Social stability	Residents' image of stability	Percentage of population satisfied
Social participation in collective affairs	Percentage of of eligible voters actually voting	

Table 35

EXAMPLE OF A GENERAL CLIENTELE GROUP CLASSIFICATION SCHEME

General population/clientele group
classification characteristics

1. Residence location
   grouped by neighbourhood, service area, precinct, etc., for local, regional, national planning level, etc.

2. Sex

3. Age
   youth and the elderly may have particular needs.

4. Family income groups
   the poor may have specific needs.

5. Racial/ethnic groups

6. Special handicapped groups
   physically, but also culturally handicapped may have specific needs.

7. Education level

8. Type of dwelling

9. Employment status

10. Family structure and size

11. Profession (farmers, craftsmen, shopkeepers, etc.).

---

258.   The most interesting methods for data collection in social evaluations are:

    -- Existing records and statistics;
    -- Interviews (with people affected, with representatives, with experts);
    -- Observation.

In these three categories many more specific methods can be found. As an example some possible sources and techniques are listed below in Table 36.

Table 36

EXAMPLES OF SOURCES FOR AND TECHNIQUES OF DATA COLLECTION

-- Questionnaires

-- Participant observation

-- Ratings

-- Psychometric tests of attitudes, values, personality, preferences, beliefs, etc.

-- Institutional records

-- Governmental records and statistics

-- Tests of information, skills, knowledge

-- Situational tests presenting respondents with simulated life situations

-- Diary records

-- Physical evidence

-- Clinical records

-- Tests of satisfaction

-- Financial records

-- Documents (newspapers, accounts of policy actions, transcripts of trials, memos)

D. PUBLIC PARTICIPATION

259.   One of the crucial parts in the process of regional development planning (in fact in all planning exercises) is the participation of the people to
whom the planning is directed and whom the planning actually affects. (There
might be a great difference between these two groups: a plan may be directed
to a certain village, but by its nature and through the reactions of a population to the plan, may in fact influence a whole region.)

260.   Neglecting the people in planning processes has been one of the main
causes of failure of many water projects from the social points of view.
Success or failure is therefore highly correlated to the degree of public involvement one chooses. However participation as such is too broad a concept
to be used directly by social scientists. Differentiation is needed. This
differentiation can take the form of a "participation-hierarchy". The
decision-maker will have to look for the most appropriate level of participation at each step of the planning process. Roughly speaking there are three
levels of participation:

-- Knowing;
-- Talking;
-- Deciding.

261. It can be seen from Table 37 that the global levels of participation (knowing, talking and deciding) might be differentiated into more detailed sub-levels. The choice of a participation level depends on many things: the scope, time span, groups involved, information required, the content of the planning process, and so on.

Table 37

LEVELS AND TECHNIQUES OF PUBLIC PARTICIPATION

Public participation		
Global level	Detailed level	Possible techniques
	Giving information after the plan has been approved (manipulation)	Presenting the plan
Knowing	Supplying and collecting straight information without interference of the public	Exhibitions Information by mass-media Surveys
	Supplying of information with cross-talks only for the purpose of "steam-relief"	Hearing Polls
Talking	Negotiations on alternatives	Action groups
	Decison-makers and participants are being treated equally (delegated power)	Referanda
Deciding	Decision-making happens on the participant level (guiding by participants)	Neighbourhood councils

262. Three points should always be kept in mind:

-- Decisions are made by politicians and policy-makers but they are shaped by a process of public participation; it should be made possible (by participation techniques) for the public to interfere -- in one way or another -- with the politicians and policy-makers;
-- The planning process includes public involvement as an integral part;

139

-- Public participation is in most cases limited primarily to leadership of relatively well-organised groups; public participation is
costly if one attempts to reach less organised groups. So there
must be a maximum feasible participation; one cannot devote 50 per
cent of the total project budget to structuring the participation to
its full extent.

263. The seven levels mentioned on Table 37 are steps in a participation
hierarchy. This does not mean that in all phases of the planning process we
have to strive for the highest level. However, in multipurpose projects crucial steps, like problem-definition and final selection of an alternative project design, should be characterised by at least one of the three highest
levels (negotiations, delegated power, self-guiding).

Chapter XIII

VARIOUS TECHNIQUES OF SOCIAL EVALUATION AT DIFFERENT STEPS OF THE PROJECT

264. At different stages of the planning process, one can make use of a variety of social research techniques. In this chapter, a few important techniques will be discussed, including those techniques related to public participation. Whenever possible the discussion should proceed according to the general agenda for studies, as defined in Chapter 2.

A. THE "SNAP SHOT SURVEY" FOR THE PRELIMINARY SCREENING OF PROJECTS IDEAS

265. The first stage of a whole multi-purpose hydraulic water project is the "preliminary screening of project ideas". In this stage specific attention has to be paid to the broad social issues likely to arise and the ways sociologists might work out these issues during the development of the project. For instance, people may not want their lands to be flooded; perhaps they do not want to leave their grounds; perhaps they do not want new methods and technologies, etc.

266. The analyses of these kinds of general social issues must be studies that will, on a broad scale, reflect the feelings of the public concerning the project ideas. Besides, they must provide some rough ideas on the most important aspects of the daily life of communities before the project starts. What is the degree of social stability in these areas? What are the income patterns? What are the health conditions? What is the scale of unemployment? How effective is the educational system?

267. At the same time, it will be necessary to identify some very general social issues at the regional level: rural poverty, unemployment, political tensions, heavy migration, inequitable access to land or other resources, health problems, are just some examples. A list of examples of general issues is provided in Table 38. The issues must be put in the perspective of the water project. Can we identify relationships between the project and these general social issues? Will the project help to lessen some of these problems? Or will they be enlarged?

268. These very general initial questions are the starting points for the

sociological analysis during the development of the project. The sociologists take these broad topics as a base for their investigations. For this reason it is worthwhile to broaden the discussions on the general social issues as much as possible. If possible, public opinion on the idea of starting a project should be heard. The sociologists could work out a snap-shot survey to sample public opinion on the project idea. The questions to be asked in this survey should be related to the general social issues which are identified by team members. At the same time however the survey can be used to bring out more of these general issues and to get more detailed information on the ways people cope with them.

Table 38

LIST OF EXAMPLES OF GENERAL SOCIAL ISSUES WHICH COULD BE
STUDIED IN THE PRELIMINARY SCREENING STAGE

Maintenance/change of social stability
Maintenance/change of religious and cultural traditions
Maintenance/change of family and group patterns
Maintenance/change in income patterns
Maintenance/change of health conditions
Migratory patterns and density
Poverty and low income
Unemployment
Low productivity
Political tensions
Resettlement
Nutrition problems
Communicational problems
Transport problems
Criminal problems
Housing problems
Educational inefficiency

269. The result of the snap-shot survey is an initial list of general social issues together with some identified relationships between these issues and the possibility of starting a project. The list of general social issues will be submitted to a first sociological analysis. In this initial analysis two general characteristics could be elaborated on:

-- The scope of the social issues;
-- The time span of the analysis of these issues.

270. Concerning the scope of the social issues, the geographical area directly affected by the project should be examined first. Which issues should be analysed during the development of the project from the point of view of this area? Changing income patterns, changing health conditions and changing religious traditions are some examples. Next a somewhat wider scope might be chosen to look at migration patterns and resettlement problems. In a still wider perspective attention must be paid to all those areas (sometimes even parts of the world) that may want to influence the development of the project.

271. Closely related to the scope is the time span of the analysis of social issues. Do we have to look at five, ten or more years of the past? How does this fit in with the empirical data available? Do we have to look for impacts during the first five years after completion of the project proper? Ten years? As a rule extensive and intensive coverage of periods have to be distinguished.

272. After the initial sociological analysis a small report can be produced on the identified social issues. It should give some general and broad ideas on the existing social situations in the area where a project might be introduced and on the ways people expect the project to change these situations. Some estimations of the willingness of people to co-operate and on the topics where resistance might be expected should be included.

273. The first report may prove helpful in the discussions with the decision-maker and other team members to make them more conscious of the project-related social issues. For this reason the issues dealt with should be covered in an accessible and easily understandable way.

B. TECHNIQUES RELATED TO PUBLIC PARTICIPATION

274. The importance of public participation has been stressed above (cf. §259 above). At least those people that are affected by the plan should have the opportunity to have a say in the planning process and hence the decision-making. This is the basic legitimation of public participation; people should have the right to build (or help building) their own environment, to create their own life-space. Planners and decision-makers therefore, being representatives of the public, have to pay attention to the initiation of structured regular public participation processes. The steps to be taken in those processes are:

a) Selection of the Relevant Groups of People to be Affected by the Project

275. This topic has already been discussed (see §255 above). The most important groups mentioned there are: the local people (directly or indirectly involved with the project), the relocatees (those people that have to be resettled), the immigrants: very diverse groups as labour forces that are needed during the construction of the project, people looking for job opportunities, people connected with industries, and so on.

b) Construction of a Participation Matrix

276. The participation matrix establishes a link between the various groups of people defined above, and the participation methods to be used at different stages of the planning process. As indicated in Table 39, columns represent the groups, and rows represent stages of the planning process. At the interaction of each row and column, the participation level to be used is indicated.

277. So for example, if the planner and the decision-makers think it of great importance that the local people as well as the relocatees discuss at

143

length the selection of the final set of alternatives, they will fill out a T (talking) in the corresponding cells. If they think that tourist organisations that are interested in, let's say, a newly created lake, should only be informed about the multipurpose project, they fill out a K (knowing) in all the cells of the column: recreational and tourist organisations.

c) Definition of the Participation Content

278. In gathering data on the participation, we are interested in questions like: which are the people that may gain? How can we trace these people? What are their incomes, their location? Are they organised in one way or another? What are their wishes and expectations? How can we reach them in order to get them to co-operate, participate and disseminate information and innovation? These questions may well be collected through, and answered by, a special part of the snap-shot survey. A number of participation-related questions may thus be added. They should at least contain an indication of the minimum and maximum levels between which people are willing to participate in the project.

279. Other questions to be answered are: What are the minimum resources we have to devote to the participation process? What level of education and attitude-building is necessary to help people participate? And at what level are people disinclined to participate? When we have this kind of information we will be able to set up a techniques-related-participation matrix. By combining the steps in the planning process in relation to participant-groups with the information needed or provided we can transform the participation matrix into a participation technique scheme (Table 40).

C. SOCIAL MONITORING

280. Monitoring is a more general activity than social evaluation study. If differs from social evaluation study because it concentrates on showing general project related changes. It does not attempt to indicate which specific activities of a project (have) influence(d) certain outputs and outcomes, and it does not separate definite project effects from changes which may have resulted from non-project efforts.

281. Monitoring is an indispensable part of every social evaluation process. By having some general ideas about trends and developments in the social system where the project is (or will be) implemented, a sound basis is created for more detailed studies. Also, because it is not very detailed and does not require large expenditures, it can provide the decision-makers with some data and insights which may be of value in helping to develop the project.

282. The usual objective of monitoring is to provide project managers and decision-makers with data which will give them an impression of how the project is going, to show if it is being run efficiently, if it is following the project guidelines, if the project staffs are competent, etc. If more detailed information is called for, more detailed social investigations must be carried out.

Table 39

EXAMPLE OF A PUBLIC-PARTICIPATION MATRIX
Cells can be filled in by indication of one of the participation levels
required e.g. K = knowing; T = talking; D = deciding

Planning steps \ Groups involved	Immigrant labour force	Local people indirectly involved (hosts)	Local people directly involved	Relocatees (Resettlers)	Immigrants	Recreational and touristic organisations
Preliminary screening						K
Selection of institutions			K			K
Preliminary project alternatives			K			K
Progressive elimination of alternatives			K			K
Selection of final set of alternatives		T	T	T	K	K
Programming						K
Construction						K
Evaluation	T	T	T	T	T	T

145

Table 40

EXAMPLE OF A LIST OF POSSIBLE PARTICIPATION TECHNIQUES
TO BE CORRELATED WITH TABLE 39, THE PARTICIPATION MATRIX

Planning step	Public participation technique
Preliminary screening of project ideas	Snap-shot survey
Selection of institutes	Consultation
Preliminary project alternatives	Meeting with the public and political leaders
	Data gathering on specific subjects (objectives, evaluation variables, Population segments)
Progressive elimination	Scenario-writing
Selection of final set of alternatives	Public meetings with community leaders and interest groups Summarising scenarios Analysing public comments Comprehensive survey Presentation to decision-makers and to the public
Programming	Procedural workbooks to be written together with the community leaders
Construction	Resettlement paper Meetings with community leader and interested community groups

283.   Social monitoring is a permanent process of information-detection and information-supply. The monitoring process should be organised in such a way that the information provided to the project-team is usable information. For this reason a list of topics must be drawn up to direct the monitoring activities.

284.   The social monitoring must be designed so as to make clear how the monitored social variables develop over time. For instance: is the general health situation of the population in the river basin area deteriorating or not? Is the educational level rising or not? Is the number of criminal violations growing or not? It is not the objective of the social monitoring process to collect very detailed data on all kinds of differentiated topics. The main purpose is to get some general views over time. The data collection

methods should not be very sophisticated or time-consuming. Existing resources should be used as much as possible. General statistical information may perhaps be found on a national or regional governmental level; newspaper analyses may provide interesting longitudinal data; strategic interviews with community leaders, politicians and administrators in the project area may point to all kinds of interesting trends. The sociological expertise and imagination of the social scientists in the project team should be applied as much as possible.

285. In the stage of the preliminary identification, design, evaluation and screening of project alternatives, this list is the first social evaluation activity needed. Logically this list will be based on the short report which was provided in the very first stage of the project ("preliminary screening of the project area") where the most important social issues were mentioned. The inventory of social topics to be covered in the social monitoring process is also the start of the ex-ante social evaluation process.

286. A special aspect of the social monitoring process must be stressed here: the monitoring of the project-related participation activities. For the monitoring of these kinds of activities we need no more than a set of rather general variables. Things to be monitored could be:

-- Kind of groups participating (characteristics included);
-- Degree of participation;
-- Success or failure of sociological techniques used;
-- Unexpected social obstacles met during the project;
-- Success or failure of communication-techniques;
-- Time needed for dissemination of information;
-- Impact of participation on the relative capacity to influence public policy, and so on.

D. SCENARIO WRITING DURING THE EX ANTE STAGE OF PROJECT PREPARATION

287. To integrate the various social aspects, the social scientist may try to use some forecasting-techniques. One of the techniques best suited to this task seems to be scenario-writing. Scenarios are paths into the future, written out in a logical and comprehensive way. Scenarios in the broadest sense contain three elements:

288. A detailed description of the present state of the subject at hand. This is a so-called base-line analysis. The aim is to give a good picture of the social situation before the project.

289. Descriptions of possible as well as desirable futures. The first case is concerned with how the future develops "spontaneously" from the present. While the second case is concerned with how people can effectively change their present situation into a different and more desirable future state. In all cases the more people, decision-makers and planners use their imagination, the greater will be the number of options looked at. In writing scenarios one is able to make those options visible.

290. The last element of a scenario is the link between the base-line

analysis and the picture one has of the (desired) future state. This link is a sequence of events which has its starting point in the present situation and which leads towards the future state. Since we are talking about the future such events have, of course, a hypothetical character.

291. Now, there are two basic forms on which one can "construct" the future: based upon the past-present situation and based upon the future. This needs some elaboration. If we want to demonstrate how a future situation will, logically and step by step, develop out of the base-line situation, we base ourselves on trends (and/or time-series) of past and present. Then, according to our expectations and assumptions on likely developments of (social) aspects, we extrapolate the trends in one way or another. In this case, past and present -- and the "laws" we discover in it -- are the mechanisms of future development. The output will be some possible future situation.

292. But we can also start at the opposite end: in the future. We then start (after having developed the base-line study) with the description of desired, normative, future states. Again, on a logical and step by step basis, we work out the sequence of events leading from that future state backwards to the present situation. In confronting this sequence of events with the possibilities (means and ends) that are given in the present situation, one can judge which desired future state is more likely to occur. The past-present approach is called projective scenario-writing; the future-oriented approach is called prospective scenario-writing.

293. Both forms of scenario-writing can be used separately or in combination. Other advantages in using this forecasting technique are:

-- Scenarios show explicitly that people themselves can shape part of the future;
-- Scenarios can make clear that present-day planning and future states are not two separate things. Planning influences our options for the future, but our future images fill out our planning schemes;
-- Scenarios can be used on different levels of participation and on different levels of specification.

294. This illustrates that scenario-writing is a valuable tool in the ex ante evaluation phase of the project-design. It may be used to develop some alternative future "images" of the social aspects of big hydraulic projects.

295. Some aspects of scenario-writing should be emphasized:

-- We always write scenarios, never one scenario; in doing so we explore the options available in the future, and at the same time draw up boundaries for future development. By choosing paths in the past and present (planning) we limit our future in certain ways;
-- Scenarios by their nature provide a relatively comprehensive picture of factors -- and their interrelationships -- which affect the future. One of the techniques that fully considers these interrelationships between factors is cross-impact analysis. This technique could be used as an auxiliary instrument during the construction of scenarios;

-- Global scenarios can be written out in small workshops within a few
   days. This means that a rapid insight may be gained, and this time-
   saving element may be very important for over-burdened people such
   as politicians.

In general it seems wise not to construct too many scenarios, but to limit
oneself to the most extreme cases. These extreme cases will give us a clear
understanding of the various ways the alternative project designs will influence the (social) future. This again will make the selection of the final set
of project alternatives much easier.

E. CROSS IMPACT ANALYSIS FOR PUTTING TOGETHER PIECES OF INFORMATION

296.   Cross-impact analysis is a collective name for a family of techniques.
With these techniques, one tries to measure the relationships between certain
changes in the probability of the performance of one set of events with
changes in another set of events. The aim is to estimate the changes in
values of the probabilities of certain forecasted events from one set, knowing
(or assuming) the occurence of certain events in the other set. The basic
principle could be formulated as: "If that event (from set No. 2) were to
occur, what would the change in probability be of this event (from set
No. 1)?". For the first set, every event has a certain forecasted probability
to start with. When confronted with the occurrence of an event from the
second set, these initially forecasted probabilities of the events in the
first set may either increase, decrease or remain unchanged. In the matrix of
Table 41 the basic principle of the cross-impact analysis is shown.

297.   The cross-impact-matrix may also be used for only one set of events.
In this case, the events of one set are confronted with one another. Table 42
provides an example of the resulting matrix.

298.   To give an example of the cross impact analysis of a sociological problem in a multipurpose hydraulic project, one might think of the influence the
occurence of the event "changing from farming to fishery for the main part of
the population" would have on the probability of a more equal distribution of
income in the primary sector. The outcome might for instance be that the initial forecasted probability changes from 50 to 80 per cent.

F. MODEL BUILDING AND ITS LIMITATIONS

299.   Model-building was (and somtimes still is) a very widespread technique
used by planners and policy-makers. In fact, it may prove to be worthwhile
for certain parts of the full social impact analysis. On the other hand, for
the purposes of social pre-evaluation highly sophisticated model-building
generally do not make a very important contribution to this evaluation process, although it must be admitted that simulation of aspects would have some
value. For example rough simulation of possible resettlement patterns could
benefit the actual planning and processes of resettlement.

Table 41

BASIC FORM OF A CROSS-IMPACT MATRIX TYPE I

If an event indicated in this column were to occur	Then the probability of the event in this row would: Increase (I), Decrease (D) or demonstrate no change (N)			
	A	B	C	D
P	N	(I)	(N)	(D)
Q	I	D	I	N
R	D	D	N	D
S	D	I	N	D

Table 42

BASIC FORM OF A CROSS-IMPACT MATRIX TYPE II

If an event indicated in this column were to occur	Then the probability of the event in this row would: increase (I), Decrease (D) or demonstrate no change (N)			
	A	B	C	D
A		D	N	I
B	N		N	D
C	I	I		N
D	D	D	D	

300. Models require a lot of quantifiable data, theoretical insight in the correlation between separate observable phenomena, modern instruments and a great deal of time and outside expertise. However if these requirements are met, there should be no problem in the application of models.

301. In most cases it would be better to use aspect-modelling or non-machine-simulation; the latter is mostly called gaming. In games, people play certain roles in for example decision-making processes, so as to gain an understanding of the possibilities and constraints involved in those processes.

302. The choice of the techniques to be used is a matter for the social scientists in the project team to decide upon. It is they who can best determine which subjects require sophisticated techniques like simulation models and which topics need less elaborate analysis.

G. EX POST ANALYSIS AND FEEDBACK

303. Once the chosen project alternatives have been implemented the social scientists can carry out their ex post social evaluation research. Ex post social evaluation research is a little less speculative than ex ante social evaluation. This is why the sociological methodology in ex post social evaluation is far more developed than in ex ante evaluation. There are four general ex post social evaluation designs available.

a) The "Before" Versus "After" Project Comparison

304. In this design the project results are "measured" at two points in time: before implementation and after implementation. The changes that are found between the before and after measurement are considered to be the effects of the project. This is the most common, the simplest and cheapest type of social information. The problem with this design is that the effects of the project are very hard to separate from other influences. The basic steps in this design are:

    -- Identify objectives, evaluation variables and population segments;
    -- Measure the values of the variables before and after implementation;
    -- Compare these "before and after" values to estimate changes brought
       about by the programme;
    -- Look for other plausible explanations for the changes that have
       occurred to estimate the effects of non-project influences.

b) The "Before" Versus "After" Project Comparison with Trends Projection

305. In this design "actual" changes after implementation are measured and compared with projection for the values of the evaluation variables. The projections are based on historical data. This design is a little more complex because of the technical expertise which is necessary for the statistical projections. It is only meaningful as a research design if an underlying trend can be made explicit; if the data are unstable this design should not be used. The basic steps in this design are:

-- Identify objectives, evaluation variables and population segments;
-- Obtain data for each variable at several intervals prior to the implementation and after implementation;
-- Use statistical methods to develop a trend projection (regression
analysis);
-- Compare actual values with the projected estimates to discover the
changes which are the results of the project;
-- Look for other plausible explanations for the changes in the evaluation variables.

c) The "Served Versus not Served" Population Segments Comparison

306.   In this design population segments which are served by the project are
compared with similar population segments not served by the project. This design tries to take influences other than those of the project into account.
If the changes in the population segments "served and not served" are nearly
identical, then it may be concluded that non-project influences were significant. A difficulty often lies in finding comparable groups. These groups are
not "planned" from the beginning of the evaluation but must be found later.
This is both time-consuming and expensive. An extra set of data also has to
be collected. The basic steps are:

-- Identify objectives, evaluation variables and population segments;
-- Identify another group of population segments, as identical as pos-
sible to the population segments served by the project;
-- Obtain data for both groups on the evaluation variables both before
and after implementation (by actual measurement or trend projection);
-- Compare the changes in the values of the evaluation variables for
both groups; compare both amount and rate of change;
-- Look for other plausible explanations.

d) The Controlled Experiment

307.   This is the most elegant, but also the most difficult and expensive design. In this design the effects of the project are estimated by systematic-
ally comparing two or more carefully separated groups. With one of these
groups the project is implemented; with the other not. The critical aspect is
that the comparison groups are pre-assigned before the project-implementation,
so that the groups are completely similar except for the project. The design
is very hard to use without violating it. All kinds of problems emerge. The
group with which the project will be implemented (the so-called experimental
group) may respond differently if they realise they are special ("Hawthorne
effect"). Political circumstances may make it impossible to provide one group
with the services and the other not. Good preparation and planning of the experimental evaluation takes time, money and highly skilled researchers. The
basic steps of this design are:

-- Identify objectives, evaluation variables and population segments;
-- Select the "experimental" and the "control" groups; the groups must
have as many similar characteristics as possible; members of the
used sample must be assigned "randomly" over the two groups;
-- Measure the values of the evaluation variables before implementation
for both groups;

-- Apply the project activities only to the experimental group;
-- Monitor the time of the project activities for both groups to find out what kind of different influences (apart from the project influences) are exerted;
-- Measure the values of the evaluation variables for both groups;
-- Compare the changes in the values of the evaluation variables for both groups.
-- Look for other plausible explanations; these will be rare because the second basic step is taken to make the groups very much alike.

308.   In reality many variants of these four ex post social evaluation designs can be found. The only reason for presenting these designs is to give an analytical insight into their procedures and the problems connected with them. In general the experimental design (d) must be recommended. Since the costs are high and the procedures may be too strict, the other designs may also prove to be worthwhile. Especially when combinations of (a), (b) and (c) are tried, the evaluation results will certainly be good enough to judge the social impacts of the project concerned.

H. FORMATIVE AND SUMMATIVE EVALUATION

309.   In this last stage of the whole planning process there are two ways in which the information from the ex post social evaluation studies can be used. In the first place the information can be fed back to "earlier" planning stages to help to improve the project. The social evaluation information is used to decide whether the project can be improved, should be redirected, should be enlarged, should be stopped, etc. This handling of social information is called formative social evaluation. It is a main aspect of planning as a learning process. The planning process must be flexible and be able to react to new information. If adjustments are needed during the construction and operating of the project, they should not be affected by fixed rules and procedures.

310.   Information from the ex post social evaluation studies can also be used as a final judgement of the project. In the case we speak of summative social evaluation. Summative evaluation studies are done after the project has ended. It provides information about the ways the project was prepared and executed and about the concrete outputs of the project. This information is not fed back to the project operation stages, but is made available to planners and decision-makers who want to start similar projects. In general, it is used to extend the knowledge about the ways these kinds of projects influence social processes and structures.

Chapter XIV

THE FULL SOCIAL IMPACT ANALYSIS

311.   The various techniques described in the preceding chapter can be used, separately or in combination, at different stages of the planning process. The degree of indepthness of social investigations (and thus, the intensity with which these methods will be used) depends upon the magnitude of the social problems which will be identified by the preliminary studies.   If no social problems are identified, then only a light monitoring will be necessary. Similarly, if only a small number of well defined difficulties emerge, the application of some of these techniques at the relevant level and time will usually solve the problems. On the contrary, whenever social problems are important, and likely to jeopardise the success of the project, a full social impact analysis is needed. Conducting this study is the subject of the present chapter.

312.   To be able to carry out such a full social impact analysis, we need an instrument for examining social aspects of multi-purpose hydraulic projects in a systematic way. It will be called the "social assessment structure" (SAS). The social assessment structure can be used as a sort of check-list (1) on possible social impacts of a multi-purpose hydraulic project. It may be used either in the ex ante evaluation or in ex post evaluation, that is, either before the definite decision to start the execution of the project, or during (and even after) execution. In the case of ex ante evaluation, forecasts should be made on the ways the alternative project designs influence the various social variables in the SAS. In the case of ex post evaluations these influences can be measured.

313.   The social assessment structure is based on the idea of an open social system and which is therefore in permanent interaction with its environment. A social system is made up of various subsystems, such as economic subsystems, the health subsystem, the religious subsystem, etc. Within each subsystem, several institutions can be found: the market, the church, the family, etc. Figure 14 shows how resources (such as physical material, knowledge, technology, values, etc.) are extracted by the subsystem from their total environment, and channelled through the social system in order to produce certain outputs in terms of individual and social well being. For assessing the impact of a change (for instance, a change brought about by the project under consideration) in this process, a number of social indicators must be defined. The most important of these are those which relate to these individual and social well being.

154

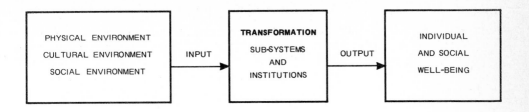

Figure 14 A SOCIAL PROCESS SYSTEM

| PHYSICAL ENVIRONMENT
CULTURAL ENVIRONMENT
SOCIAL ENVIRONMENT | INPUT → | TRANSFORMATION
SUB-SYSTEMS
AND
INSTITUTIONS | OUTPUT → | INDIVIDUAL
AND SOCIAL
WELL-BEING |

A. INDIVIDUAL WELL-BEING

314. <u>Individual well-being</u> could be defined if we could establish the nature of individual human needs. This would enable us to evaluate the "<u>quality of life</u>" of an individual in a specific social setting. Although several publications on these topics have appeared, there is still no definite set of basic individual human needs. Nevertheless we may distinguish two general categories of human needs.

315. The first category is formed by the so-called <u>biogenic needs</u>. Biogenic needs are supposed to be essential requirements for individual survival. They are:

1. Nutrients (minimums vary by body size, age, amount of activity)
   -- Vitamins
   -- Minerals
   -- Proteins
   -- Carbohydrates
   -- Calcium
   -- Fats
2. Bodily warmth and coolness (range of acceptable temperature without artificial protection is 60° - 85°F)
3. Water (absolute minimum is one pint per day per person) (2)
4. Oxygen and carbon monoxide release
5. Bodily hygiene
6. Invocation of "striped musculature" (exercise)
7. Rest of "striped musculature" (rest and sleep)
8. Expulsion of bodily wastes (bladder and colon release)
9. Avoidance of noxious stimulation (avoidance of fear and injurious conditions)
10. Avoidance of inclement environmental conditions (avoidance of wind, waves, earthquakes, tornados, etc.)
11. Sexual tension maintenance.

316. Besides biogenic needs a second category can be distinguished: the

so-called learned needs, that are mentioned as essential basic human needs in
several publications. Learned needs (or acquired needs, derived needs) are
the results of learning processes of individuals in society. Of course the
biogenic needs (or natural needs, formal needs) also appear only in modified
social-cultural forms. Nevertheless it seems important to make a distinction
between the two categories of biogenic and learned needs on the level of individual well-being. Learned needs are learned in the social setting in which
the individual participates. Learned needs include personal as well as
psychological individual needs. They are (3):

I. Personal needs

    1. Prestige;
    2. Acquisition of knowledge and skills (education);
    3. Explanation of the meaning of human existence;
    4. Creature comfort (goods and services, above and beyond subsistence,
       including recreation);
    5. Income;
    6. Employment.

II. Psychological needs

    1. Affection;
    2. Interaction (both in formal and informal settings);
    3. Communication and transport;
    4. Protection (from the social misdeeds of others);
    5. Self-esteem and self-actualisation.

B. SOCIAL WELL-BEING

317. Social well-being may be defined in different ways. First, according
to the "level of living" of the population. The level of living refers to the
living conditions of the population as a whole. It is an evaluation index of
the ways the basic human needs are satisfied for the whole population. For an
indication of the basic human needs of a whole population the same basic needs
as those that were identified at the individual level can be used. It should
be pointed out however, that for the establishment of the level of living of
the population, we cannot confine ourselves to the averages on needs satisfaction per head; we must also take the distributions of satisfaction levels
over the population into account.

318. Social well-being can also be defined by the way the different subsystems and institutions of a social system are able to fulfil basic human
needs. Here we are mainly concerned with the co-operative efforts of individuals and with the development of collective actions, structures and programmes to attain specified goals, related to specific basic human needs. In
order to evaluate the social well-being by focusing on the subsystems and institutions we need an overview of these subsystems and institutions. Such an
overview will be presented later on.

319. Social well-being can finally be looked upon from the perspective of the social system as a whole. The social system as a whole is both the result of the processes of needs satisfaction which are organised to fulfil basic human needs, and the conditioning total structure within which these processes have to take place. The social system as a whole is the social process system we typified earlier, and the conditioning factors are concretised in the three types of environment (physical, cultural and social) mentioned above. Looking from the perspective of the social system as a whole, we may identify some very abstract "basic needs" of a social process sytstem that have to be fulfilled to keep the social system sound and alive. These needs are different from the needs we identified earlier because of their abstract and general character and the typical focus which goes beyond the level of basic human needs. Perhaps we could speak of basic social system needs. Included in these needs are:

1. Development and growth (necessary for the viability of the system as a whole);
2. Consciousness (ability to set and pursue collective goals;)
3. Participation (opportunities available to people to participate in the whole system);
4. Stability (certain amount of change resistancy as a necessary aspect of the capability to function as a whole system);
5. Legitimacy (ability to attract loyalty and motivation of the people participating in the whole system);
6. Competence (ability to be effective, i.e. to use resources from environments to enhance individual and social well-being.)

320. It may be concluded from the statements above that the concept of "needs" can be analysed at different levels. First there is the individual level, where the quality of life of an individual in his social setting is evaluated in terms of the satisfaction levels of the basic individual human needs. Secondly there is the level of the social well-being, where three different approaches are distinguished. At the social well-being level we can concentrate on the level of living of the population involved, using the same basic needs we identified at the individual level, but adding distributional aspects. Besides that we can look at the different sub-systems and institutions that exist within a social system and that are directed at pursuing some collectively valued goals. These collectively valued goals and the structures and processes that exist to pursue them can be evaluated in the way they fulfil basic human needs. Finally there is the perspective of the social system as a whole, which is fundamentally different from the other perspectives, but which may give us some valuable additional information on the social well-being of the social system we are concentrating on.

321. The general structure of the way we may look at individual and social well-being may be summarised as indicated in Table 43.

322. The lists of individual basic human needs and of social system needs presented above are certainly not complete lists; their only purpose is to suggest the kinds of needs which are involved on the different levels in the analysis of a social system. The same holds true for the list of subsystems which will be presented below.

Table 43

INDIVIDUAL AND SOCIAL WELL-BEING

Individual well-being	Social well-being
Quality of life of the individual by measuring the fulfilment of his biogenic and learned individual basic human needs.	Level of social well-being of the population by measuring the fulfilments of the biogenic and learned basic human needs of the individuals and the distributional aspects of these fulfilments.
	The various subsystems and institutions that are directed at collectively fulfilling basic human needs.
	The social system as a whole where some social system needs have to be fulfilled to keep the social system "sound" as a social process system.

C. THE COMPONENTS OF THE SOCIAL ASSESSMENT STRUCTURE

323.   The Social Assessment Structure looks at two types of social impacts of big policy-decisions: beneficial impacts and adverse impacts, both in relation to the levels of basic needs. Beneficial social impacts are those results of big policy-decisions which contribute to increases in the satisfaction levels of basic needs. Adverse social impacts are those results of big policy-decisions which either reduce the satisfaction levels of the basic needs, or which do not contribute to the increases of the satisfaction levels of the basic needs, although the opportunities for such increases may be available.

a) The Individual Level of the Social Assessment Structure: the Quality of Life Concept

324.   This first component corresponds with the individual level of basic needs: individual well-being. In the literature we usually find the concept "quality of life" as a general name for this component. Quality of life refers to the overall nature of impacts of big policy-decisions on individual well-being, and on the well-being of his or her family. An individual's and his or her family's quality of life is of course very hard to measure. The stage of life, the place an individual occupies in a community, the overall economic situation and several other factors influence the specific quality of life of one specific individual. Burdge (1973) summarises a few sociological findings concerning the quality of life concept:

-- Quality of life impacts will be different if one is displaced or not displaced;
-- Quality of life impacts will be different depending on who is involved and what they value (e.g. younger people may value recreation, farmers the certainty of crop development, the elderly a sense of security);
-- Quality of life impacts will be different if one is in a position of strength (e.g. economically, in terms of age, legally) rather than a position of weakness (e.g. poor, elderly, unable to secure legal help);
-- Quality of life impacts will be different if one is able to maintain one's sense of community and have neighbours who share one's beliefs, as compared with a situation where one is thrust into a new community, especially if that community has a new life style (e.g. rural to urban, comfortable economic circumstances to marginal existence);
-- Quality of life impacts will be different if one is leaving a situation with which one has only marginal attachment rather than leaving a place where one has strong roots and deep attachment;
-- Quality of life will be different depending on whether one is anticipating a favourable future in his or her new circumstances or whether one is anticipating a personal or family crisis in a new situation.

325.   The quality of life concept will be used in this text to depict the overall nature of the individual and family well-being as a result of the satisfaction levels of the basic individual needs. Both biogenic and learned needs will be incorporated in the component "quality of life" of the Social Assessment Structure. For reasons of convenience the biogenic needs will be aggregated into four categories: "nutrition", "life and health", "clothing and shelter" and "safety". The learned needs will be categorised under seven headings: "social economic status", "education", "income" (and goods and services), "employment", "affection and interaction", "communication and transport" and "personal satisfaction" (Table 44).

Table 44

QUALITY OF LIFE CATEGORIES

Nutrition	
Health	Related to biogenic
Clothing and shelter	individual needs
Safety	
Socio-economic status	
Education	
Income (and goods and services)	Related to
Employment	learned needs
Affection and interaction	
Communication and transport	
Personal satisfaction	

Central in the quality of life concept is the fact that the individual and/or the family is the unit of measurement. The impacts of policy-decisions are evaluated in terms of the beneficial or adverse impacts on the individual well-being.

b) The Social Level of the Social Assessment structure: the Level of Living Concept

326. The level of living concept is very much akin to the quality of life concept. The only difference is that in the level of living concept attention is focused on the whole population of a certain area or of a certain community. The level of living is the level of satisfaction of the needs of a population attained per unit of time as a result of the goods, services and living conditions which that population enjoys in that unit of time (Drewnowski, 1974). It should be pointed out that as the level of living refers to a population, not only is the average level per head of the satisfaction of needs important, but also its distribution. In other words, if we look at the overall nature of impacts of big policy-decisions on the well-being of a population, we also have to pay attention to the extent to which the beneficial and adverse social impacts would be distributed among the members of the population involved.

327. In considering the distribution of social impacts, special measures have to be used. In the various categories of the quality of life the distributional aspect must be taken into account when a certain population is the main focus of attention in evaluating policy-decisions. Using the same categories in the level of living index as in the quality of life index (individual level), we also pay attention to the distributional aspects of the satisfaction levels of these needs.

328. The general way of measuring the distribution of need satisfaction levels can be presented in the following way (after Drewnowski, 1974). First the whole range of individual need satisfaction levels is determined per category. Then each category is divided into a number of sub-ranges, and the percentage of the population within the various sub-ranges is computed. The larger the number of sub-ranges, the more exact the distribution picture becomes (cf. Table 45).

c) The Social Level of the Social Assessment Structure: the Level of Subsystems and Institutions

329. On the level of subsystems and institutions we are concerned with the ways in which social subsystems and institutions are able to fulfil basic human needs. Big policy-decisions may influence these ways of fulfilling human needs, so within the Social Assessment Structure we will have to try to assess the impacts of policy-decision on the functioning of subsystems and institutions.

330. Depending on the subjects the policy-decisions are dealing with, some specific subsystems can be distinguished. Below we present a list of subsystems, which is adapted from a study by Fitzsimmons et al., 1977, in a social assessment manual for planning water resource projects (Table 45).

331. We shall briefly typify each of the 16 subsystems mentioned:

1. Demographic relates to the structure of the social system in terms of size, ethnicity, marital status, age/sex distribution, etc. of the population.

2. Education deals with the educational institutions within the social system (primary, secondary, post-secondary and post-academic education as well as vocational training), and with their activities and capacity.

3. Government operations and services deal with the structure, size and complexity of the different levels of goverment (local, regional, national) and the services which goverment provides to the population.

4. Housing and neighbourhood concerns the quality and quantity of housing facilities for the population (seen from the local, regional and national perspective), as well as the conditions of the neighbourhoods.

5. Law and justice deals with the criminal justice system in the social system and the possible impacts in terms of criminal and civil violation, which might result from the policy-decisions concerned.

6. Social services concerns the public and private sector services available to various population groups.

7. Religion deals with the religious structure of the social system and the extent to which religion affect the lives of the members of the population.

8. Culture concerns the ethnic composition of the population and its associated values and folkways, as well as "cultural materials" (e.g. archeological sites, cultural manifestations, etc.).

9. Recreation relates to public recreational facilities, their uses and the changes in uses.

10. Informal groups concerns groups which are not a part of the formal governmental and institutional structure (e.g. fraternal organisations, religious and ethnic minority groups, environmental groups).

11. Employment deals with the means by which various population groups earn their living.

12. Income concerns the amount of money population groups receive for their labour efforts.

13. Welfare and financial compensation deals with the quality and quantity of benefits (including money and services) provided to people who, for various reasons, are unable to support themselves.

14. Communications discusses various personal and media methods for communication.

15. <u>Transport</u> deals with private and public transport methods, their conditions, locations and costs.

16. <u>Economic base</u> concerns the overall economy of the social system, including types of industry and agriculture, the changes and developments within these types and social impacts these changes may have.

Table 45

LEVEL OF LIVING CATEGORIES

Level of living	
Categories	Distributional aspects
Nutrition	Different groups receiving various quantities and qualities of food.
Health	Different groups receiving various quantities and qualities of health services.
Clothing and shelter	Different groups receiving various quantities and qualities of clothing and housing.
Safety	Different groups receiving various quantities and qualities of protection services.
Socio-economic status	Pattern of traditional placement in specific status categories.
Education	Different groups having different accessibility to educational opportunities.
Income (and goods and services)	Distribution of income and distribution of services provided.
Employment	Pattern of job opportunities
Affection and interaction	Distribution of interaction patterns in formal and informal settings.
Communication and transport	Different groups having different accessibility to communication and transport facilities.
Personal satisfaction	Different categories of measured satisfaction levels.

Table 46

LIST OF SUBSYSTEMS POTENTIALLY INVOLVED IN WATER PROJECTS

Subsystems
Demographic
Education
Government operations and services
Housing and neighbourhood
Law and justice
Social services
Religion
Culture
Recreation
Informal groups
Employment
Real income
Welfare and financial compensation
Communications
Transport
Economic base

d) The Social Level of the Social Assessment Structure: the Level of the Social System as a Whole

332. This component of the Social Assessment Structure is concerned with the possible beneficial and adverse social impacts of big policy-decisions on the basic needs of the social system as a whole. The effects of policy-decision are now assessed in terms of the ways the social system as a whole will be able "to grow and develop itself" (as the most general social system need). Among other so-called social system needs already mentioned: consciousness (ability to set and pursue collective goals), participation (opportunities available to people to participate), stability (certain amount of change consistency), legitimacy (ability to attract loyalty and motivation) and competence (ability to be effective).

333. Social system needs are very abstract and hard to measure. Nevertheless the items mentioned here are important evaluative dimensions of social impacts of big policy-decisions on a social system and in one way or another should be incorporated in the Social Assessment Structure.

334. Now the main components of the Social Assessment Structure have been identified, we can present the complete structure in the Figure 15.

e) Indicators for the Social Assessment Structure

335. In this section we will concentrate on some examples of possible social indicators for the forecasting and measurement of the impacts on the satisfaction levels of the levels of needs which have been distinguished in the Social Assessment Structure. The social indicators mentioned are only examples, and

163

more indicators could probably be found. Since our aim is only to illustrate, we are not attempting to present a comprehensive picture.

336. A social indicator can be defined as a direct and valid statistical measure which monitors levels and changes over time in a fundamental social concern. An indicator must have the form of a variable whose values can be observed. Sometimes these observations can take the form of a series of continuous numbers; if these numbers can be treated as cardinal numerals we speak of cardinal indicators. Sometimes we cannot have series of cardinal numerals and we must be satisfied with numerals, dividing the variable into sub-ranges by ordinal numbers (e.g. first, second, third, etc., or very adequate, adequate, inadequate, etc.). We then speak of ordinal indicators. Tables 47 to 49 list such possible indicators.

337. The social assessment structure is an instrument which of course requires much technical skill in the techniques of social forecasting and a solid knowledge of sociological theories. In general a full social impact analysis can only be carried out by a team of experienced social scientists, who may fall back on the use of scenarios (cf. supra, §294 and following).

338. The social scientists will have to rely heavily on the information that was collected during the earlier stages of the whole planning process. Information from public consultations, from mobilised existing sources, from the social monitoring process and from additional sociological investigations should be integrated to give a complete and detailed picture of the ways the project alternatives are expected to influence the categories in the social assessment structure.

NOTES

1. See for instance those provided by the Water Resources Council (1973).

2. But such norms are always disputable and vary from case to case, in France, it is considered that the absolute minimum is two litres per day per person, and vital needs are estimated at 20 litres per day per person.

3. Maslow 1954.

Figure 15 **THE SOCIAL ASSESSMENT STRUCTURE**

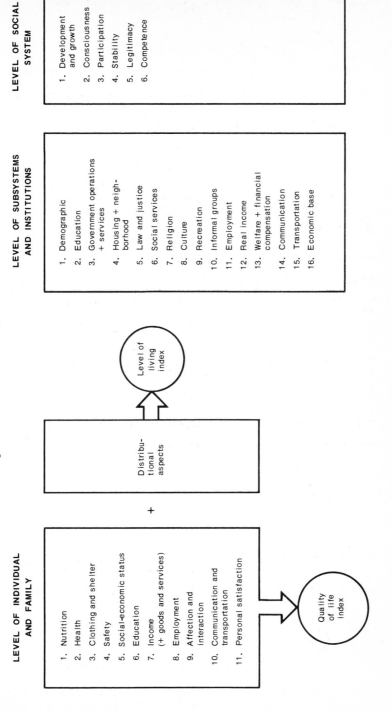

LEVEL OF INDIVIDUAL AND FAMILY

1. Nutrition
2. Health
3. Clothing and shelter
4. Safety
5. Social-economic status
6. Education
7. Income (+ goods and services)
8. Employment
9. Affection and interaction
10. Communication and transportation
11. Personal satisfaction

Quality of life index

+

Distributional aspects

Level of living index

LEVEL OF SUBSYSTEMS AND INSTITUTIONS

1. Demographic
2. Education
3. Government operations + services
4. Housing + neighborhood
5. Law and justice
6. Social services
7. Religion
8. Culture
9. Recreation
10. Informal groups
11. Employment
12. Real income
13. Welfare + financial compensation
14. Communication
15. Transportation
16. Economic base

LEVEL OF SOCIAL SYSTEM

1. Development and growth
2. Consciousness
3. Participation
4. Stability
5. Legitimacy
6. Competence

Individual well-being

Social well-being

Table 47

INDICATORS FOR THE INDIVIDUAL LEVEL COMPONENT

Categories	Examples of indicators	Examples of units of measurement
Nutrition	Calories intake level	Calories intake per day as percentage of norm
	Protein intake level	Protein intake per day as percentage of norm
Health	Level of prevention of infection and parasitic disease	Chance of dying due to infection of parasitic disease
	The probability of a healthy life through all stages of the life cycle	Life expectancy at age 1
Clothing and shelter	Cloth consumption level	Amount of cloth bought for clothing per year
	Housing facilities level	Number of m^2 or rooms available per inhabitant
Safety	Disaster risk level	Chance of loss of life due to natural disasters (ordinal indicator)
	Personal security level	Ordinal indicator
Social-economic status	Index (combination of indicators) of educational level, income number and quality of consumer goods	Type of schools visited (ordinal indicator), income per year, amount of cloth per year, quality of cloth per year (ordinal indicator)
Education	Educational achievement level	Number and types of schools and classes visited (ordinal indicator)
	Educational facilities level	Number and types of schools accessible and available (ordinal indicators)
Income (+ goods) and services)	Income available	Income per year
	Cultural facilities	Number of theatres within walking distance
Employment	Job continuity	Number of days without a job per year
	Labour relations	Quantity of tension during work (ordinal indicator)
Affection and interaction	Atmosphere in core family	Ordinal indicator
	Atmosphere in community	Number of interactions with inhabitants of community per unit of time
Communication and transport	Communication facilities	Number, type and quality of communication types available (ordinal indicator)
	Methods of transport	Number, type and quality of transport available (ordinal indicator)
Personal satisfaction	Level of satisfaction (index of perception of social, physical and cultural environment)	Ordinal indicator

Table 48

INDICATORS FOR THE SUBSYSTEMS AND INSTITUTIONAL LEVEL COMPONENT

Categories	Examples of indicators	Examples of units or measurement
Demographic	General demographic make-up of the population -- size -- density -- migration trends -- age/sex distribution -- marital status -- ethnic groups	Number of people; Number of people per geographic unit
Education	Number of enrolments	Number of new pupils
	Number of dropouts	Number of pupils leaving
	Level of education of general population	Number of people having visited or visiting certain types of schools
	Diversity in school types and courses offered	Number of types of schools available
Government operations and services	Types and qualities of services provided by government	Number of police agencies, fire protection agencies, sewage systems, garbage collection services, etc.
	Budgets of governmental organisations	Quantity of money per operation and service provided
Housing and neighbourhood	Housing quality level	Per cent of persons living in substandard and overcrowded housing
	Housing occupancy level	Number of dwelling units occupied year round
	Housing costs level	Median monthly contract rent construction costs
	Diversity of housing types in neighbourhood	Number of apartments, one-family units, studios, etc.
Law and justice	Civil and criminal code violations	Number of violations
	Judicial efficiency	Number of arrests as per cent of reported crimes
Social services	Quantity of services provided	Number of persons receiving social services, by type of service received; Number of social service agencies
	Quality of services provided	Ordinal indicator
	Accessibility of social services	Distance in relation to dwelling units
	Public acquaintance level with social services	Number of people (per geographical unit) having right to services, but unaware of it
Religion	Size of church membership, by denomination	Number of people having membership
	Attendance rate	Number of people attending churches as a percentage of membership
Culture	Ethnic composition of population	Number of people belonging to various ethnic groups
	Types of traditional behaviour, values and folkways	To be established after social research has been carried out
Recreation	Use of recreation facilities	Number of people using facilities per unit of time
	Recreational diversity	Number of recreational facilities available

Table 48 (continued)

Categories	Examples of indicators	Examples of units or measurement
Recreation (cont'd)	Recreational accessibility	Distance in relation to dwelling units:
		Costs of recreational facilities in relation to financial situation of population
Informal groups	Number and types of informal groups	To be established after social research has been carried out
	Cohesion and solidarity within informal groups	To be established after social research has been carried out
Employment	Unemployment ratio	Number of persons unemployed as a per cent of total labour force
	Employment structures	Percentages of employed population by occupational category
Real income	Income structure	Percentages of families and unrelated individuals by income level
	Average income	Mean income by class of worker or recipient
	Poverty level	Per cent of people below certain income level
Welfare + financial compensation	Quantity of welfare services provided	Number of persons receiving welfare services of different types as a per cent of total population
	Quantity of financial services provided	Number of persons receiving financial services of different amounts and types as a per cent of total population
	Accessibility of welfare and financial services	Distance in relation to dwelling units
	Public acquaintance with welfare and financial services	Number of people (per geographic unit) having right to services, but unaware of it
Communications	Quantity of communications available	Number of households with at least one television set, radio or telephone; number of radio and television broadcasting stations; number of newspapers being published per geographic unit
	Public acquaintance with communication pathways	Circulation of newspapers per certain number of people per geographic unit; number of people knowing different communication facilities
	Communication pathways	To be established after social research has been carried out
Transport	Transport use patterns	Percentages of travellers using different types of transport
	Availability of transport types	Number of cars and licensed drivers per geographic unit; number and density of public transport systems
Economic base	Economic structure	Number of persons employed in industry, agriculture and service sector as a per cent of total labour force
	Economic production level	Total value of industrial, agricultural and service sector products
	Economic consumption level	Total consumption per head at current and constant prices

Table 49

INDICATORS FOR THE SOCIAL SYSTEM LEVEL COMPONENT

Categories	Examples of indicators	Examples of units or measurement
Participation	Participation level	Percentage of people directly or indirectly voluntarily involved in political processes of decision-making as compared with a norm
	Subsystem residents' or participants' image of participation level	Percentage of people satisfied with participation level as compared with a norm
Stability	Stability level	Number of changes in institutional and organisational forms during a certain unit of time, as percentage of a norm
	Subsystems residents' or participants' image of stability level	Percentage of people satisfied with stability level as compared with a norm
Legitimacy	Legitimacy level	Percentage of actions by residents or participants of subsystems to point at illegitimacy of the status of the subsystems as compared with a norm
	Subsystems residents' or participants' image of legitimacy level	Percentage of people satisfied with legitimacy level as compared with a norm
Competence	Competence level	Percentage of effective and efficient actions within the subsystems (in relation to specific subsystems' goals) as compared with a norm
	Subsystems residents' or participants' image of competence level	Percentage of people satisfied with competence level as compared with a norm

Chapter XV

HEALTH CONSIDERATIONS IN WATER RESOURCES PLANNING

339.   Water is a basic need of man. This well known fact causes many problems for those deprived of sufficient water supply for everyday needs: drinking, washing, waste disposal, watering crops. Food is a basic need as well.
In executing multi-purpose water projects mankind is trying to satisfy, in one
way, those basic needs. Water projects like dam building, the setting up of
irrigation systems and river-basin flood-control have an important impact on
health conditions. By changing the ecological, environmental and social (economic) structures of large regions, disease patterns are changed and new
diseases are introduced. Without prior planning and application of health
measures at all stages of planning, any project will result in losses of
lives, loss of workdays, health degeneration of people and unnecessary attacks
on the world health situation. Although water projects are a part of every
nation's daily routine the potential threats to human health come from those
projects that are situated in the tropics and sub-tropics. This is not a reason for countries outside those regions to be less careful. Although some
diseases may appear to be eradicated, the ever-increasing mobility of mankind
and the tremendous import of foreign labour-forces to Western Europe and the
Middle East could well be the cause of the rebirth of those diseases. The
case of malaria may prove this.

340.   In this chapter some health aspects associated with multi-purpose water
projects will be dealt with. As a general example of those projects it seems
suitable to take the so-called man-made lakes. In addition to the health aspects there will be some remarks made on the relation between health and food
on the one hand and health and planning on the other hand. In the last section an indication will be given of the kind of studies and measures which
should be undertaken to fulfil the needs of a modern planning process, where
people are no longer treated as objects to which planning is directed, but as
subjects who are highly involved in shaping their own future.

A. HEALTH ASPECTS TO BE CONSIDERED

a) Physical and Mental Health Effects

341.   The main factors most likely to influence the patterns of disease are
urban growth, population movement, agricultural development, engineering

projects and social and behavioural change. Most of these factors play a role in the water projects dealt with in this book. The same can be said of a man-made lake as a specific facet of multi-purpose water projects. Especially in areas in which human communities frequently suffer from overcrowding, poverty, endemic infectious disease and a low rate of economic development, the combined effects of the construction of the lake and the named factors on health conditions may be disastrous. Large scale water-project development planning is considered vital for the economic progress of many countries, and can contribute significantly to improvement in health and welfare. Feasibility studies should include consideration of the <u>impact</u> of the <u>project on the transmission and the severity of several diseases.</u> Although we mainly focus on physical health effects some of the most serious health effects may be mental. These mental defects will arise when people are uprooted from an environment around which their way of life was organised. This environment has an important social and psychological significance. When people have to be moved into a different physical and social environment, social conflicts and psychological stress, resulting in mental defects and illness, will be a regular (and predictable) phenomenon.

b) <u>Spatial Location</u>

342. The transmission, severity and changing pattern of diseases are directly connected with the changes in the social and ecological environment caused by the construction and the use of the project. The partly foreseeable harmful developments occurring as a result of the construction and use of a man-made lake may be associated with the spatial location and the temporal stages of the planning. Under the first category we will find:

1. <u>Impoundment of the lake itself</u>

343. The health hazards associated with spatial-location aspects are found in all kinds of water projects in all parts of the world. The broadest categories of diseases are snail-borne infection and arthropod infection. The well-known bilharziasis (schistosomiasis) is an example of the former, the latter includes malaria, onchocerciasis (sometimes called river blindness) trypanosomiasis (sleeping sickness), etc. Even in ancient times there are striking examples of technical marvels versus poor health consequences: the irrigation system of Anuradhapura in Sri-Lanka wiped out one-third of the population through malaria introduced by man. In the following pages we will try to gain a rapid insight into the causes of the spatial-location-associated health hazards and into the relationship of those hazards to the reference groups mentioned in the resettlement section.

344. All man-made lakes create the problem of what should be done about the natural vegetation along the shoreline of the flooded area. The type of plant growth along the shoreline, and at times in the lake itself will influence the incidence and development of vector-borne diseases. The effects of clearing are different and highly dependent on intermediate factors. So the absence of clearing in the Brokopondo-area in Surinam did not affect health aspects, as the acid waters of the Surinam River, which feeds the Brokopondo impoundment, were apparently unfavourable for the development of snails. However most of the time the effects are considerably more serious, as was noted in Kainji Lake and Lake Nasser, where the clearing radically altered the insect and

snail populations. Obviously the decision to clear trees and other vegetation from areas that will form the bed of a man-made lake calls for the inclusion of cost-benefit assessment in the initial planning for any project. These are of course highly technical matters for which local health planners, consultants and technical engineers are responsible. Besides this we have to consider the construction period and the actual use of the lake. From several studies it seems to be clear that immigrant labour-forces are in many respects the first and most potent source of new diseases. It is highly advisable to draw attention to this fact especially during the campaign to attract labour forces. In most cases the social guidance of multi-purpose water projects is for the greater part directed towards social and health aspects of resettlement. But all good efforts are of low value, if insufficient attention and funds are given to health-improving and sickness-prevention of the pioneers in the field, the construction workers.

345. Domestic water-supply, not directly taken from the lake, a sewage disposal system and sufficient housing amenities could avoid the coming out of hitherto "not-known" diseases. The actual occupation of the lake's shoreline as a settlement ground depends on the economic and political structure of the region. Unsupervised resettlement near the lake, especially by migrants trying to improve their economic position in the new situation through fishery, contributes to the spread of filiariasis. Inadequate (or non-existing) drainage and sewage-disposal systems will result in more contamination of the lake with secondary effects in the irrigation systems and the river below. Good housing and settlement planning providing the most elementary hygienic amenities can do a lot against the dangers outlined above, although there will always be a certain percentage of uncontrolled settlement. The third group of invaders are the day-recreationists and the tourists. This group may be responsible for the introduction or spreading of new diseases. Not only the ecological damage, but also the health hazards associated with mass-tourism must be taken into account. From several points of view -- cultural, social, ecological and health -- the exploitation of tourism should be only gradually developed. The steering of this process is difficult and will be counteracted by the desire for economic process. Anticipation of infections, movements of people, tourist booms, and so on, requires a lot of data that can be collected by (local) experts in public health sanitation, demography, anthropology, biology and recreation.

2. Spillways, irrigation waters and the river downstream of the dam

346. These matters will be discussed briefly as they derive from the impoundment of the lake. Approximately the same problems arise here as under point (a). Since spillways from dams provide ideal breeding grounds for the development of the river-blindness infection, devices such as automatic siphonic spillways and submerged pass pipes should be used wherever possible to prevent breeding. Irrigation systems have long been known as areas of schistomosiasis insofar as they increase the availability of water and consequent human contact with it. (It is however becoming apparent that the lakes themselves produce similar effects). The definitive host of bilharziasis, man, is responsible for the dissemination by contaminating the aquatic environment which in turn becomes a source of infection for man. It is within the range of possibilities for scientists to predict the ideal breeding grounds for vectors and the circumstances under which those vectors will cause severe damage to people, as the Volta drainage shows. Man being the host of more than one

vector brings us to the idea that health education is a key factor in improving health care. In the long run health education is personal and community hygiene will probably prove to be more effective than any attacks on the intermediate vector hosts. Ecological changes will be felt not only in the lake itself but also downstream where they may affect the hea- lth of the river dwellers. Actions taken in the lake for biological or chemi- cal control will result in dead vegetation in the river below, which may well be the source of the water supplies of several communities.

B. HEALTH AND FOOD

347. There is a basic need for providing supplementary health control measures for man and livestock where they are moved to a different environment. Besides the "normal" disturbances in health conditions caused by resettlement (see under that heading) there is an amplifying effect caused by the food supply. The productive capacity of resettled people will be far lower during the first period after resettlement. Unless there is a planned food supply on a very large scale this decreasing productive capacity will result in more health problems as there is a vital link between nutrition and health conditions. The World Health Organisation (WHO) can provide figures on a comparative basis on what costs are involved in providing food to tide resettlers over until they are able to produce crops on their own new land. For example, at Lake Volta some 80,000 people in more than 50 settlement areas were provided with approximately $4 million worth of food for daily consumption; other food aid includes school feeding and feeding in professional and training institutions. A thorough examination of possibilities and costs of food-aid in relation to diminished economic activity and health conditions is a necessary, although often underestimated, step in the ex ante evaluation of project designs. Hidden in the food-aid area are secondary dangers. A community that has been fed gratis for a year or two may have little inclination to revert to the hard labour of farming. Here socio-psychological experts are needed to guide the planners in tackling their problem.

C. HEALTH PLANNING

Data and studies

348. In this section we will make a distinction between data-gathering studies to be undertaken and health education as part of the planning process. Data collection, analysis and interpretation are inputs to the planning process itself. The first data that are needed in case of health will be so-called base-line data. Rough data at first that can be compared with future survey results. Those baseline data will consist of:

-- Population stock and flow marks;
-- Current disease patterns;
-- Figures on housing, sanitation and sewage disposal systems;
-- Expected impact from changes in the vegetation in relation to the development of future intermediate hosts;

173

-- A list of new events, for example the influx of migrant labour forces or the temporary housing of those forces;
-- Data related to the employment, food and resettlement situation.

Roughly speaking it can be said that the collection of these data has
to precede the evaluation stage of the project design. Without these elementary data it is unwise to take health aspects in the ex ante evaluation into
consideration. One reason for this is that in the evaluation period an effort
must be made to estimate costs of, say, sewage collection and disposal systems
or health education programmes, weighed against the expected benefits resulting from those systems and programmes for the prevention of the outbreak of
diseases such as cholera, typhoid and dysentry. The data needed can easily be
fitted into the benchmark approach of Drewnowski's lists on Quality of Life
concepts.

349. At the same time as data-gathering of the existing situation begins,
several detailed studies will probably also be undertaken. These studies
might well include:

-- Specific ad hoc limited surveys to indicate the trends and transmis-
sion of parasites;
-- Longitudinal epidemiological studies in the area as a whole;
-- General studies of the mistakes and strategies of comparative lake-
planning-processes in the past;
-- Study of relevant problems in the future.

D. HEALTH EDUCATION

350. Education, like human health, must also be considered early in the
planning process. Education is a key factor. Medical care without basic
health education of the population, of the community, in particular the children, is wasted effort. We learn from studies that the control of insect vector ultimately depends on an educated human community. But local precautions
are not enough. In the long run, confronted with waves of foreign "invadors",
national and even international co-operation and health education will be
necessary. As we have seen, problems of health are highly interconnected with
problems in the field of resettlement and food supply. This means that health
planning can never be a case on its own: especially at a regional level there
should be tendency towards joint health planning. Health education systems
based on local health planning, with personnel trained in anticipation of the
needs of resettled (or local but interfered) people are preferable to the use
of outside experts and consultants. The local staff can far better understand
the cultural, social, economic and, in some cases, even the religious aspects
of water utilisation. It is quite a job for example to teach people not to
store drinking water in jars they always used, which often harbour the mos-
quito vector of yellow fever. Special attention should be given to this kind
of ground-level innovation because those innovations are the basic instruments
for a better health-care planning.

Chapter XVI

DEALING WITH RESETTLEMENT

INTRODUCTION

351. Resettlement problems arise mainly with very large water projects in developing countries. The present chapter has been written with this kind of situation in mind, however similar problems of a lesser dimension, can also be encountered in developed countries, in particular with the building of large dams. So far some research (1) has been done on these questions but very little is still known about it. Resettlement is a transition process which may take up to ten years. This process starts as soon as the first rumours about the possibility of relocation begin to be heard. It peaks when the people are officially informed, when the moving takes place and during the time immediately following the relocation. It ends when the relocatees have adjusted to their new environment. Four broad categories of groups of people who are likely to be relocated as a consequence of a multi-purpose hydraulic project may be distinguished:

-- Those who must relocate, because their homes will be flooded;
-- The residents of the future lake shores whose homes will not be flooded; they will be the hosts of the relocatees, because most of the relocatees prefer to resettle as close to their former habitat as possible;
-- Immigrants who will enter the lake basin area to seek new economic opportunities;
-- Transients who come along for recreation or as tourists.

352. A big hydraulic project may improve the standard of living of the re-locatees, the hosts and the immigrants and at the same time may make the environment more suitable for tourists and daily recreationists. In doing this it will certainly contribute to national development.

A. RESETTLEMENT ASPECTS

a) Compulsory replacement

353. The resettlement transition process is a very complex multi-dimensional process, which has to be handled with extreme caution. First of all we have

to be aware of the fact that resettlement is <u>compulsory</u> and that compulsory relocation may be a traumatic experience for a large majority of the people that have to be relocated. People probably will resist; they will see the resettlement agency as an enemy and intruder, which can lead to severe conflicts. The resettlement agency must start as early as possible with its planning regarding this complex transition process; people have to be informed, initial surveys are necessary, relations with the people involved have to be established. There have been too many cases where such planning started after the construction of the dam was already in full operation, and led to the tension-laden, underfinanced so-called crash programmes.

b) Whole Communities

354.   A second aspect of resettlement which has to be kept in mind is that usually <u>whole communities</u> have to be relocated. In Africa for instance about 56 000 people were relocated during the 1950s in connection with the Kariba dam in Zambia and Rhodesia, over 70 000 people were resettled because of the Volta Dam in Ghana and 42 000 people were moved as a result of Nigeria's Kainji Dam. In Egypt and the Sudan more than 100 000 relocatees had to leave their homes when the Aswan Dam was constructed. Within such a community all kinds of formal and informal relationships exist which all have their specific meaning for the members of such a community. Kinship, religion, agriculture are only a few topics that the resettlement agency will have to be aware of. A lot of the special characteristics of a community may be tied to the land and geographical setting in which people live. Because of the resettlement local people often have to change their habits completely and adjust to new and different environments and living conditions. Farmers may have to become fishermen. The dead must be left behind. Religious customs may have to be changed.

c) Stress

355.   A resettlement agency must be aware of the kinds of difficulties that a moving community might experience. A lot of research will be necessary to find out which changes will be acceptable to the community, which will not, and which will be catastrophic. The traumatic experiences with compulsory mass resettlement will probably lead to different types of <u>stress</u>. Stress is the third aspect of resettlement to which attention should be paid. Stress resulting from compulsory relocation can be divided into <u>psychological, physiological and socio-cultural</u> components, which are of course intricately interrelated.

356.   The two main types of psychological stress are first: increased anxiety and uncertainty, and secondly "grieving for a lost home". Anxiety and uncertainty concern both the worrying about the relocation which is going to take place and the worrying about what may happen in the uncertain and new future. The grieving is related to having to leave a well-known territory, personally built houses, gardens and (especially) graves. The elderly appear to be particularly susceptible to psychological stress; they are of course most closely attached to a specific territorial setting.

357.   Physiological stress may result in higher morbidity and mortality rates. There is good reason to expect that during a complete transition

process physiological problems occur more often than before or after such a process. The main factors which influence this growing physiological stress are: increased population densities, inadequate food supplies, inadequate water supplies and changes in the nature and incidence of disease.

358.   Socio-cultural stress can be inferred from several sociological processes that occur during a transition process. Resettlement for instance may very well lead to an undermining of local authority. If the local leaders co-operate with a resettlement agency, they will very quickly be associated with the hated resettlement authority, and their influence will be reduced. But if they do not co-operate with the resettlement agency they will appear not to be able to stop the removal, which will also lead to a diminishing of their authority.

359.   Another socio-cultural stress indicator is the simplification of the socio-cultural system directly following the relocation. Since the relocatees will have to give up some habits which were attached to the old habitats, their cultural inventory will be reduced. Moreover, the new circumstances may reduce this inventory even further, if the relocatees are afraid of their new neighbours or of their new habitat. Only very slowly will a simplified cultural inventory grow into a new, more complex socio-cultural system again, a process which starts when the transition process ends.

360.   As may be concluded from these remarks, resettlement must be handled with extreme subtility and caution. Resettlement planning is one of the most difficult sub-processes of the planning of a multi-process hydraulic project.

B. RESETTLEMENT PLANNING

361.   A major part of multi-purpose hydraulic project planning is the planning of the resettlement process. Resettlement planning is a complex, time-consuming and expensive process. Data must be accumulated, the administrative structure must be set up, new settlements and a new infrastructure must be planned.

a) Resettlement Timing and Finance

362.   The experience with resettlement processes show us that up to now the time allocated for planning and executing resettlement has been completely inadequate. Planning for resettlement is seldom initiated at an early enough stage. In connection with the Kossou dam in the Ivory Coast the agency responsible for the resettlement planning was not established until the dam was already half a year under construction. In such circumstances it is hard to avoid tension-laden crash programmes and traumatic experiences.

363.   Resettlement planning is expensive. It is expensive in terms of finance, personnel and equipment. It is not unusual for the total final cash costs to be 2 times greater than the original estimates. At Aswan the total costs amounted to $2 000 per capita. Resettlement of 50 000 people at $2 000 per capita amounts to $100 million. Besides these costs there are of course the human costs that are a result of the resettlement process. Human costs

are hard to measure, but they must be taken into account. Resettlement planning must be set up in such a way that these costs are minimised. Tension and stress cannot be completely avoided, but ways to cope with them must be incorporated into a resettlement planning process.

b) Information and Communication

364. Resettlement planning has to start early. Resettlement planning has to start at the same time as the other preinvestment feasibility surveys. The first step of resettlement planning must be to define the exact future maximum lake margins in order to find out which and how many people must be evacuated. Surveys must be used to register who these people are, what kind of lives they lead, what occupations, what kind of houses, properties, families structures they have. Such surveys are time-consuming and may be delayed by all kinds of circumstances.

365. The surveys give as much information as possible on the project and its consequences. People have to be convinced that they will be displaced. Since people often find it hard to believe that they will have to leave their homes, this is also a time-consuming process.

366. The future resettlers must be given information on what the future holds in store for them. Early initiation of educational and training programmes is necessary. People have to be educated for the evacuation and the resettlement.

367. Both relocatees and hosts must be involved in a continual two-way communication process, which must be the basis of the whole resettlement planning process. Conflicting behavioural patterns and goals must be understood, so that severe conflicts can be avoided. Special sociological research will have to make clear what these possible conflicts may be, and how they can be handled.

368. Resettlement planning must provide a framework to make this two-way communication effective. Resettlement planning must be organised in a way that those who are most directly affected can be informed so that they are not suddenly confronted with the loss of homes and lands. Resettlement planning must also be open to local opinions and initiatives. Local individuals and groups must be able to make a meaningful contribution to the total effort. Communication facilities must be created: the resettlement agency should be receptive to ideas coming from future resettlers, hosts and immigrants. At least some local leaders should be involved in the planning. Effective resettlement planning can only be open participatory planning.

c) The Evacuation

369. The movement of people to new areas is a difficult and hazardous process, which should be prepared in an extremely cautious way. People do not like to leave their homes and land and compulsory removal leads to all kinds of stress. Although information and communication may be very well organised, several problems may complicate the evacuation. At Kariba for instance many of the women and children had never before travelled by motor vehicle, with the result that a significant number were sick en route. Evacuation does not

always have to take place with government assistance. In some situations a proportion of the population in the area to be flooded may be able to reestablish themselves. A considerable number of the Tonga people of the Zambian valley were resettled in this way. Mostly however government assistance will be necessary. This assistance must take the form of careful planning.

370. First of all the moment of transfer must be chosen judiciously. Usually the best moment for moving to new areas will be after the farmers have harvested their crops. Then they can take the largest possible supply of food. Food shortages are well-known problems which are directly related to the evacuation process. During the time preceding the actual relocation people tend to reduce their productivity, especially when the planners warn them that evacuation will soon take place. However if the timing of the evacuation is not optimal and the moment of transfer is postponed, food resources will be lower than was the case in other years.

371. The second aspect of evacuation planning therefore must be a food relief policy. Immediately before, during and after evacuation, government-sponsored food assistance will be necessary. But food-relief must be kept to a minimum once relocation has taken place. Production and self-sufficiency must again be stimulated and a dependency relationship must be avoided.

372. A third aspect in evacuation planning in connected with the health problems which arise from major resettlements. Mass movement may be followed by catastrophic epidemics. Everything possible must be done to control the spread of infection and the outbreak of disease. Prevention will be better if the incipient medical and health problems are perceived early in the whole resettlement planning process and not when discovered become imminent. Preliminary health surveys make it possible to recognise potential medical problems before evacuation begins. In Thailand leptospirosis was discovered in the areas scheduled for irrigation by the Nong Wai dam, before the dam was built. After the evacuation medical control surveys must be continued and the health facilities of the evacuation stage will have to be phased into the health facilities of the new settlements.

373. A last important aspect of the evacuation is the mode of transport for the resettlers and their belongings. Will trains be used, as was the case in the Sudan? Or are buses and trucks more appropriate? Do we know how many people have to be relocated and how far? What do they take with them? At Volta the settlers were accompanied by 2 594 cattle, 11 600 chickens and 42 000 sheep and goats. Who will assist in this enormous operation? If the army is used, it is important to note that conflicts may arise from special military attitudes and measures.

d) Resettlement Areas

374. Very important for a successful resettlement planning is an integral programme for the planning of the resettlement areas. Such an integral programme should embrace several aspects which will briefly be mentioned below. First of all the project authorities have to take the responsibility for developing new economic opportunities for the relocatees. An important part of these opportunities will be related to agriculture. For most of the relocatees agriculture is usually the basic form of life and resettlement planning cannot be carried out without attention being paid to the

179

agricultural development of the new settlement areas. Special assistance is to be provided for those who wish to use resettlement as a chance to change their occupations.

375. Land use planning is another major aspect of the integral programme for the planning of resettlement areas. The main parts of land use planning are agricultural development and intensification, housing and the provision of service facilities. As far as <u>housing</u> is concerned, a system with "core" houses, which gives the relocatees the opportunity for extension and design, is to be preferred to the provision of expensive ready-built houses which are not very attractive for their new inhabitants, because of their modern and unfamiliar design. If possible, pilot studies should be undertaken even before the construction starts, to find out what the most appropriate forms of housing may be. Past experience has also shown "site and service" planning to be necessary and successful.

376. <u>Service facilities</u> cannot be completely ready at the moment the relocatees arrive. But the resettlement planning should be able to provide at least the vital needs, such as water supply, sanitary facilities, roads and health facilities. Later other facilities like schools, shops and markets can be developed in close co-operation with the wishes of the new and old inhabitants. Immediately after the evacuation, <u>famine relief programmes</u> must be organised in the new settlement areas. A careful planning to reduce these programmes in connection with the stimulation of new economic opportunities is an important task which should be connected with the other aspects of the planning of the resettlement areas.

e) <u>Concluding Remarks</u>

377. A final aspect of the integral programme for the planning or resettlement areas is the attention which has to be paid to the <u>relationships between relocatees and hosts</u>. All kinds of problems can arise when relocatees are settled in areas where hosts are already living, usually in long-established settlements. Land conflicts and problems of ritual authority are very common. The best thing a resettlement agency can do is to obtain the legal authority to intervene in disputes that may threaten the development. Another way of lessening the conflict potential is to involve the hosts in the whole resettlement planning process as soon as possible and to facilitate the communication between relocatees and hosts. This too is an important task for a resettlement agency.

378. The comprehensive planning of the different aspects of the resettlement area is a very complex process; the success of such planning depends to a large extent on the type and quality of the <u>administration</u>. In such an administration professional knowledge of planners, architects and social scientists must be related to a broad participation of the different groups involved. A continuous dialogue between planners and people, explaining the plans and programmes and encouraging participation is essential. The administration has to be based on a process of community development. Community development will provide the natural form of administration, which will be characterised by a system of local government. In Zambia and Ghana local government is becoming more viable now that the initial problems have been dealt with. Local government can exist in a framework which is provided by specialised agencies of central government.

379.   Once a satisfactory form of administration is created, it is possible to begin on the important task of co-ordinating the comprehensive planning. The success of this co-ordination will to a large extent be decisive for the success of the resettlement planning.

NOTE

1.   In particular see Fernea and Kennedy (1966) as well as Scudder (1979).

Part IV

ENVIRONMENT

Chapter XVII

THE BASIC ENVIRONMENTAL QUESTIONS IN WATER PLANNING PROJECTS

A. THE ENVIRONMENTAL PROBLEM

380. The growth of concern and positive interest in the conditions of the natural environment is one of the most striking phenomena of our times. The increased concern about environmental degradation stems from an increasing awareness of the high costs in terms of human health of air, water and radio-active pollution, as well as the high levels of damage to property and crops. The positive interest in maintaining a high quality environment stems from increased appreciation of the natural environment from recreational and aesthetic points of view and this has arisen from a general improvement in living standards.

381. Large multiple-purpose water projects will change the environment in the project region, both directly and indirectly. However, these changes can be both positive and negative unless one takes the attitude that all changes are bad. Anyone who has visited a reservoir in a hot, dry region and noticed the heavy participation in water-based recreation by local residents must accept the high value which such recreational services can have. At the same time, certain local ecosystems may have been damaged or irreversibly changed -- a cost not often counted or even noted.

382. Many types of environmental change are associated with water projects. Table 50 provides a preliminary listing by major environmental categories.

383. The importance of particular trade-offs among the environmental categories (1) and between environmental changes and the economic outputs of a project is largely a matter of the environmental balance found in the project region. If the river valley flooded by a reservoir is very similar to many other miles of nearby river valley, the loss from an environmental viewpoint is probably not very great. If the area flooded is unique to the region, the loss must be counted as much greater. These judgements must be made with a view to the entire project region and not just to the project itself.

384. Environmental changes originate from certain sources, they are trans-mitted through environmental media, and then impact certain receptors, either animal, plant or human or all three. The simplest examples are those of air and water pollution, but all forms of environmental change involve these three factors, and all three must be considered in environmental evaluation. If a

Table 50

ENVIRONMENTAL COMPONENTS AND CATEGORIES

Component Group	Evaluation Category
Areas of Natural Beauty and Human Enjoyment	Open Space and Greenbelts Streams and River Systems Lakes and Reservoirs Beaches and Shores Wilderness, Primitive, and Natural Areas Estuarine and Wetland Areas Other Areas of Natural Beauty
Archeological, Historical and Cultural	Archeological Resources Historical Resources Cultural Resources
Biological, Geological and Ecological	Biological Resources Flora Fauna Geological Resources Ecological Systems
Quality	Water Quality Land Quality Visual Quality
(Considerations related to all component groups)	Uniqueness Considerations Irreversibility Considerations

reservoir permits the accumulation of nutrients from agricultural return flows, so that massive algae growth occurs in the reservoir destroying its recreational value and reducing dissolved oxygen to a point at which fish die, the agricultural return flows constitute the sources, the reservoir and its contents constitute the medium, and the persons who would otherwise use the reservoir for fishing and other forms of recreation are the receptors of the effects.

385.   The basic environmental questions(2) which must be asked about each water project are:

1. What categories of the environment will be changed by the project, and which of these changes will be positive and which negative?
2. What irreversible changes may occur (e.g. loss of plant or animal species or spoliation of unique valley features)?
3. What steps can economically be taken to mitigate negative environmental impacts or to enhance positive impacts?
4. What is the distribution of environmental benefits and costs among relevant social groups?
5. What is the nature of the general strategy to be followed in the environmental assessments?

a) Dimensions of the Environment

386. The simplest way of answering this question is to present a more complex table of dimensions which may be important. Experienced environmental engineers will be quickly able to identify the parameters likely to be important in a particular project setting, although this depends not just on technical judgement but on the inventory of environmental resources in the whole project region and on the value judgments of society (Cf. Table 51).

b) Possible Irreversible Environmental Changes

387. In general, it is in society's interests to avoid irreversible changes of any type since, in the future, it may become highly desirable to restore the initial conditions. The desirability may result from predictable or unforeseen future conditions. For example, if it is known with certainty that fusion power will be cheaply available in the year 2050 and that the value placed on natural scenery will be very high by that time, it might be highly desirable to dam some unique canyons for hydro-electric power until that time, and then to restore the canyons to their original condition for aesthetic enjoyment. Unfortunately, the changes brought by the dams will irreversibly change the canyons, partly filling them with silt, staining the walls, and causing physical deterioration of rock formations, so that such a project would have to be ruled out.

388. From a more general point of view the eradication of plant and animal species continually becomes more serious from a world viewpoint, both from an aesthetic point of view for humans and from a scientific viewpoint. Species of little apparent importance may contain genetic characteristics which will be medically or agriculturally important in the future.

c) Steps to Mitigate Negative Impacts or to Enhance Positive Impacts

389. Negative environmental impacts may be sufficiently bad to cause a project to be rejected by the decision-makers or even by members of the technical team during preliminary screening. However, it is often possible to lessen negative impacts by changes in or additions to project design. For example, the salmon fishery on the Columbia River (United States) was threatened with extinction by the construction of electric power dams in the 1930s. Fish ladders permitted the fish to survive, although in much lesser numbers (3). The extent of investments to mitigate negative effects is a matter for economic evaluation, extending such steps not until all negative effects are eliminated but just until marginal benefits justify the marginal costs.

390. Positive environmental effects or potentials can often be enhanced by modifications or additions. The most obvious example is the preparation of a reservoir shoreline for recreational use, with the preparation of beaches, picnic-sites, camping grounds, etc. Such investments may be quite small relative to the benefits. If commercial fisheries are planned, clearing of the reservoir bottom to avoid de-oxygenation and interference with fishing gear is likely to be a good investment. The aesthetic value of the reservoir can often be enhanced by avoiding unsightly road cuts (even at higher cost), the careful selection of powerline routes, and the choice of natural architectural styles.

Table 51

ENVIRONMENTAL CATEGORIES TO BE INCLUDED IN THE EVALUATION OF
ALTERNATIVE PROJECT DESIGNS

1. Water quality	Dissolved oxygen. Biochemical oxygen demand. Total organic carbon. Biomass. Phosphates. Nitrates. Salinity. Specific toxicants. Temperature. pH suspended solids. Bacteria, viruses, parasites (human and fish).
2. Water quantity	Flow rates. Seasonal variations. Flooding.
3. Amenity/Recreation	Clean water: turbidity; colour/odour: surface appearances (debris, oil films) + water quality parameters.
4. Land quality	Soil erosion. Sedimentation. Protection of beaches. Solid waste disposal. Derelict land, unrestored, after construction. Soil acidification -- leaching. Salination, alkilinisation, water logging.
5. Air quality	Sulphur oxides. Nitrogen oxides. Other volatiles (hydrocarbons, fluorides) particulates). Carbon monoxide.
6. Aquatic ecosystems	Breeding, migration. Maintenance of natural and genetic heritage, specially rare and endangered species and systems.
7. Terrestrial ecosystems	Breeding, Migration. Maintenance of natural and genetic heritage, including rare and endangered species and systems: and vegetation types.
8. Undesirable and/or irreversible changes	Salination, Poisoning (of soil or water) Eutrophication.
9. Exposure to natural hazards	Earthquakes, Tidal waves Hurricanes, Geological anomalies (vulnerability of dams)
10. Aesthetics	Loss of rare and valued scenery, historical, cultural and archeological sites.
11. Micro-climate	Reduction of frost/ice. Incidence of fog. Reduction of temperature ranges experienced.
12. Noise	Construction activity. Industry. Power plants. Traffic.

d) The Distribution of Environmental Benefits and Costs

391.   Just as with the quantifiable benefits and costs, the distribution of environmental benefits and costs can be an important consideration in project evaluation. Suppose it is proposed to trade-off some irrigation benefits to achieve a superior water quality for recreational purposes. The decision-makers will certainly be interested to know who will lose the irrigation benefits and who the recreationists will be. That decision on the project design might well depend on whether the farmers were smallholders and the recreationists upper income townspeople, or whether the farmers were well off while the recreationists were expected to be low income townspeople.

e) A General Strategy for Environmental Assessment of Project Alternatives

392.   The following pointers will be useful in developing an overall strategy:

1. Environmental assessment requires forecast of impacts and evaluation of those predicted impacts against public values and regional environmental inventories;

2. Environmental impacts are measured in physical and ecological dimensions where accepted methods of measurement exist, otherwise in qualitative descriptive ways;

3. Environmental descriptions must be prepared for the "with" and "without" project situations;

4. Dimensions of environmental quality may not be independent and may require joint assessment, e.g. nutrient factors relating to eutrophication;

5. Each project may involve unique environmental problems;

6. Public input regarding environmental values is exceptionally important to successful planning.

B. AGENDA FOR ENVIRONMENTAL STUDIES

393.   The various steps in the design and the evaluation of a project have already been discussed in Chapter 2 above. Each of these five phases therefore permit the progressive weeding out of less attractive alternatives with the help of economic and social analyses. It should be emphasized that environmental considerations should be part of the project planning process from its conception. Project siting, in particular, should be greatly influenced by environmental considerations. Environmental analysis should not be left simply to the evaluation of an already chosen alternative. Paragraphs 21 to 29 above give the environmental steps to be taken at each stage of the project evaluation.

C. ENVIRONMENTAL REGULATIONS IN VARIOUS COUNTRIES

394.   The use of, and form of, environmental impact analysis for large projects such as multipurpose water projects vary greatly from country to country -- nearly every nation today has established laws and regulations regarding environmental protection, environmental standards, and environmental conditions for project feasibility. The team obviously must know these laws and regulations in detail. Often, there may be room for improving the existing laws and regulations as experience is gained. The team should remain alert to the opportunity of suggesting improvements in laws and regulations through appropriate channels.

395.   Some nations require an "environmental impact statement" for each public (and sometimes private) project. This EIS statement often is supposed to assess the environmental impacts (positive and negative) that a particular project will have, quantifying these as far as possible, and looking especially for irreversible environmental changes. Such a statement would correspond very closely to the evaluation procedures proposed in this chapter. Some nations require even more of the statement, to identify and evaluate a set of reasonable alternatives to the project, including the "no project" alternative. Such steps constitute parts of the overall planning process developed here and should not have to be included in the environmental impact statement if the planning process is well designed.

396.   In those countries using formalised environmental impact analyses (and statements) the procedures and ground rules for conduct of the analyses are laid down in legislation (which is not necessarily environmentally inspired). The factors to be taken into account are detailed, and the degree of public participation and involvement is specified. Finally, a useful overview of OECD Member country practices and legislation entitled "Analysis of the Environmental Consequences of Significant Public and Private Projects" (1977), has been diffused by the Environment Committee of the OECD. Canada has produced a simple guide to its system in "A Guide to the Federal Environmental Assessment and Review Process", Fisheries and Environment Canada, 1977. The guide to current United States practices is the Principles and Standards documents and represents the most detailed guidelines available. In France, ministerial recommendations on impact analysis have recently been introduced into project design procedures.

NOTES

1. For example, the trade-off between recreational quality of a reservoir shoreline, which requires little fluctuation in reservoir level, and the downstream water quality, which may require a uniform reservoir release pattern -- implying fluctuating reservoir levels.

2. See especially Maler and Wyzga (1976) and OECD (1977).

3. In the same project, another major problem of the super-saturation of the water below the dams with nitrogen, causing large fish kills, was totally unanticipated.

Chapter XVIII

GENERAL TECHNIQUES FOR ENVIRONMENTAL STUDIES (1)

A. BASIC DEFINITION, AND PHILOSOPHY OF THE ENVIRONMENTAL STUDIES

a) The Prediction of Environmental Change: the "With-Without" Approach

397.   The "with-without" approach has been described in detail in Chapter III (paragraphs 53-54).   That approach also underlies environmental evaluation. The starting point must therefore be a set of baseline data on the relevant dimensions of the environment as they exist before any project activity starts.   For example, water quality, plant and animal communities in the project vicinity, groundwater, fish life, sites of cultural value, etc., should all be inventoried in advance of all construction activity.

398.   Starting with the baseline data, we must project the likely future values of the environmental variables with and without the project alternative being evaluated.   Projections cannot be simple trend extrapolations, for many environmental variables are too complex to be forecasted this way.   The environmental members of the team must have an understanding of the physical and ecological systems involved to be able to make the required qualitative and quantitative projections.   For example, the creation of a reservoir will affect hydrologic flows, groundwater levels, water temperatures and rates of re-aeration.   Given the oxygen-demanding waste loads likely to enter the stream above and below the reservoir, what will be the future dissolved oxygen levels in the reservoir and below the dam?   This is a complex question, requiring an understanding of the processes by which wastes are oxidised in quiet and flowing water.   Those processes depend upon water temperature, water turbulance, volumes and flow rates, each of which must be predicted.

399.   These complex computations can be made informally or by using appropriately calibrated computer models.   Each approach will be appropriate for certain planning situations.

400.   It must be remembered that water projects can have both positive and negative effects on the environment.   Public attention today is centered on environmental problems such as air and water pollution, but we must remember that projects can have positive effects.   In the design of projects, we must remain alert to modifications which will enhance positive impacts as well as modifications which will mitigate negative impacts.

b) Evaluating Predicted Environmental Changes

401.   In multi-objective planning, decisions are finally made by weighting the various economic, environmental, and social impacts of the project alternatives so that the project alternatives can be compared.

402.   Three types of environmental criteria exist in this respect:

1. Physical and life-system criteria;
2. Legally set environmental standards; and
3. The broad concept of regional environmental balance.

403.   Physical criteria would include critical values of certain environmental variables beyond which problems can be expected to occur, even if the exact nature of those problems cannot now be specified. In the water quality area, we know that water users will encounter problems if the total dissolved solids load exceeds 800 or 900 parts per million. If turbidity becomes too high, all forms of marine life will be adversely affected. If the pH factor becomes too low (acidity too high), marine life will be adversely affected and the usefulness of water for potable and industrial uses (especially cooling) will be seriously impaired. These criteria might not mean much to decision-makers, but the technical team must use them in the early design and evaluation stages.

404.   Life system criteria would include the presence, absence, abundance, and mixtures of aquatic life forms or even terrestrial species dependent upon the water system. A diverse aquatic community represented by the presence of, say, clams, mussels, oysters, numerous fish species, and micro plant and animal forms is indicative of a healthy water system which will generate human benefits as well. Limits on water quality parameters such as turbidity and dissolved oxygen are crucial to maintaining such life-system diversity.

405.   Environmental standards have been established by law in some countries, and it may be mandatory that these standards be observed. In the water quality area, standards have been set for suspended solids, total dissolved solids, dissolved oxygen, heavy metals, and various chemical compounds. In the design and selection of project alternatives, the team must insure that these standards will be met with high productivity. It should be noted, however, that many of these standards have been quite arbitrarily set. The possibility of requesting changes in the standards must be kept in mind. One reason for such a request might be an extremely high cost of meeting a standard. Davis (1968) showed for example that maintaining a 5 parts per million dissolved oxygen standard during a 7 day summer low flow period on the Potomac River would cost (2) twice as much as maintaining a 4 ppm standard. The advantages of the higher standard were not clear.

406.   Regional environmental balance is a concept relating to the uniqueness of the resources affected by the project being evaluated. For example, if a proposed dam would eliminate the last natural river in the project region or a very unique stretch of river, the regional balance would be impaired. On the other hand, if the characteristics of the area inundated are very common to the region, balance would not be impaired. The same concept can be usefully applied to all environmental resources.

407.   The ultimate impacts of environmental changes must be evaluated in

terms of their human impacts. Thus, while water quality changes will affect marine life, we will want to know how these changes are valued by human society. If herds of wild animals are affected by the presence of a reservoir, how are those changes valued by society? If clear water is aesthetically valued by people who live near the stream, or if water clear of infectious bacteria or viruses permits the water to be used for swimming, how much are these features worth? How much additional project cost would be justified to achieve these goals?

408.   The monetary valuation of changes in environmental conditions is a task on which some progress has been made. Walsh et al. (1977) have made use of sample survey techniques to determine peoples' willingness-to-pay for improved water quality. Techniques for the quantification of water-based recreation benefits have been developed (e.g. Knetsch, 1974). However, the relationships of the various measures of water quality to recreation participation and to the value of the recreational experience to the participants have not been established.

409.   Thus, this is an area in which the environmental team members must co-operate closely with the economists and sociologists on the team, the former providing measures of the changes in environmental conditions and the latter translating these changes into changes in human activities and (if possible) values. Many persons remain sceptical of trying to assign monetary values to these changes, so it may be decided that the analysis should stop with descriptions of how humans are likely to be affected.

B. BASIC TOOLS IN ENVIRONMENTAL STUDIES

a) Units of Measurement for Environmental Variables

410.   Some of the early methods of environmental quality evaluation utilised the construction of indexes as ways of summarising the entire environmental picture. For example, Leopold (1969) constructed an "index of the uniqueness of riverscape" to assist in making river project decisions (3). Dee et al. (1972) constructed a weighting scheme for many measurements of water quality, biological productivity, and aesthetics which resulted in a scalar measure of "environmental desirability" so that alternative projects or project designs could be compared. The construction of indexes has not been standardized, however, and they tend to be very hard to understand Dunn (1974). They can easily be misleading, for they depend on the analyst's concept of environmental quality.

411.   Since the evolution of multiple-objective planning and decision-making processes which typically call for the participation of many parties, there has been a trend away from indexes and back toward physical measures of the various dimensions of environmental quality. Leopold et al. (1971) have proposed a qualitative matrix approach for evaluating environmental impacts. The practices for constructing environmental impact statements in several countries now call for quantification of the physical or life-system changes likely to be caused by a project. Thus, it is recommended that natural physical dimensions be utilised in recording and reporting conditions of the environment.

b) Monitoring and Modelling

412. Monitoring refers to the processes by which we know the physical attributes of our environment. It could involve casual, ad hoc observations and measurements, but usually monitoring refers to a planned, regular process of taking and recording environmental measurements. Monitoring may involve the installation of a network of permanent recording instruments such as recording water flow pages and water quality instruments, or it may involve simply sending technicians to take measurements at scheduled times and places, like taking daily "grab samples" for water quality measurement.

413. Modelling refers to the mathematical and/or computerised representation of a water resources system or sub-system such as a reach of river, a complete river system, a particular dam with its inflows and releases, or the hydrology of a drainage basin. Models are formal, explicit representations of systems as opposed to the intuitive pictures we may use in our minds as we think about water systems. Among the advantages of formal models are the following:

a) Models force the analyst to be explicit about the assumptions being made concerning the system;
b) Models provide direction in data gathering by identifying the variables that are needed for model calibration and utilisation;
c) Models assist in analysing systems which are too complex for intuitive analysis or for non-computerised calculations;
d) Models permit "sensitivity analyses" to be carried out to determine the relative importance of the accuracies with which various parameters or variables are measured.

414. These remarks on monitoring and modelling make it clear that the two activities are highly complementary. At a minimum, there must be a sufficient data base to permit estimation of the model's parameters (i.e. calibration) and verification or testing of the model. However, new projects will sufficiently change the hydrologic regime of the river that some variables after the project will assume values outside the range of historical observations. For this reason, monitoring must be continued after the project is in operation to check model projections made during planning and to take corrective action if the system behaves in unexpected ways.

415. For example, maximum and minimum flows below the dam will fall in a narrower range than before the dam was constructed, but suspended solids, dissolved oxygen, and temperature may extend beyond the ranges used in calibrating the model(s). Since the model(s) have not been tested beyond the data of record, continuing monitoring is needed.

C. TYPES AND CHARACTERISTICS OF WATER MODELS IN COMMON USE

416. We have spoken of models without indicating what types of models are in common use. As will be noted below, one criterion for deciding whether or not to utilise formal models is knowing how well established and proven are the uses of a particular type of model.

417. For any type of model, decision will have to be made concerning the following model characteristics:

a) Number of environmental variables to be included;
b) Region or area to be covered;
c) Degree of precision to be utilised (e.g. grid size, number of segments to be used in modelling a river, etc.);
d) Range of management strategies or technologies which can be varied within the model (e.g. release rules for a reservoir, changing rainfall-runoff relationships through charges in ground cover, changes in locations and rates of waste loading, changing instream reaeration rates, etc.);
e) Choice of time interval and length of model runs to be made (e.g. short time intervals for flood routing and forecasting, monthly intervals for irrigation planning, annual flows or ten year average flows for long-term land use planning.)

a) Hydrologic Models (4): An Overview

418.   The basic model for water project planning must be some type of hydrologic model which generates and routes flows through the river system. Such models of flow volumes are extremely useful in the design stages of planning in estimating best reservoir size, spillway size, levee height, channel dimensions, and navigation channel measurements. Water quality models are always constructed as additions to an underlying flow model. The time dimension of the flow model must be mentioned. Traditionally, the primary use of hydrologic techniques has been for the design of control works. Especially when flood control was an important purpose, a "design flow" or "design flood" was assumed as the basis for design. This was generally an extreme event of undetermined frequency. Its use was rationalised by the extreme damages that would result from structural failure. When floods are not the dominant problem, it is important to use the entire distribution of flows since the frequencies of all flows determine what will be available for economic uses. Thus, flow simulation models have been developed to permit the simulation of monthly, seasonal, and annual flows for project planning purposes (5).

b) A Few Flow Models

419.   The simplest type of flow model is known as a routing model. These models convert specified runoff to hydrograph form, but they usually don't include any procedure for estimating runoff rates. Sometimes they are augmented by infiltration loss functions to transform rainfall into runoff.

420.   Continuous water balance models represent an improvement over the routing model in that they maintain a continuous accounting for all water in the drainage area from rainfall to stream-flow. Their evaporation and infiltration loss functions are related to current conditions of the watershed and thus permit detailed, continuous simulations of flow for long periods of time. An example is the Stanford Watershed Model (SWM), version IV (6). The LANDS module of SWM IV generates simulated channel inflow, land runoff and groundwater flow from input data on precipitation, temperature and radiation. A second module then uses a routing procedure to transform these channel, overland, and groundwater flows into streamflow patterns.

421.   The calibration of such models is, of course, a major task requiring a good data base. Calibration of large models is usually carried out by trial

and error processes, although optimal parameter estimation procedures can be carried out for small models if optimality can be defined through an appropriate objective function.

422.   Given a basic streamflow simulation model, the simulation of other factors can be added, including especially sediment transport, dissolved salts, dissolved oxygen, algae, etc.

c) Continuous Simulation Models

423.   Once water quality modules have been added to the basic streamflow model, a distinction must be made between steady-state models and continuous simulation models.   Most models developed to date are of the steady-state variety in which a fixed flow rate and fixed pollution rates are assumed while the quality variables (like dissolved oxygen) are calculated as functions of time and downstream distance.   The steady state assumption leaves more computer memory space for the complex quality computations and can also greatly simplify those computations -- as with the linear steady-state solution to the Streeter-Phelps differential equations for dissolved oxygen.   However, continuous models have obvious advantages and are necessary is stochastic flows or pollution rates are to be used.

d) Surface Water Quality Optimisation Models

424.   The preceding paragraphs described simulation models of water quality, i.e. models capable of generating values of water flows and quality, starting from inputs of historical flows, runoffs, or precipitation.   Once water quality is recognised as an objective of water management, the question of optimising water quality management arises, i.e. how can the difference between water quality benefits and costs be maximised, given the values of the other objectives?   Benefits from water quality levels are generally not quantifiable, so water quality optimisation generally takes the form of achieving specified water quality standards at the lowest possible costs.   When a new water project is being designed, water quality will be affected and the maintenance of the desired standards may require one or more of the following actions:

      a) Modification of project design (e.g. allowing for aeration of water released from the reservoir);
      b) Waste load reductions;
      c) Treatment of wastes prior to discharge into the river;
      d) In-stream reaeration;
      e) Piping of waste loads to other points on the river.

425.   The number of combinations of such steps, for maintaining standards can be very large, and hence finding the least cost combination can be very difficult.   Such a problem calls for the use of an efficient search technique such as those contained in water quality cost minimisation models.   Since the search procedures are mathematically complicated, computer limitations require that such models use simplified representations of the physical system.   Such simplifications generally prevent such models from finding the true minimum cost solution.   Nonetheless, these models are extremely helpful in screening alternative solutions, i.e. reducing the number of alternatives which are to

be studied in greater detail. The following references will be useful for the environmental evaluator: Sobel (1965); Loucks, Revelle and Lynn (1967); Shih (1970); Jacoby and Loucks (1972).

e) Other Types of Water Quality Models

426.   Estuarial problems have long defied analysis because of their irregular geometry, unsteadiness of flows, and the complexity of natural and man-made physical, chemical, and biological interactions which take place in estuaries. Physical hydraulic models have been used to evaluate physical changes, but these models cannot include quality dimensions. In recent years, computerised mathematical models of estuarial systems have become useful planning and management tools. A good introduction to these models is found in Orlob et al. (1969).

f) Ecological Models

427.   The majority of water quality models have simply been extensions of the basic work on organic decay and dissolved oxygen by Streeter and Phelps in 1925.   More recent advances include nitrogenous oxidation processes, to account for the oxygen depleting effects of organic nitrogen, as well as ammonium nitrite and nitrate ions (7).   Now, because of the problems of large algae blooms and eutrophication in reservoirs, lakes and estuaries, models have developed in the direction of predicting algae densities and dissolved oxygen levels, especially as these respond to changing organic and nitrogenous waste loads. Some of the models attempt to include fish life, although such models have not proven reliable. Major applications of ecological models have been made to the Delaware Estuary (Kelly, 1975), the southern bight of the North Sea (Nihoul, 1975), and the Potomac River estuary (Di Toro, et al., 1975).

D. DESIGN AND UTILISATION OF MONITORING NETWORKS

428.   Monitoring is designed to measure water quantity, water quality, and other dimensions of the physical and life environment. Water quantity and quality monitoring are the most highly developed in terms of experience, instrumentation, and methods for designing efficient networks, i.e. networks generating the most useful information per unit of expenditure. The monitoring of a wide variety of non-aquatic ecosystems has long been practiced for research purposes, but only in recent years has ecosystem monitoring been considered as a tool of resources management.

429.   Environmental monitoring is used initially to establish the baseline conditions in the project area prior to the start of construction. This initial set of conditions would cover not only water quality and marine life but terresterial plant and animal populations in the project area and in areas affected by the project.

430.   Yet, a set of baseline conditions is not enough. Our objective in environmental analysis is to project the state of the environment with and without the project. Both sets of projections require that we have knowledge of

the trends which would occur if the project were not constructed. Thus, our required pre-project monitoring must be sufficient to let us establish these without project trends.

431. The most highly developed monitoring procedures are for water flows. Obviously, information on the probability distributions of short-term, monthly, seasonal, and annual flows is vital to the design and management of water storage projects. The greater the certainty with which we know these distributions, the greater the probability that our project designs will be close to the optimum. Our knowledge of these distributions comes from the gauging (or monitoring) of streamflows at different points in the system over some period of time. If the underlying hydrologic regime is stationary (i.e. if its probability parameters don't change over time), the longer the period of record, the better our estimates of flow distributions will be.

432. When flow distributions are not known with certainty but only estimated from short periods of record, there is a risk of over-designing or under-designing projects, with resultant losses relative to optimum design. However, the optimal length of hydrologic record is finite for two reasons:

a) Continued gauging of flows costs money, while marginal information gains fall with increasing length of record;
b) Delaying project design and construction to obtain longer flow records delays the generation of any net benefits the project might produce (whether optimally designed or not).

433. These ideas are represented in the following two figures. Figure 16 pictures the costs of the data gathering period (DC), as well as the initial construction costs (IC), the operating and maintenance costs (OM), and the project delay caused by the initial data-gathering period. Figure 17 shows that the present value of expected net benefits of a project is a function of the length of hydrologic record underlying the project design.

434. When the existing length of flow records is inadequate for estimating flow distribution with the desired level of certainty, procedures other than simply waiting to accumulate more data are available - namely the "regionalisation of hydrologic parameters" (Benson and Matalas, 1967). This technique takes the form of regressions of flow parameters (such as means and standard deviations) against drainage basin characteristics (such as area, forest cover, slope, soil types, etc.). It is thought that the accuracy of these regressions can be improved by increasing the number of basins from which data are collected to estimate the regression function. The standard error of the regression line can be transformed into a measure known as the "equivalent years of record" (8), a concept defined as the expected length of time and ungauged site would have to be gauged before the accuracy of flow parameter estimates derived from at-site observations becomes as great as estimates derived from the regression functions. Other important references to these techniques include Maddock (1973), Moss (1970).

435. These procedures can be applied to environmental parameters other than water flow parameters. For example, water quality data records are likely to be quite short, perhaps too short to accurately estimate current average levels or trends. Data from other basins can be transferable to the project basin via the "regionalisation" technique. The sample areas and the variables in the regression would have to be carefully chosen for such transfers to be valid.

E. CRITERIA FOR UNDERTAKING MODELLING

436.   Some hydrologic modelling will almost surely be undertaken during the project design and evaluation phase for all but the smallest barrages. If nothing more, a simple digital computer model which permits routing historical flows through the project structures to test their adequacy and to derive operating rules will be utilised. If it is desired to use the more modern techniques of synthetic hydrology (see Fiering and Jackson, 1971) to test the project more adequately, a relatively sophisticated computerised model is required. Questions naturally arise concerning how far modelling should be carried, what expense is worthwhile, and how many environmental dimensions can be modelled? After all, modelling is expensive.

437.   Three criteria are suggested which will help in answering these questions:

    a) Has the type of model under consideration demonstrated success in similar applications and what is the degree of professional acceptance of such models?
    b) What is the likelihood of continued use of the model beyond the initial project design and evaluation stage?
    c) Will it be possible to build the model in-house, and if not, are competent consultants available to assist not only on model construction but for assistance on applications and up-dating?

438.   The criteria are self-explanatory, but a few comments should be made. Surface flow models using historical data or synthetic hydrology are well established and widely available. Dissolved oxygen models for rivers and estuaries are also well established and available, and generally are modules which can be added to the computerised flow model. Sediment transport models are well established, as are concentration models for stable pollutants such as salts. Models dealing with algae and eutrophication are much newer and more difficult to find but are proving to be useful management tools in some settings. Aquatic ecological models extending up the food chain to fish are still experimental in nature, as are terrestrial ecology models.

439.   Continued use is an important issue, since the initial construction, calibration, and verification are costly, while running and maintaining the models are relatively cheap. It is frequently desirable to plan to continue these models as management tools during the project's operating life. Such uses of models have educational and training values to the users who thereby learn much about the system they are managing.

440.   The question of who will build the model is important, for one wants to be sure that in-house expertise is increased as a result of the model-building work and that an in-house capability of using the model is developed. Capable consultants can be of great help, but they should be required to train in-house staff as part of the modelling work. Incentives should be offered for doing this training work well, and penalties should discourage attempts to ignore the training function. Many "counterpart" programmes involving consultants in a planning role have been failures because of too-tight time deadlines, unfamiliarity with training techniques, and low quality counterpart personnel.

Figure 16 **COST AND BENEFIT STREAMS OF A WATER PROJECT**

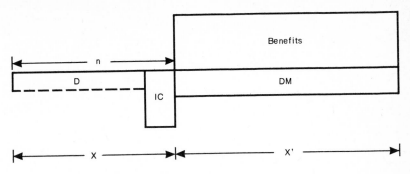

Source : M.R. Karlinger, 1976.

Figure 17 **PRESENT VALUE OF A PROJECT AS A FUNCTION OF LENGTH OF HYDROLOGIC RECORD**

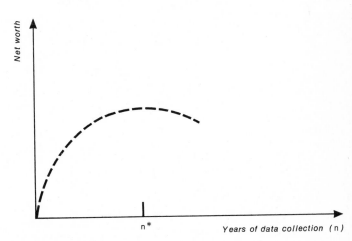

Source : M.R. Karlinger, 1976.

F. SPECIAL ENVIRONMENTAL PROBLEMS DURING PROJECT CONSTRUCTION AND EARLY OPERATING LIFE

441.   The construction period is likely to be the most damaging from an environmental point of view: new roads are built; vast social surfaces are bared; the dam site is blasted and rock and earth fill materials are excavated from their natural sites; tunnels are built and the river is diverted; men and machines intrude into new or primative areas; new air-borne and water-borne wastes are generated, etc. Naturally, all of these impacts should be anticipated and estimated in magnitude during planning, but many simple steps can be taken to minimise these impacts. Then, each impact must be monitored during construction to be sure it is not exceeding anticipated values.

442.   The scars from construction may remain forever, so care and prevention of unnecessary environmental disruption during construction can pay large dividends.

443.   Early operating life may have special environmental problems, too. The reservoir fill period first totally breaks wildlife migration patterns as well as human travel patterns. After filling, the reservoir dissolved oxygen and temperature regimes may be very unstable. Changes in adjacent groundwater systems may induce other rapid environmental changes. These should all be monitored.

G. DISCOVERY AND USE OF EXISTING DATA BASES

444.   Efficient project planning requires effective use of all existing data bases which relate to the project alternatives under consideration. It is often tempting to start a programme of data gathering without carefully investigating what data sets may be available from the planning agencies themselves or from other sources. Since data gathering is both expensive and time consuming, all possible sources (both public and private) should be checked.

445.   The nature of the data needed will, of course, suggest where to look. The most obvious source will be public agencies with continuous data gathering programmes. The national meteorological service will have precipitation, temperature, and wind data. If no weather stations are close to the project sites, special studies may have been carried out in the past for previous projects, local radio stations and aiports may have maintained records, etc. Many countries have permanent networks for surface water gauging of all major streams, sometimes including water quality data. Water quality data may also be collected by public health agencies at sub-national levels.

446.   Universities often have research programmes or extension programmes which involve gathering data on environmental variables. Crop and forestry research require detailed meteorological observations. Water science, ecological, and environmental institutes may have collected extensive data set.

447.   International organisations frequently compile data from many national sources and may even gather new data for international projects. The United Nations agencies such as the World Meteorological Organisation, the Food and

Agricultural Organisation, and UNESCO compile extensive data for publication. Non-government international organisations such as the Scientific Committee on Problems of the Environment (SCOPE) of the International Congress of Scientific Unions (ICSU) also organise collaborative international studies which generate extensive and unique data sets. Examples include the International Hydrological Programme, the Man and the Biosphere Programme, and the Global Atmospheric Research Programme. Studies carried out by OECD (1977) should also be mentioned.

448. Private organisations such as industrial companies, transport companies (air, surface, and maritime), power companies (electricity and gas), communications organisations, and co-operatives or collectives may regularly compile data on environmental, economic, and demographic variables in their regions which could be of use in water project planning.

NOTES

1. Mr. Michael Proctor, expert of the Water Management Group, collaborated -- during the conceptual phase of this Chapter -- in the work done by the team responsible for writing this document.

2. The cost of waste treatment, low flow augmentation, and other quality maintenance measures.

3. To test the usefulness of the index, Leopold applied it to various streams in the State of Idaho. In that lovely, underdeveloped setting, the most "unique" stream turned out to be a small, highly polluted one.

4. This discussion draws heavily on the excellent papers in the book edited by Asit K. Biswas (1976). See also Clarke (1973).

5. Different "real time" models have been developed for short-term critical events such as flood forecasting and forecasting the dispersion of critical pollution events.

6. See Crawford and Lisley (1966).

7. For instance, see Thomann et al., 1970.

8. See Hardison, 1969.

Chapter XIX

PRESENTING THE RESULTS OF THE ENVIRONMENTAL STUDIES

449.   Table 50 (cf above §382) and Figure 18 (hereafter) suggest a taxonomy of environmental dimensions. It is intended that, under each of the environmental categories, an inventory of that particular type resource (e.g. streams) in the project impacted area be constructed. Each resource in that inventory (e.g. each stream) would then be evaluated in terms of five evaluation factors:

    a) Quantity;
    b) Quality;
    c) Human influence;
    d) Uniqueness;
    e) Possible irreversible changes in the resource as a result of the
       project.

450.   Under each factor, a number of measures may be taken. For example, for "quantity" of a stream, length of stream, width and depth by river mile, seasonal flows, etc., might be recorded. Some measures may be qualitative and judgemental (especially those under "quality" or "uniqueness") and may best be recorded on an ordinal scale of 0 to 10.

451.   After detailed inventories and evaluations of environmental resources have been completed along these lines, summaries will have to be prepared for use by decision-makers. Useful tables for compiling both the initial inventories and the summaries are listed in Section B below. Section A provides a suggested list of measures that might be taken on each resource in the initial inventory.

    A. A LIST OF RELEVANT ENVIRONMENTAL MEASURES TO BE COMPILED FOR
       ENVIRONMENTAL RESOURCES IN THE RELEVANT PROJECT AREA (1)

452.   a) Open Space and Greenbelts

    1. Quantity factors:

        i) Acres designed as parks;
       ii) Acres serving wildlife purposes;
      iii) Agricultural lands   (already irrigated
                                 (non-irrigated

iv) Rangelands;
   v) Forest land;
  vi) Areas of lands administered by the various levels of government;
 vii) Wetlands and marshes.

Figure 18 **HIERARCHICAL STRUCTURE FOR ENVIRONMENTAL DIMENSIONS**

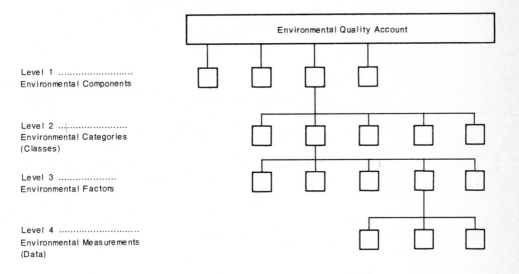

Level 1 ....
Environmental Components

Level 2 ....
Environmental Categories
(Classes)

Level 3 ....
Environmental Factors

Level 4 ....
Environmental Measurements
(Data)

2. Quality factors:

    i) Special land features;
    ii) Extent of variety in topography, soils, and groundcover.

3. Human influence factors: human influence runs both ways, from current human influence <u>upon the resources</u> and the <u>significance of the
resources for human well-being</u>.

    i) Relationship to the population. The degree that the area can
or does receive use. Consider time and distance factors relative to origin of users and location of resource;
    ii) Public access. The degree or extent of area open to public
use, considering existing or proposed transport systems;
    iii) Public amenities. The degree to which public use facilities
are developed in the area. Consider picknicking, camping,
fishing, hiking, riding areas, overlook, scenic viewpoints,
golf courses, etc.;
    iv) Legal and/or administrative protection. The degree to which
the area is reserved from encroachment by industrial or residential developments;
    v) Legal and/or administrative restrictions to public use. Con-
sider both positive and negative effects. (i.e., overuse may
be detrimental to the resources, whereas too many restrictions
may preclude satisfaction of recreation demands);
    vi) Physical protection. The degree of change expected to occur
as a result of natural processes, considering the amount of
land management practices expected;
    vii) The ability of the area to accommodate the anticipated use, or
its durability, without degradation of natural values. Use in
this situation would refer to human impact, including recreation, urban or industrial development, etc.;
    viii) Effect of climate on public use of area.

b) <u>Streams and River Systems</u>

1. Quantity factors:

    i) Total miles of stream with sustained and intermittent flows;
    ii) Miles of undeveloped stream that have wild, scenic, and/or re-
creational potential;
    iii) Stream dimensions: width, length and depth;
    iv) Amount of fluctuation in streamflow, seasonal (climatic) -- up-
stream releases (power, irrigation, etc.).
    v) Acres adjacent to shoreline with scenic quality characteristics.

2. Quality factors: (Consider quality from viewpoint of an observer in
or on the stream.)

    i) Water quality: turbidity, debris, chemicals, odour, algae,
temperature;
    ii) Capability of supporting aquatic life;

iii) Type of flow: placid, turbulent, rifles, rapids, falls, or no flow (intermittent);
  iv) Characteristics of stream bottom: muddy, gravel, rocks, etc.;
   v) Outstanding water features: scenic, biotic, geologic;
  vi) Specific uses of stream: river boat trips, fisheries, boat races, etc.;
 vii) Land features along stream: land forms such as steep cliffs, deltas, beaches, etc.;
viii) Biotic features along or in stream: riparian vegetation, special wildlife habitat, fisheries, etc.

3. Human influence factors as listed above.

c) Lakes and Reservoirs

454.   This includes both natural and manmade lakes and reservoirs and other areas of standing water (except those areas classed as wetlands or estuaries).   Any water impounded behind a dam or other structure where the quantity of water is materially increased should be included.   The minimum size of lakes and reservoirs to be included in this analysis should be determined for each study. Area of influence should consider recreation potential and satisfaction, plus fisheries and wildlife habitat relative to project area.

1. Quantity factors:

    i) Total maximum surface area of natural lakes;
   ii) Total maximum surface areas of manmade lakes and reservoirs;
  iii) Total number of natural and manmade lakes;
   iv) Average surface area of natural and manmade lakes during the prime recreation season;
    v) Maximum depth of the lake;
   vi) Amplitude of surface level variations.

2. Quality factors:

    i) Water quality: turbidity, debris, chemical components, odour, algae, temperature;
   ii) Scenic setting: narrative description;
  iii) Related land features;
   iv) Faunal and floral desirability: presence of insects, nettles, poison oak, algae, aquatic plants (these may be detrimental to swimming or boating, but enhance wildlife or fisheries);
    v) Productivity: degree to which or reservoir sustains desirable faunal or floral communities;
   vi) Fluctuation: impact on reservoirs and adjacent land;
  vii) Depth: adequacy for sustaining year-round fish populations.

3. Human influence factors: as listed above.

d) Beaches and Shores

1. Quantity factors:

    i) Total miles of shoreline.
    ii) Total acres of support land for beach and shore recreation.
    iii) Total acres of land in use or available for use for swimming beaches, fishing access points, boat ramps or marinas, etc.

2. Quality factors:

    i) Water quality: suitability for recreation use;
    ii) Scenic setting: line of sight from shoreline area;
    iii) Composition of beach material (of particular importance for swimming);
    iv) Effect on biota (pests, poison oak, etc.) on use of beaches and shorelines.
    v) Type and morphology of shoreline (rocky, cliff-likem sandy, flat, steep, etc.).

3. Human influence factors: approximately as listed above.

e) Wilderness, Primitive, and Natural Areas

456.   Wilderness and primitive areas are those areas defined as lands included within or having the potential for inclusion within the National Wilderness Preservation System, or have similar qualities and characteristics. Such areas should be undeveloped land retaining primeval character and influence, without permanent improvements or human habitation, which is protected and managed (or has the potential for so being) so as to preserve its natural conditions. The area should be of sufficient size to make practicable its preservation and use in an unimpaired condition. The area may contain ecological, geological, or other features of scientific, educational, scenic or historical value. Prairie grass lands and desert areas, as well as forested mountain areas, could be included in the above category. Natural areas are those areas defined as containing rare and/or unique biotic, geologic, pedologic, or aquatic characteristics, forms and processes. Such areas may range in size from less than 1 acre to many thousands of acres. Areas may be set aside for scenic aspects (Grand Canyon National Park) or as Research Natural Areas for scientific and educational purposes. Area of influence should consider the significance of natural values to project area, particularly any impacts on the resources by project development or increased use induced by the project.

1. Quantity factors:

    i) Wilderness and primitive areas: total acreage of wilderness and primitive areas;
    ii) Natural areas: total number of natural areas that have scenic, scientific or educational value; total acreage of natural areas.

2. Quality factors:

    i) Land features. Topography;
   ii) Water features;
  iii) Living natural resources of the area;
   iv) Significant size or visual impact.

3. Human influence factors:

    i) Relationship to population: the degree that the area can or does receive use. Consider time and distance factors relative to origin of users and location of resource;
   ii) Public access: the degree to which area is open to public use;
  iii) Public amenities: the degree to which public use facilities are developed in the area, camping, fishing, hiking, riding areas, overlooks, scenic viewpoints, etc.;
   iv) Legal and/or administrative protection;
    v) The ability of the area to accommodate anticipated changes in use without degradation of natural values;
   vi) Effect of climate on public use of area;
  vii) Scientific value;
 viii) Educational value: the degree the area can contribute to general understanding of wilderness or natural areas.

457.   f) <u>Estuarine and Wetland Areas</u>

1. Quantity factors:

    i) Total number of wetland areas;
   ii) Total acres of estuarine area;
  iii) Total acres of intermittent wetlands;
   iv) Total acres of wetlands that contain standing water during most years.

2. Quality factors:

    i) Water supply: availability of water to serve wetlands; availability of fresh water for salinity gradient in estuary;
   ii) Water quality: the degree to which natural values are preserved, degraded, or enhanced;
  iii) Related land features;
   iv) Desirability of the plant and animal species of the area.

3. Human influence factors: as above.

g) <u>Other Areas of Natural Beauty</u>.

458.   These include any examples of nature's <u>visual</u> and scenic grandeur not accommodated in the other categories. Consider the maximum areas of influence utilised in evaluating the other environmental categories.

1. Quantity factors:

    i) Number of each type (e.g. waterfalls, canyons, etc.);
   ii) Number of acres of river miles related to each type of area;

2. Quality factors:

     i) Land features.
    ii) Water features;
   iii) Biotic features;

3. Human influence factors: as above.

h) Archeological Resources

459. This category considers those material remains such as occupation sites, work areas, evidence of farming or hunting and gathering, burial sites, artifacts, and structures of all types of past human life and activities during prehistoric periods.

   1. Quantity factors:

       i) Total number of sites: places, with locations and descriptions;
      ii) Total number of sizable structural remains with locations and descriptions;
     iii) Summary of scattered artifactual material if widely dispersed;
      iv) Total number of sites displaying petroglyphs, pictographs, or pictorial or symbolic graphic modification of the earth surface, with locations and descriptions;
       v) Total number of burial places -- or other sites of religious significance not covered above, wuth locations and descriptions;
      vi) Miles and number of prehistoric trails, steps carved into cliffs, etc., with locations and descriptions.

   2. Quality factors (as determined by professional evaluation):

       i) Conditions of preservation of material;
      ii) Uniqueness of resources, as illustrative of the associated cultures and/or time periods;
     iii) Worthiness for preservation and/or restoration and interpretation to the public compared to potential contribution to knowledge expected from salvage excavation.

3. Human influence factors: as above.

i) Historical Resources.

460. This category includes those remaining evidences of the origins, evolution, and development of the nation, state, or locality. It also encompasses

recognition of places where significant historical or unusual events occurred even though no evidence of the event remains, or places associated with a personality important in history.

1. Quantity factors:

    i) Total number of sites with locations and descriptions;
    ii) Total number of trails and historic roads with locations and descriptions;
    iii) Total number of historic farms, fields and other sites with locations, sizes, and descriptions.

2. Quality factors (as determined by professional evaluation):

    i) Historical significance of resources;
    ii) Condition or preservation of structures, extent of deterioration, extent of change from historic period, etc.;
    iii) Record of past investigation or preservation of sites and structures;
    iv) Worthiness for preservation and/or restoration.

3. Human influence factors: as above.

461.   j) <u>Cultural Resources</u>

1. Quantity factors:

    i) The number of individuals associated with each type of culture;
    ii) The extent and geographic distribution of the cultures and of their lands.

2. Quality factors (as determined by professional evaluation and the testimony of members of the culture): extent of culture change intruded or imposed from outside.

3. Human influence factors: the ability of the culture to retain its identifiable characteristics and unity.

462.   k) <u>Biological Resources: Flora</u>

This category includes beneficial and adverse effects on individuals, species, and populations of living plants.

1. Quantity factors:

    i) Species that are rare or in danger of extinction;
    ii) Area dominated by tree species;

iii) Area where shrub species dominate;
iv) Area where grass species dominate;
v) Area where other species dominate.

2. Quality factors:

i) Degree that the plant communities are in good condition and tend to remain stable;
ii) Diversity of species within the community.

3. Human influence factors:

i) Scientific value;
ii) Educational value;
iii) Recreational value;
iv) Physical (bioenvironmental) protection;
v) Legal and/or administrative protection.

1) Biological Resources: Fauna

463.   The subcategory of fauna includes all major types of animals and their habitats within the areas of potential impact for each. At least eight groupings of animals should be considered on separate work sheets (Table 52) for existing condition, without the project and the various project alternatives. Each of the animal groups is composed of species having generally similar life cycles or habitat requirements or otherwise logically fitting together for purposes of analysis. Threatened species should be treated individually. Areas of impact for each animal species may vary in size and location. Habitat base will be expressed quantitatively (in acres, sections, or other appropriate units) and qualitatively (high, medium or low value). The population dynamics (relative condition analysis) will be subjectively rated and expressed using the appropriate 0 to 10 scale as previously described. Similar subjective ratings will be made of factors selected to show human influence (values, accessibility and protection). A summary display (Table 53) will reflect only subjective ratings of the factors which are materially affected by one of the plans.

1. Quantity factors:

i) Habitat and carrying capacity for individual threatened species;
ii) Habitat and carrying capacity for big game species;
iii) Habitat and carrying capacity for upland game species;
iv) Habitat and carrying capacity for fur bearing species;
v) Habitat and carrying capacity for waterfowl species;
vi) Habitat and carrying capacity for other bird and mammal species;
vii) Habitat and carrying capacity for fish species.

2. Quality factors: the population dynamics (relative condition or stability of habitat and populations) expected under each condition (existing, no project, and project alternatives).

212

Table 52

ENVIRONMENTAL EVALUATION WORKSHEET FOR FAUNA

Prepare separate sheets for existing conditions without plan and for each alternative plan considered

Planning setting _____

Category _____

Area evaluated _____

	Quantitative factors					Qualitative factor	Human Influence Factors				
	Habitat base (in units and capacities or standing crops (in number or pounds/unit)						Resource Value/Accessibility			Resource Protection	
	High value (units)	Capacity crop (per unit)	Medium value (units)	Capacity crop (per unit)	Low value (units)	Capacity crop (per unit)	Dynamics (summary)	Scientific and Educational	Recreational value	Accessibility or visibility to public	Legal and Administration	Physical	Summary
1. Threatened species											
2. Big game											
3. Upland game											
4. Fur bearers											
5. Miscellaneous birds and animals											
6. Waterfowl											
7. Fish											
8. Other											

Table 53

ENVIRONMENTAL EVALUATION WORKSHEET FOR FAUNA SUMMARY

Planning Setting: _____

Category: Fauna Summary

Area Evaluated: _____

	Display summary							
	Present conditions		Without plan		Plan A		Plan B	
	Dynamics	Value/Acc/Prot	Dynamics	Value/Acc/Prot	Dynamics	Value/Acc/Prot	Dynamics	Value/Acc/Prot
1. Threatened species								
2. Big game								
3. Upland game								
4. Fur bearers								
5. Miscellaneous birds and mammals								
6. Waterfowl								
7. Fish								
8. Other								

214

3. Human influence factors: as above.

m) Geological Resources

464. This category covers areas of importance as future mineral supplies as well as those areas of interest in studying or displaying the development of the earth.

1.) Quantity factors:

   i) Approximate grade and volume of important mineral deposits;
  ii) Number of locations where fossil beds occur;
 iii) Number of locations where exposed rock formations illustrate the structure of the surface composition of the earth.

2. Quality factors:

   i) Uniqueness of the geological formations and processes in the area;
  ii) Conditions of preservation in natural conditions.
 iii) Chance for fossil or mineral recovery.
  iv) Presence of seismic risk.

3. Human influence factors: as above.

n) Ecological Systems

465. This category covers the identifiable communities of organisms and the physical conditions in which they exist. Each natural area, such as a water-shed, a vegetation and soil type, a tidal salt marsh, a swamp, a lake, or a stream complex, represents an ecosystem, an interdependent physical and biotic environment that functions as a continuing dynamic unit. Beneficial effects resulting from preservation of ecological systems include the maintenance of a natural environment, the provision of aesthetic contact with nature, and scientific understanding derived from the study of natural ecological sys-tems. In some cases cultivated areas can also be added to the list of ecolo-gical systems of interest. For instance, meadows can be of interest as a breeding habitat for water birds, etc.

1. Quantity factors:

   i) Size in hectares of forest ecosystems;
  ii) Size in hectares of shrublands and desert ecosystems;
 iii) Size in hectares of grassland ecosystems;
  iv) Size in hectares of lake and river ecosystems;
   v) Size in hectares of bog, marsh, swamp, and estuarine ecosystems.

2. Quality factors: (i) degree that each ecosystem is in good condition and tends to remain in a state of equilibrium.

3. Human influence factors: as above.

o) Water quality

466. This category includes the chemical, physical and biological aspects of fresh, brackish, and salt water. The effects of a project on water quality may extend well beyond the immediate project area. An example would be an irrigation project from which the effects of salinity may extend far downstream.

1. Quantity factors:

i) Type, number, and quantity of wastewater sources. For reconnaisance reports identify waste sources by broad categories, e.g. municipal, agricultural, industrial. For implementation studies, source identification should be expanded to specific source locations which should be shown on a map;
ii) Miles of river not meeting established water quality standards, indicating which standards are violated;
iii) Number and area of diffuse sources of pollution such as agricultural lands.

2. Quality factors:

i) Extent to which water supports desirable aquatic regions;
ii) Extent to which water quality impairs or enhances aesthetics;
iii) Extent to which desired or existing uses are limited by water quality: irrigation, municipal and industrial water supply, and recreation.

3. Human influence factors: the extent to which technology is available to meet water quality standards.

p) Land Quality

467. Land areas with identifiable existing and/or potential quality problems are to be evaluated under this category. Among the types of lands evaluated would be farmland areas, rangeland areas, forest areas, other (alpine, desert, etc.), urban and industrial land areas.

1. Quality factors:

i) Naturalness. Extent that the viewer appears to be in a natural landscape;
ii) The degree that manmade structures or changes to the natural landscape blend into or add beauty to the scenic setting;

216

iii) The degree that manmade structure or changes to the natural landscape detract from the beauty of the natural setting.

2. Human influence factors:

    i) Degree that the public has access to view the scenic qualities;
   ii) Degree that public access influences the quality of the scenic setting;
  iii) Presence and influence of public amenities (visitor centres, campgrounds, restrooms, etc.).

q) Uniqueness Considerations

468.   Some environmental resources are of particular significance in that they are rare, unusual or extraordinary in the nation or in the region. The degradation or destruction of such a resource may deprive future generations of the opportunity of viewing or otherwise enjoying it. Those resources rated under the other categories which are considered to be unique should also be identified and evaluated under the uniqueness category. The uniqueness of a resource will be evaluated in relation to its frequency of occurrence in the nation or region. The following scale may be useful:

1-2: Unique in the planning setting but occurs in abundance throughout other parts of the region;

3-4: Unique in the region but occurs in abundance in other parts of the nation;

  5: Unique in the region but examples occur frequently in other parts of the nation;

6-7: Rare throughout the nation but several examples occur within the region;

8-9: Very rare throughout the nation and region with one of few examples occurring in the planning setting;

10: The only one of its kind or only population of a species occurring in the nation;

The effect of the project on the environmental resource considered in the uniqueness category is to be measured in relation to the degree of degradation or destruction of the resource. The following scale may be helpful:

  0: Resource totally destroyed;

1-4: severely affected;

  5: moderately affected: a portion of the resource degraded or destroyed but an adequate portion remaining to preserve the resource on a reduced scale;

6-9: minor effect;

10: no measurable effect on the resource;

Table 54 may be useful in assembling these data.

r) Irreversibility Considerations

469. Irreversibility is evaluated by identifying each natural, physical and cultural resource likely to be irreversibly changed by the project. Table 55 is suggested for use in evaluating actions to be taken under each future condition. A summary index, ranging from 0 to 10 for each resource listed may be used in the last column. The higher the value, the greater the likelihood of a significant irreversibility. Amongst the irreversible phenomena to be considered, the pollution of freshwater aquifers by seawater is especially hazardous. While coastal freshwater aquifers are generally im equilibrium with sea water, the piezometric pressure of the former can fall due to excessive pumping of coastal wells. The resulting invasion by seawater causes the immediate destruction of the freshwater aquifer.

B. THE PRESENTATION OF SUMMARY DATA AT DIFFERENT STAGES OF PLANNING

470. The data outlined in Section A are extensive and, to the layman, quite complex and even confusing. As stated earlier, some of the data will not be of interest to the decision-makers and may be retained by the technical team for internal uses. However, at each major step of the co-ordinated action plan, an efficient and attractive summary of relevant environmental data must be compiled for communication to decision-makers and the public.

471. The initial screening is to be carried out mostly with data already available from general sources although, of course, site visits must be contemplated even at this stage. The data being arranged according to the classes listed in Section A and qualitative judgments will be made by the environmental team members concerning the environmental conditions without a project and with each of the several alternative projects. These alternative judgments could be summarised as in Table 56 below.

472. In the intermediate stages of the environmental assessment, it will probably be necessary to present several more advanced summaries of the evaluations, presenting increasing amounts of quantified data of increasing detail and accuracy. This process leads to the most detailed presentation in the environmental impact statement constructed for the chosen project alternative. For these various summaries, tables similar to Table 57 below may be useful.

Table 54

ENVIRONMENTAL EVALUATION WORKSHEET FOR UNIQUE RESOURCES

Planning Setting: _____

Category: Unique Resources _____

Area Evaluated: _____

Description and measure of resources	Uniqueness	Magnitude of effects of alternative conditions			
		No plan	Plan A	Plan B	Plan C

Table 55

ENVIRONMENTAL EVALUATION WORKSHEET FOR IRREVERSIBILITY

Planning Setting: _____

Category: Irreversibility Considerations(1) _____

Area Evaluated: _____

Resource (type and quantity)	Nature of occurrence	Inter-relationships	Reversibility	Effect on remaining resources	Mitigatory actions	Summary of irreversibility

1.   Prepare separate sheets for existing conditions, without plan, and for each alternative plan considered.

Table 56

PRELIMINARY SCREENING EVALUATION OF THE ENVIRONMENTAL EFFECTS OF ALTERNATIVE PLANS

Environmental category	No Plan					Alternate A					Alternate B					Alternate C				
	Major adverse	Minor adverse	None	Minor beneficial	Major beneficial	Major adverse	Minor adverse	None	Minor beneficial	Major beneficial	Major adverse	Minor adverse	None	Minor beneficial	Major beneficial	Major adverse	Minor adverse	None	Minor beneficial	Major beneficial
Open space and greenbelts	X						X							X					X	
Streams and river systems	X							X						X						X
Lakes		X						X						X					X	
Beaches and shores		X						X						X					X	
Wilderness, primitive, and natural areas		X					X							X					X	
Estuaries and wetlands		X						X						X					X	
Other natural beauty areas	X						X					X					X			
Archeological resources		X					X				X					X				
Historical resources		X					X					X					X			
Cultural resources	X							X						X					X	
Biological resources -- plants	X						X					X					X			
Biological resources -- animals	X						X							X		X				
Geological resources		X					X							X					X	
Ecological systems	X						X					X					X			
Water quality	X									X			X							X
Land quality		X						X						X					X	
Uniqueness considerations		X					X							X		X				
Irreversibility considerations		X					X							X					X	

221

Table 57

ENVIRONMENTAL EVALUATION OF ALTERNATIVE PLANS: QUANTITATIVE/QUALITATIVE SUMMARY

	Alternatives		
	A	B	C
AREAS OF NATURAL BEAUTY AND ENJOYMENT			
BENEFICIAL EFFECTS			
Create reservoirs:			
Number	2	4	4
Combined surface area (acres)	3 470	6 360	5 580
Total shoreline (miles)	36	74	70
Create minimum pool, Mckay Reservoir, 10,000 acre-feet	Yes	Yes	Yes
Enhance quality of open and green space with diversified new irrigation (acres)	11 240	42 730	31 490
Create 3-mile greenbelt, Pendleton (200 acres)	No	No	Yes
ADVERSE EFFECTS			
Inundate intermittent streams, scenic rivers, and adjacent shorelines (miles)	10	20.4	19.5
Reduce open space because of project and associated population increase (acres)	5 000	10 000	7 000
ARCHEOLOGICAL, HISTORICAL, AND CULTURAL ELEMENTS			
BENEFICIAL EFFECTS			
Assist Umatilla Indian culture with:			
Minimum riverflows for fish enhancement	Yes	Yes	Yes
Irrigation for Reservation areas (acres)	No	21 000	21 000
Special upland game habitat in Reservation areas (acres)	No	No	1 260
ADVERSE EFFECTS			
Inundate Thomas-Ruckles Stage Station	Yes	Yes	No
Inundate part of Thomas-Ruckles Toll Road	Yes	Yes	Yes
Inundate known archeological sites	17	18	17
BIOLOGICAL, GEOLOGICAL, AND SOCIOLOGICAL ELEMENTS			
BENEFICIAL EFFECTS			
Enhance quality of flora with diversified new irrigation (acres)	11 240	42 730	31 490
Enhance waterflow habitat (areas)	2	4	4
Enhance upland game habitat (relative magnitude)	1%	3%	5%
Enhance anadronous fishery (No. fish)	96 760	96 760	96 360
Enhance resident fishery (No. fish)	1 375 800	1 744 800	1 824 800
Enhance lake ecosystems with reservoirs (surface areas)	3 470	6 360	5 580
Enhance river ecosystems with increased flows in summer and flood control measures	Yes	Yes	Yes
Enhance quality of land ecosystems (relative magnitude)	1%	4%	5%
ADVERSE EFFECTS			
Eliminate natural flora and land ecosystems with reservoir inundation, other project features, and irrigation development (acres)	5 000	15 000	12 000
ENVIRONMENTAL QUALITY CONSIDERATIONS			
BENEFICIAL EFFECTS			
Improve water quality	Yes	Yes	Yes
Provide minimum flows and temperature control in Umatilla River	Yes	Yes	Yes
Trap silt in project reservoirs	Yes	Yes	Yes
Provide flood control measures			
Reduce air pollution from dust storms through irrigation of lands (relative effectiveness)	1%	3%	2%
Reduce soil erosion with new irrigation and flood control (relative magnitude)	1%	4%	3%
Enhance esthetics with development of reservoirs (No.)	2	4	4
Create a 3-mile greenbelt along Umatilla River	No	No	Yes
ADVERSE EFFECTS			
Average drawdown during the recreation season, May through September:			
Ryan Reservoir (feet)	84	88	88
Snipe Reservoir (feet)	13	13	1
Beacon Reservoir (feet)	NA	21	1
Stage Reservoir (feet)	NA	37	37
12-mile Hidaway Canal in area of high scenic quality	Yes	Yes	Yes
IRREVERSIBILITY CONSIDERATIONS			
Inundate free-flowing perennial streams at Ryan Reservoir (miles	6.0	6.6	6.4
Inundate known archeological sites (No.)	17	18	17
Inundate Thomas-Ruckles Stage Station	Yes	Yes	No
Inundate Thomas-Ruckles Toll Road	Yes	Yes	Yes
Eliminate natural flora and associated land ecosystems (acres)	5 000	15 000	12 000
Reduce open and green space because of project and associated population increase (acres)	5 000	10 000	7 000
UNIQUE RESOURCES LOST			
Inundate Thomas-Ruckles Stage Station	Yes	Yes	No
Inundate part of Thomas-Ruckles Toll Road	Yes	Yes	Yes
Inundate known archeological sites	17	18	17

Annex I

SKETCHES OF REPORTS TO BE COMPLETED AT EACH STEP
OF THE DECISION PROCESS

As stated in Chapter I, these sketches are only intended for illustrative purposes. It is important to note, however, that they have been used in the elaboration of benchmark studies. (cf. Annex 2).

Five sketches are proposed according to each type of report, as defined in Table 1.

SKETCH OF REPORT TYPE 1

"Preliminary evaluation report"

Introduction

Mention:

a) The limits (usually administrative limits) of the area considered for the project (should be larger than the final project area). Join a map of the region;
b) Underline water problems in this area (Is there any problem of irrigation? of food control? of drainage? etc.)

Tables to be given in annex: population, income and income distribution in the area. Main cities. Importance of agriculture, industry and services in the regional CNP. Estimates of the corresponding items in 20 years ahead.

Possible solution

Describe briefly the kind of waterworks that could be imagined. Summarise them all in a table giving:

-- The identification of the waterworks (dam of X, drainage system of the plan of Y, etc.);
-- The capacity of the waterwork (million of M^3 of the reservoirs, area drained, etc.);
-- A rough estimation of the nominal costs with a range for the estimation (estimates should be justified in the text).

Expected advantages

Discuss the possible purposes of the waterworks. Summarise the results of this discussion in a table showing:

-- The nature of benefits (irrigation, drainage, domestic water, etc.) (according to the items listed in Table 10);
-- The corresponding physical quantity (expected value and range) in appropriate units (number of irrigated ha, number of M^3 supplied for domestic purposes, etc.);

-- The corresponding values at nominal prices (expected values and ranges).

Give, on these basis, a rough estimate of the IRR or of the benefit/cost ratio.

Links with regional and national plans

Discuss the insertion of the project within regional or national plans, if any. Discuss its influence on the balance of payments (if any) (cf. Chapter V). Mention briefly its possible influence on income distribution (cf. Chapter XI)

Possible environmental problems

1. Review national laws and regulations regarding environmental standards, restraints on environmental quality changes, and required analyses and reports (paragraphs 21-22 and 394-396);
2. Review the concept of regional environmental balance and consider its relevance to the region involved in current water development. Review the list of potentially relevant environmental factors (cf. Chapter XIX);
3. Make a quick diagnosis of likely negative major environmental impacts. It will be helpful to review the environmental factors listed in paragraph 471;
4. Evaluate the possibility of taking steps of modifying project designs to lessen these negative impacts;
5. Make a quick diagnosis of likely beneficial environmental impacts;
6. Using existing maps, environmental inventories of plant and animal life, wind data, etc., make a preliminary estimate of the geographic extent of these impacts;
7. Recommendations regarding further consideration of project ideas.

Possible social problems

The following questions must be answered, as far as possible:

a) General

1. Do national regulations exist regarding the social aspects of the evaluation of multipurpose hydraulic projects?
2. Are these general social issues which may be important for the project identified? Some examples: rural poverty, unemployed, migrations, health problems, etc. (cf. paragraph 242);
3. Are these general social issues related to the project idea?
4. Are scope and time spans of these issues taken into consideration? (cf. paragraphs 269-273).

b) Participation

1. Is the public opinion heard? By which instrument? (e.g. snapshot survey paragraphs 265-273);
2. Is a list of general social issues set up? Are new issues brought up by the public taken into account?
3. What kind of differentiations regarding participation are or could be used (cf. paragraphs 274-275)?
4. Which kind of participation techniques are or could be used? (cf. Tables 37, 39 and 40, and paragraphs 277-279).

c) Institutional possibilities

Discuss the institutional arrangements that could be made in order to realise the project. Especially, from a social point of view, try to answer the following questions:

1. How is the project team put together? (paragraphs 70 and 71). Are there institutionalised relationships between the various levels of government, the private sector, the public and the project team? How are the team-members recruited? Is there an advisory team formed (experts? political representatives?) (Chapter IV);
2. Is there a specific organisation structure developed?
3. What kind of data are used for the selection of the institutional arrangements?

d) Financial problems

1. Discuss the order of magnitude of expenses of any kind in relation to the project (Chapter X);
2. Set up a tentative list of agencies which are interested a priori in the project (Ministries, local communities, etc.). Evaluate the possible amount of their participation (this part of the report may be confidential). Try to build formal links between the technical teams of the project and the possible funding agencies.

Conclusion

Recommend and define further studies -- Define the framework of these studies, and the composition of the team to be set up for pursuing the work of planning and evaluation. Evaluate the corresponding budget.

SKETCH OF REPORT TYPE 2

"Examination of variants report"

Introduction

Delimination of the area involved and sketch of main water problems in the region (as for report type 1).

Technical description of variants

a) Description of the "central variant" (usually, that which gives the highest economic benefit). Type and location of waterworks and their main purposes (provide a map);

b) Description and identification of variants, according to the same criteria.

Economic analysis

a) Sources of data and estimations. Assessment of their values - their range of variation (See especially chapter VI). Justification of shadow prices, if any. Brief description of models used, if any. Discussion of any methodological choice;

b) Presentation of results. For each variant, fill in Tables 10, 11, 12 and 15. Optionally, fill in Tables 13 and 14 whenever possible. Comment these results;

c) Additional information. Consequences of the "central variant" for income distribution (using eventually Tables 27 to 32. Corrections, if any, brought about to this situation by other variants;

Degree of risk associated with each variant. Sensitivity analysis for each variant or, eventually, simulation analysis (cf. Chapter VI).

d) Plans for further studies. Indicate gaps in the available information: Suggest studies for filling them (with indication of cost and resources needed).

Environmental analysis

1. Discuss the criteria used for the initial design and evaluation of project alternatives, including the critical values of any parameters that may be specified by law or practice. Consult paragraph 405;
2. Summarise the initial data base, including data gathered by sampling procedures (e.g. water quality). Indicate all available sources;
3. For each variant as well as for the situation "without project", present initial projections of the criteria selected in point 1 above, and covering both the construction period and the operating life of the project. Many projections will be qualitative in nature at this point, and will be displayed using a format like Table 56;
4. Discuss the economic and ecological feasibility of steps to mitigate negative impacts that have been predicted;
5. Design and initiate monitoring systems that will be needed for more detailed evaluations, e.g. flow and quality gauging stations and networks, migration and cropping pattern trends, etc. Consult Chapter XVIII;
6. Consider the benefit of formal computer modelling (see paragraphs 436-440) and state the resources (in terms of manpower and data) necessary to continue the studies.

Analysis of social problem

For each variant, check briefly the following points:

1. Is a list of topics drawn up to direct monitoring activities? (paragraphs 280-286). Is there a relationship with the general social issues mentioned in step I?
2. What kind of project objectives are identified? What kind of evaluation variables are formulated (cf. §251-254)?
3. What kind of population segments are identified (cf. §255-256)?
4. How was the participation organised (cf. §259-263)?

In addition provide examples of questions used for identification of objectives, variables and population segments. Discuss methods of data collection used if any.

Conclude by discussing:

1. Are additional detailed sociological studies suggested?
2. Are specific screening criteria formulated?

Financial considerations

-- Evaluate the total amount of money available from various sources;
-- Set up a financial plan for the "reference variant" (cf. Tables 25-26);
-- Check that other variants could be financed in the same framework, or that additional funds could be eventually raised;
-- If some variants are significantly less costly than others, indicate the way adjustments should be done. (Requesting funds which will not be used is just as troublesome as being short of money!);

-- Check that no firm (including the project manager) can be financially hurt by the existence of the project, under each variant.
Otherwise, prepare _ad hoc_ plans for compensation.

Conclusion

Summarise by a table showing:

-- The list of variants;
-- The main advantages;
-- The main drawbacks;

Make the choices clear that are open to the decision-maker.

SKETCH OF REPORT TYPE 3

"Selection of variants report"

Introduction

History of the project: how did it reach this stage? What amount of work has been already spent? (give the references of the corresponding studies). What are the main interests involved in the project?

Technical description of variants

Describe the main waterworks. Provide a map of the region showing their location, and the areas involved.

Economic analysis

The plan made for report type 2 applies here, except that the notion of "central variant" is probably no more relevant, since the number of variants is reduced to 4 at the maximum. Each variant should therefore be treated here as the "central variant" in report type 2.

Of course, the content of the report will be quite different from that of the report type 2, since data and models will be more accurate, and the number of variants is reduced.

Environmental analysis

Basically, this part of the report will be similar to that of report type 2, except that quantitative, instead of qualitative projections will be obtained in most cases. They should be presented according to the framework of Table 57.

In addition, a description of the computer models (if any) used during the study would be necessary.

Social studies

1. Describe the social monitoring process (cf. §280-286) which should

have been started at this stage. In this social monitoring process both the general issues studied in the first step and more specific topics delimited in the previous studies should be included. Depending on the scope and time-span of the project, the social monitoring process could be more or less elaborated. Is special attention given to the monitoring of project-related participation activities?

2. Describe more detailed sociological investigations done since preceding steps. Are new evaluation variables extracted from these investigations?

3. To integrate the various social aspects, the evaluation variables, topics, etc., a specific technique may be used: the scenario-technique (cf. $287-295). This technique has various advantages in working towards the final set of project alternatives. The report should summarise briefly the main results of this exercise (detailed descriptions of the sociological studies can be put in annex).

Finally, it must be stressed that public participation Tables 39-40, and §277-279) must be taken care of at this stage. Therefore, the report should indicate to what extent the evaluation team will be able to:

1. Assist in planning public participation in keeping with national practice to determine reactions to surviving project's alternatives.

2. Re-evaluate the list of criteria being used in the assessment, extending or contracting it as indicated by public concerns and initial analyses.

Financial considerations

A full financial plan (cf. Chapter X) is needed for each remaining variant (eventually, it is the same for all variants with the same cost). Refer to the "Guide to the Economic Evaluation of Irrigation Projects" for an example of table to be filled in this respect.

Discuss the financial consequences of each variant on each economic unit involved in the project (cf. Tables 17 and 18). These economic units comprise:

-- The agency in charge of the project;
-- Any user of water resources;
-- Public or private agencies in charge of any equipment (such as road, harbour, etc.) linked with this project;.
-- Household (especially, collective households, such as hospitals, school, etc.).

(This discussion involves at least some rough knowledge of the pricing system of the projects' outputs. Since the pricing system is probably not yet defined, make use of likely assumptions).

Discuss possible consequences of inflation cf. §162 and 207).

Conclusion

Summary of each remaining variant, according to the following table:

	Variant 1	Variant 2	Variant 3
Identification (name)			
Total nominal cost			
Total discounted cost			
Duration of construction period			
TIR or benefit/cost ratio			
Total discounted benefit			
Breakdown of benefits by purposes, in %			
purpose No. 1			
purpose No. 2			
....			
purpose No. n			
Main environmental drawbacks			
Main environmental advantages			
Main social drawbacks			
Main social advantages			
Main risk taken with the variant			

For each variant, indicate the reasons for which it could be retained and those, on the contrary, for which it could be rejected. Indicate the recommendation of the technical team, based upon its own preference, with respect to the variant which should be finally retained.

"Final ex ante Report"

Introduction

Short history of the project - Summary of variants examined and rejected. Reasons for their rejection. Presentation of the variant retained. Main characteristics of the waterworks. Indication of the purposes served by the project. (Give reference of previous studies).

Economic and financial analysis

a) General presentation

Summary of previous economic studies. Reference to any model or data bank used for the project. Short methodological summary (detailed methodological discussion should be put in annex).

b) Main results

Presentation of Tables 10 to 15 (Chapter VII). Justification of each figure, including especially shadow prices (if any).

Discussion of the events which could in the future necessitate modifications in the plans as they are presented here.

c) Pricing policy

Discuss the intended pricing system, according to Chapter X.

Examine possible consequences of this tariff for the financial equilibrium of customers (cf. Tables 17 and 18), as well as for the general income distribution among the beneficiaries of the project.

d) Distributional effects

As far as possible, fill up Tables 27-32, Chapter XI. Discuss and justify.

e) Risk analysis

Sensitivity analysis (Chapter VI). Description of any decision rule decided upon.

Social analysis

1. Social assessment structure (Chapter XIV)

The impacts of the project can be evaluated by the social assessment structure (SAS). This instrument often used for most detailed forms of social evaluation is developed in Chapter XIV. The social assessment structure can be used as a sort of check-list of possible social impacts of multipurpose hydraulic projects.

2. Public participation (§259-263 and 277-279)

How are consultations with the public organised (public meetings, summaries of scenarios presented to the various groups, etc.).

3. Conclusion

State any suggestions in preparing detailed procedural workbooks on the topics covered by the studies undertaken, e.g. resettlement, together with the impacted groups of people, so as to guarantee the optimal course of public participation (Chapter XVI).

Environmental analysis

This chapter corresponds to the "environmental impact statement" as called for existing regulations in most countries.

In the absence of such regulations, filling in Table 57 for the retained variant, and justifying each figure by reference to the ad hoc study will provide a good starting point for the redaction of this chapter.

Any model or data bank used must be outlined, and the reference of a least one more complete report should be given.

In addition, a detailed statement of every measure taken in view of future monitoring will be needed. Describe carefully these measures. Eventually, if operating hand books or regulations have been drafted by the project, give them in the annex.

Financial analysis

Describe financial arrangements taken with each fund supplier. Complete a table of future receipts and payments, as in report type 3.

Conclusion

Summarise again the reasons for which the project should be undertaken.

SKETCH OF REPORT TYPE 5

"Ex post evaluation Report"

Introduction

Historical sketch of the project, explaining how it reached its present state.

Present state of the project.

Its planned future (according to the feasibility report).

The problems which are encountered now, and which justify the publication of this report.

Description of new alternatives

As for report type 2 "technical description of variants".

Economic analysis

Present and discuss Tables 10 to 15, slightly modified in order to show the differences between what was expected in the feasibility study, and what is observed now.

Indicate the main reasons for these discrepancies (revision in price or quantity forecast, new technology available, etc.).

As far as possible, interpret these results in the light of econometric models which should have been built during the preceding steps. Do not forget to take account of inflation.

Discuss the value of the new forecast (revised value of the IRR, etc.).

Evaluate the possible alternatives for improving the situation – this presentation of new alternatives should be done according to the plan of report type 2.

Social evaluation

1. Execute formative social evaluation studies and feed back information to improve the quality of the _ex ante_ evaluation methodology. For example, by comparing the forecasts of the social assessment structure (Chapter XIV) with the real outcome, one can judge the usefulness of the forecasting-techniques that were used.
2. Discuss the new actions to be undertaken in the light of these findings. Discuss new monitoring systems to be set up and, more generally, the means of alleviating the consequences of the errors which have been made previously.

Environmental evaluation

Recall the criteria which were decided upon in the feasibility report. Compare actual values with forecasted values (use Table 57 modified in order to put in light "forecasted" and "actual" values). Report investigations made for discovering the sources of possible discrepancies, especially undesirable ones.

Examine the actions proposed, and make use of the experience gained in previous studies to assess their chances of alleviation or the elimination of the difficulties encountered (if any).

Financial evaluation

Compare the _ex ante_ financial plan with values observed _ex post_. Discuss the reasons for the discrepancies. Propose solutions for improving the situation.

A financial plan, presented under the form of a table showing "expected" and "actual" receipts and expenses would be helpful.

Pricing considerations

Often, the cause of bad financial results is in an inadequate pricing policy. Compare estimates of demand with actual sales. Discuss the possibility of changing the pricing policy in order to meet effective demand (this should be discussed in close connection with financial analysis). Indicate the methodology which was used to reestimate the demand parameters.

Conclusion

Summarise the main errors made during previous steps of the project's design and execution. Not, of course, to put the blame on anybody responsible for these errors, but in order that they could not be reproduced elsewhere.

Present the new courses of actions that can be envisaged. Summarise their advantages and drawbacks (as in report type 3).

Recommend the choice of one of these solutions.

Annex II

APPLICATIONS

1.   National experts from OECD Member countries prepared reports on the evaluation they had made of specific projects, applying, fully or in part, the present document.

2.   These contributions proved valuable in refining the methodologies and drawing up the final version of this document, and provided a first illustration of its applicability, of problems and difficulties encountered and possible consequences on management practices, within a brroad range of institutional contexts. The country reports vary considerably, depending on the size and the scope of the projects, their implementation stage, the evaluation objectives and the surrounding institutional framework. Four of them, those of Finland, Italy, Portugal and Turkey, follow more or less closely the procedure and pattern laid down in this document, and even include examples of tables filled according to its models; the others treat of particular aspects of evaluation and refer to interesting specific projects.

3.   The Finnish report deals with the economic, social and environmental evaluation of the Vuotos reservoir project, whose main purposes are energy production and flood protection. This case is a vivid example of public sensitivity on environmental issues. The report also illustrates a case of active public participation in water management and planning.

4.   The application of the present document by the French national team was limited to the selection of alternative technical solutions for the development of the Oise watershed through flood control, regulation of the water supply for various purposes (agriculture, industry, domestic use, etc.), improvement of water quality. The report also deals at some length with public participation procedures.

5.   The Irish national team presents a preliminary evaluation of the Corrib-Mask drainage and flood protection project. Given the simple features of the project, the use made of techniques proposed in this document was limited to a cost-benefit analysis and a review of environmental effects and relevant protection measures.

6.   The Italian case study refers to the economic, social and environmental evaluation of a complex interregional project for the utilisation of the water resources of the Appennins through the construction of 37 dams and other water development works. The project objectives are: energy production, flood

237

control, water supply for irrigation, industry and domestic use and tourism. It concerns 16 provinces with a total area of 37 000 km², and a population of 8 million people. The dimensions of the project, the multiplicity of its objectives, the variety of regional conditions and technical features and the long-term perspectives of its implementation make it quite exceptional. For this reason, although the general pattern and approach presented in this document were followed, the evaluation techniques had to be adapted to the complexity of the project and to its specific requirements.

7.   The Dutch report refers to an original project, the closure of the eastern Scheldt estuary by a series of dikes and storm surge barriers to protect land and population against storm-driven floods and to preserve the natural environment. The exceptional scope of the project, whose main objectives are human safety and the preservation of ecological balances excluded any literal application of the present document in the fields of economic and social analysis. On the other hand, the evaluation of environmental impacts largely followed the proposed patterns. A report on the evaluation methods developed in the Netherlands for land consolidation projects, including an example of practical application, was also presented by the Dutch team. These projects can be considered as multipurpose (they comprise several technical actions, among which the improvement of water management) and their different effects have to be assessed from an economic, social and environmental viewpoint. The evaluation method, which is similar to the approach, proposed in the present document provides policy-makers with a basis of comparison between land consolidation projects or between such projects and other public investments. The particular interest of this report lies in the fact that it demonstrates the possibility of extending the proposed approach to projects other than the standard large hydraulic ones.

8.   The Portuguese report applies the methodology of this document to the economic evaluation of the Mondego Hydraulic Scheme. The project has several objectives: energy production, flood prevention and water supply to industry, irrigation and domestic use. The report discusses the difficulties found in the estimation of certain parameters required by economic analysis. An evaluation of the social aspects of the project was also undertaken, with special reference to the agricultural sector. The method employed was that of the "social assessment structure". The report estimates the influence of the project on various social factors affecting different types of farming households as well as the overall farming sector and attempts to integrate the project aims within the general planning options of the region.

9.   The Turkish case study is the ex post evaluation of the Kapulukaya Project, whose main purposes are the regulation of the river regime, the production of energy and the supply of industrial, domestic and irrigation water. The economic analysis follows quite closely the patterns laid down by this document; the social evaluation makes an assessment of social conditions and establishes the link between social problems in the project area and the overall regional economic development; environmental evaluation, in accordance with the approach proposed in this document, makes a systematic assessment of the potential impacts of the alternative project plans.

10.   Two documents compare the principles and procedures followed in the United States to plan water development projects and the methodology of the present document, discussing the different perspectives from which large projects can be viewed and judged, as well as the growing trend to use

multi-objective approaches for their evaluation. The documents draw a step-by-step parallel between the evaluation of the Animas-La Plata project, in Colorado, the United States, and the methodology suggested, pointing out similarities in the action plan and in the techniques used. They conclude that the interest of this document lies in its comprehensive view of evaluation issues and in the decision-oriented character of the methods used.

BIBLIOGRAPHY

Acres, H.G. (1972), "Water Quality Management Methodology and Its
    Application to the Saint John River, Niagara Fall, Ontario.

Arrow, K.J. et Lind, R.C. 1970, "Uncertainty and the Evaluation of Public
    Investment Decision", American Economic Review (June 1970); (reprinted as
    Chapter 11 in: Arrow, K.J., Essays in the theory of risk bearing, North
    Holland Publishing Co., Amsterdam, 1971).

Bell, C, et Hazell, P.B.R. (1980), Effects of Agricultural Investment Project,
    AJAE 62(1) February, pp. 75-86.

Benson, M.A. and Matalas, N.C. (1967), "Synthetic Hydrology Based on
    Regional Statistical Parameters", Water Resources Research, Vol. 3, No. 4.,
    pp. 931-935.

Bergmann, H. and Boussard, J.-M. (1976), Guide to the Economic Evaluation of
    Irrigation Projects, OCDE, Paris.

Biswas, A.K. (editor) (1976), System approach to water management,
    McGraw Hill, New York.

Börlin, M. (1971), Econometric Model for River Basin Planning, OCDE, Paris.

Bruce, C. (1976), "Social Cost Benefit Analysis: A Guide for Country and
    Project Economists to the Derivation and Application of Economic and
    Social Accounting Prices" World Bank Staff Working Papers, n° 239,
    Washington D.C. (August).

Burdge, R.J. (1973), A Summary of Sociological Studies of Water Resources,
    Dealing with Social Goals and the Quality of Life, The University of
    Kentucky Press, Lexington.

Bussery, A. (1973), Méthodes d'appréciation des projets dans les pays moins
    développés, OCDE, Paris.

Chervel, M. (1974), "L'évaluation des projets de production en économie sous
    développée : Essai de typologie des méthodes", Tiers Monde, 15 (59-60)
    July-December, pp. 771-804.

Chervel, M. and Le Gall, M. (1976), Manuel d'évaluation économique des
    projets : la méthode des effets. Ministère de la Coopération, Paris.

Clarke, R.T. (1973), Mathematical models in hydrology. FAO, Roma, 1973 (Irrigation and drainage papers N° 19).

Clawson, M., and Knetsch J. L. (1966), The economics of outdoor recreation. The Johns Hopkins press, Baltimore.

Crawford, N.M. and Lisley, R.K. (1966), Digital simulation in hydrology: the Standford watershed model (IV), Stanford University technical report 39, Stanford (Cal.).

Dasgupta, P., Marglin, S. et Sen, A. (1973), Directives pour l'évaluation des projets, Nations Unies, série formulation et évaluation des projets, N° 2, New York.

Davis, R.(1968), The Range of Choice in Water Management: A Study of Dissolved Oxygen in the Potomac Estuary, Johns Hopkins Press, Baltimore (1968).

Dee, N., Baker, J.K., Drobny, N.L. (1972), Environmental evaluation system for water resource planning. United States bureau of reclamation, Washington.

Di Toro, D.M., O'Connor, D.J. et Thomann, R.V. (1975), "Dynamic water quality forecasting and management", mimeo, Manhattan College, N.W., Ecological research series report, ERA/660/3-73-009.

Drewnowski, J. (1974), On Measuring and Planning the Quality of Life, The Hague.

Dunn, M.C. (1974), Landscape evaluation techniques: An Appraisal and Review of the Literature, Birmingham Centre for Urban and Regional Studies, Birmingham, United Kingdom.

Eckstein, O. (1958), Water resource development: the economics of project evaluation, Harvard University Press, Cambridge, 1958.

Fernea, R.A. et Kennedy, J.G. (1966), "Initial Adaptations of Resettlement -- A New Life for Egyptian Nubians". Current Anthropology, Vol. 7, No. 3.

Fiering, M.B. et Jackson, B. B. (1971), "Synthetic Streamflows", Water Resources Monograph 1. American Geophysical Union, Washington, D.C.

Fisheries and Environment Canada (1977), A Guide to the Federal Environmental Assessment and Review Process, Ottawa.

Fitzsimmons, S.J., Stuart, L.I., et Wolf (P.C.) (1977), Social Assessment Manual, Boulder, Westview Press.

Gum, R.L. et Martin, W.E. (1975), "Problems and solution in estimating the demand for and value of outdoor recreation", A.J.A.E., 57 (4), November, 1975, pp. 558-566.

Hanke, S.H., Carver, P.H. et Bugg, P. (1974), "Project evaluation during inflation", Water resources research, Reprint in Zeckhauser.

Hardison C.H. (1969), The accuracy of streamflow characteristics, Geological survey, Washington D.C.

Howe, C.W. et Lineaweawer, F.P. (1967), "The impact of price on residential demand", Water resources research 3 (1).

Howe, C.W. et Easter, K. (1970), Inter basin transfers of water: Economic issues and analysis, Baltimore, the Johns Hopkins Press.

Howe, C.W. et Cochrane, H.C. (1976), "A decision model for adjusting to natural hazard events with application to urban snow storm", The Review of Economics and Statistics. Vol. 58, No. 1, pp. 50-58.

Hufschmidt, M.M. et Fiering, M.B. (1966), Simulation Technics for Design of Water Resource Systems. Harvard University Press, Cambridge, Mass.

Jacoby, H.D. et Loucks, D.P.(1972), "Combined Use of Optimisation and Simulation Models for River Basin Planning, "Water Resources Research (United States), 8 (6), pp. 1 401-1414.

Kalinger, M.R. (1976), Economic Worth of hydrologic data in project data design: an application to regional energy development, United States Geological Survey open-file, Report 76-316.

Kelly, R.A. (1975), "The Delaware estuary" in Russel (C.S.): Ecological modelling in a resource management framework, Resources for the future, Washington, D.C.

Kendall, H. et Moglewer, S. (1975), "Preliminary Review of Reactor Safety Study" in Zeckhauser, R. et al., Benefit cost and policy analysis, Aldine, Chicago.

Kendall, M.G. et Stuart, A. (1973), The advanced theory of statistics, London, Griffin.

Knetsch, J.L. (1974), "Outdoor recreation and water resources planning", Water resources monographs, No. 3, American Geophysical Union, Washington. D.C.

Knetsch, J.L. (1977), "Displaced facilities and benefit calculations", Land Economics; 53, February 1977, pp. 123-129.

Lal, D. (1975), Appraising foreign investment in developing countries, Heinemann, London.

Leopold, L.B. (1969), Quantitative comparison of some aesthetic factors among rivers, United States Geological survey.

Leopold, L.B., Clarke, F.E., Hanshaw, B.B., et Balsley, J.R. (1971), A procedure for evaluating enviornmental impact, United States Geological Survey, Circular No. 645.

Little, I.M.D. et Mirrlees, J.A. (1974), Project appraisal and planning for developing. Heinemann, London, (first edition, OCDE, Paris, 1972).

Loucks, D.P., Revelle, C.S. et Lynn, W.R. (1976), "Linear Programming Models for Water Pollution Control", Management Science (USA), Vol. 14, No. 4.

Loucks, D.P. et al. (1969), "Stochastic Methods for Analyzing River Basin Systems", Cornell University Water Resources Center Technical Report 16, August.

Loughlin, J.C. (1977), "The Efficiency and Equity of Cost Allocating Methods for Multipurpose Water Projects", Water Resources Research, Vol. 13, N° 1, pp. 8-14.

Maddock, T. (1973), "Management Model as a Tool for Studying the Worth of Data", Water Resources Research, Vol. 8, N° 2, pp. 995-1 005.

Mäler, K.G. and Wyzga R.E. (1976), La mesure économique des dommages dans le domaine de l'environnement, OCDE, Paris.

Marks, D.H. et de Neufville, R., (1974) Systems Planning and Design, Prentice-Hall, Inc., Englewood Cliffs, N.J.

Marshall, H.E., "Economic Efficiency Implications of Federal-Local Cost Sharing in Water Resource Development". Water Resources Research, Vol. 6, N° 3, pp. 673-682.

Moss, M.E. (1970), "Optimum operating procedure for a river gauging station established to provide data for design of a water supply project", Water Resources Research 6 (4), pp. 1 051-1 061.

Nihoul, J.C.J. (1975), "Effects of the tidal stress on residual circulation and mud deposition in the southern bight of North Sea", Pure applied Geophysics 113, (4), pp. 577-581.

OCDE (1974), Process for the Treatment of Waste Waters for the Removal of Phosphorous and Nitrogen, Paris.

OCDE (1975), Strategies for Urban Noise Abatement -- an overview, Paris.

OCDE (1977), Analysis of the Environmental Consequences of Significant Public and Private Projects, Paris.

Orlob, G., Evenson, D.E. and Monser, J.R. (1969), "Preliminary selection of waste treatment systems", Journal of water pollution 41 (11), pp. 1 845-1 858.

Pouliquen, L.Y. (1970), "Risk analysis in project appraisal", World Bank Staff Occasional Paper, N° 11, Johns Hopkins University Press, Washington.

Rasmussen, W.C. (1974), Reactor Safety Study. An Assessment of Accident Risks in the United States Commercial Nuclear Power Plants, United States Atomic Energy Commission, Washington.

Reutlinger, S. (1970), "Technics for project appraisal under uncertainty", World Bank Staff Occasional Paper, N° 10, Johns Hopkins University Press, Washington.

Riordan, C. (1971a), "Multistage marginal cost model of investment pricing decisions: application to urban water supply treatment facilities", Water Resources Research 7 (3), pp. 463-478.

Riordan, C. (1971b), "General multistage marginal cost dynamic programming model for the optimization of a class of investment pricing decisions", Water Resources Research 7 (2), pp. 245-253.

Roberts, K. et Weitzman, M.L. (1981), "Funding criteria for research development and exploration projects". Econometrica Vol. 49, N° 5, September, pp. 1 261-1 288.

Roesler, T.W., Lamphear, F.C. et Beveridge, M.D.(1968), The economic impact of irrigated agriculture on the economy of Nebraska, University of Nebraska, economic and business report, N° 4, September.

Scudder, T. (1979), "An alternative scenario for river basin development in African woodland savanas", FAO Fisheries Technical papers, FAO, Rome.

Shih, C.S. (1970), "System Optimization for River Basin Water Quality Management", Journal Water Pollution Control. (United States) (42), 10, Octobre.

Sobel, J.J., (1965), "Water Quality Improvement Programming Problems" Water Resources Research (American Geophysical Union, Washington, D.C.).

Squire, L. et Van Der Tak, H.G. (1976), Economic analysis of projects, Johns Hopkins University Press, Londres.

Thomann, R.V., Di Toro, D.M. and O'Connor, D.J. (1970), "A dynamic model of the phytoplancton population in the Sacramento-San Joaquin delta" in: Non equilibrium systems in natural water chemistry, symposium of the American chemical society, Houston, Texas, pp. 131-180.

Turvey, R, (1974), "How to judge when price change will improve resources allocation", Economic Journal, 34 (336), pp. 825-832.

Walsh, M.R. et al. (1977), "Dredged material as a natural resource", Journal of the Waterways, ports, coastal and ocean division, American Society of Civil Engineers, 103 (WW3) pp. 303-319.

Walters, C. (1975), Foreclosure of options in sequential resource development decisions -- IASA internal paper, Laxenburg, Autriche.

Water Resources Council (1973), "Principles and standards for planning, water and related land resources", Federal Register, 38, (174) Sept. 10.

Zeckhauser, R. (1975), Aldine benefit cost and policy analysis, Aldine, Chicago, 1975.

INDEX

Numbers refer to paragraphs

OECD SALES AGENTS
DÉPOSITAIRES DES PUBLICATIONS DE L'OCDE